Shadowing the White Man's Burden

America and the Long 19th Century

GENERAL EDITORS
David Kazanjian, Elizabeth McHenry, and Priscilla Wald

Black Frankenstein: The Making of an American Metaphor
Elizabeth Young

Neither Fugitive nor Free:
Atlantic Slavery, Freedom Suits, and the Legal Culture of Travel
Edlie L. Wong

Shadowing the White Man's Burden:
U.S. Imperialism and the Problem of the Color Line
Gretchen Murphy

Shadowing the White Man's Burden

*U.S. Imperialism and
the Problem of the Color Line*

Gretchen Murphy

NEW YORK UNIVERSITY PRESS

New York and London

NEW YORK UNIVERSITY PRESS
New York and London
www.nyupress.org

© 2010 by New York University

Library of Congress Cataloging-in-Publication Data

Murphy, Gretchen, 1971–
Shadowing the white man's burden : U.S. imperialism and
the problem of the color line / Gretchen Murphy.
p. cm. — (America and the long 19th century)
Includes bibliographical references and index.
ISBN-13: 978-0-8147-9598-9 (cl : alk. paper)
ISBN-10: 0-8147-9598-6 (cl : alk. paper)
ISBN-13: 978-0-8147-9599-6 (pb : alk. paper)
ISBN-10: 0-8147-9599-4 (pb : alk. paper)
1. American fiction—19th century—History and criticism.
2. American fiction—20th century—History and criticism.
3. Race in literature. 4. Racism in literature. 5. Imperialism in
literature. 6. United States—Race relations—History—19th century.
7. United States—Foreign relations—19th century. I. Title.
PS374.R32M87   2010
813'.4093552—dc22   2009046690

New York University Press books are printed on acid-free paper,
and their binding materials are chosen for strength and durability.
We strive to use environmentally responsible suppliers and materials
to the greatest extent possible in publishing our books.

Manufactured in the United States of America

c   10 9 8 7 6 5 4 3 2 1
p   10 9 8 7 6 5 4 3 2 1

Contents

Acknowledgments

A number of people and institutions helped me complete this book. Thanks to Eric Zinner at New York University Press; Shelley Streeby and the other anonymous reader who offered suggestions; and the series editors, David Kazanjian, Elizabeth McHenry, and Priscilla Wald, with special thanks to Priscilla for believing in my work. Grants from the National Endowment for the Humanities, the University of Minnesota, and the University of Texas provided travel expenses and financial support. Many librarians helped with this project along the way, including staff at the National Archives, the Library of Congress, the Schomburg Center of the New York Public Library, the British Columbia Archives at the Royal BC Museum, the Oregon State Supreme Court Library, and Special Collections at the University of Calgary, Washington State University, and Fisk University; the incredibly resourceful interlibrary loan office of the University of Minnesota–Morris; and the University of Texas's Harry Ransom Center and wonderful library system.

Colleagues at the University of Minnesota–Morris were influential in the early stages of conceptualizing this manuscript; thanks to Roland Guyotte for team-teaching an interdisciplinary course on the Spanish American War with me, and to Brad Deane for so many smart insights on Kipling, literature, and empire. Colleagues at the University of Texas read drafts and provided crucial feedback during the later stages; thanks especially to Phil Barrish, Coleman Hutchison, John Gonzales, Martin Kevorkian, Evan Carton, Ann Cvetkovich, José Limón, the American Literature Interest Group, and the Women and Gender Studies New Faculty Colloquium. Heather Gardner, Kathryn Hamilton, and Tekla Schell provided research support, and students at both institutions helped by providing new perspectives on texts that I discuss here. I've also benefited from John Cullen Gruesser sharing my enthusiasm for recovering Steward's writing. Thanks to Julia Lee and Argie Manolis for personal support and friendship, and to Rich Heyman for being there through it all: my personal geographer, proofreader, and best friend, he has truly been a partner in this endeavor.

Introduction

Writing Race on the World's Stage

In a 1901 essay for the *Overland Monthly* titled "Red, Black and Yellow," John T. Bramhall noted a timely coincidence marking the 1899 publication of Rudyard Kipling's poem "The White Man's Burden." Originally subtitled "The United States and the Philippines" and published in a popular U.S. magazine, Kipling's poem urged Americans to take up the burden of joining Europe in what the poem represents as the thankless task of colonial administration. But for Bramhall, the poem spoke to more than just the question of overseas expansion; it was also a statement about U.S. race relations. Bramhall rhetorically asks, "When Rudyard Kipling wrote 'The White Man's Burden,' was it a coincidence that the Americans were just going into the Philippines, and that we were confronted at the same time with the necessity of furnishing employment to our red men, and of solving the negro problem in the South?" For Bramhall, the simultaneity of these two moments—of becoming a "world power" and at the same time having to work out new political and social relationships among white, African, and Native Americans—prompted a new application of Kipling's poem. As Bramhill explains, if "the white man's burden is his dark-skinned brother," that duty takes on a different form in the multiracial United States than it would in Kipling's England.[1]

Bramhall's comment about interpreting Kipling in the United States introduces a cultural phenomenon that I set out to explore in this book: the ways in which U.S. Americans reexamined domestic racial conflicts in light of a newly perceived global mission of overseas commercial, military, and cultural expansion at the turn of the twentieth century. If empire was viewed as a "white man's burden," or more generally justified with reference to notions of racial inferiority or superiority, then what role should the "the red, black, and yellow" peoples inhabiting the United States play

1

in the new world mission? Bramhall proposes a solution that in its divergent impulses exhibits some of the culture's uncertainty surrounding this question. He calls for enlisting African and Native American men in the U.S. military, where they will be uplifted morally by military discipline and politically by the national honor of service, and where all the while they can assist with uplifting Filipinos and other peoples across the Pacific. He pitches this idea as a call to overcome racial prejudice and inequality: "Our new possessions are making us broader minded and less provincial than we were before 1898. . . . Let us, then, break down the narrow prejudices of race and admit, though late, our red and yellow wards and our black fellow citizens to equal rights and equal glory as American soldiers." Predictably, however, Bramhall's solution retains clear signs of racial hierarchy, as when he invokes racial stereotypes about loyal African Americans and warlike Apaches, or when he explains that an influx of men of color in the military will free up many whites "who are better fitted to administrative service or productive occupation."[2] And yet, his proposal raises an ambivalent but clear challenge to the notion that the United States acting as an imperial world power could be identified as a force of whiteness. The white man's burden in the United States could not entirely remain the white man's burden.

In this book I examine cultural debates surrounding the relationship between whiteness and empire, highlighting the literary responses of four multiethnic U.S. writers: Frank R. Steward, Pauline Hopkins, Winnifred Eaton, and Ranald MacDonald. These writers used literary forms such as novels and personal narratives to complicate the popular association of whiteness with national mission or global progress. On the surface, their literary strategies for doing so may look like Bramhall's argument, because each writer describes a racially ambiguous figure who could be defined as nonwhite (such as a mixed-blood African American, American Indian, or Japanese man) taking up the project of furthering U.S. world power. In their writings, nonwhite soldiers, scientists, explorers, and diplomats travel abroad, altering the racial scripts of empire by revealing the U.S. national mission for global power and leadership to be, instead of white, potentially multiracial. And yet, in ways that are more complicated and interesting than Bramhall's, these writers also detach race from empire by challenging whiteness itself as a social, scientific, and legal category.

I call these strategies "shadowing the white man's burden." I do so for two reasons. First, because in them a nonwhite figure literally "shadows" or follows routes of U.S. global power; second, because whiteness itself is shadowed or called into question by these authors' categorical challenges to racial definitions. Using opportunities afforded by new global fields of imagination and conflict, these writers demonstrate that the fragile social construct of whiteness is always in danger of swerving into its dark opposites.

I emphasize this period between 1890 and 1914 because at this time many U.S. Americans perceived themselves as entering a new era of national importance and global status that they viewed with a mixture of pride and discomfort.[3] Along with this new understanding of the United States as a modern "world power" came opportunities and conditions for rethinking U.S. racial identities on a global scale.[4] Science and law were two places where definitions of whiteness that had evolved according to historically specific colonial practices and local social conditions were being systematized and adapted to changing patterns of global migration and changing narratives of America's place in the world.[5] Courts and legislators struggled to interpret the 1790 statute restricting U.S. citizenship to "white persons" in light of new influxes of questionably white immigrant groups such as European Jews, Syrians, and Chinese. Ethnologists developed provisional theories of affiliation and difference among "races" around the world, trying to reconcile traces of millennia of human migration with existing prejudices and power relations. In popular, academic, and policy forums, new notions of race were used to explain color lines, not only between Euro-American colonizers and colonized people around the world but also among those Euro-American colonial powers. Commonly appealed to as a totalizing system explaining global and local power relations, race remained a battleground of varying theories as Americans attempted to chart the relative racial identities of Euro-American colonial powers and to identify the people and places that they hoped would provide links to new global markets, new fields for nationalist fantasy, and new sources of immigrant labor.

The kinds of racial theories these ethnologists, courts, and policy experts struggled with are the heart of this book, because they form the material that the literary writers I discuss exploit in their stories of shadowing the white man's burden. One such theory regarded Anglo-Saxonism as a transnational racial identity. Other theories speculated about the relative whiteness of new colonial objects, partners or rivals such as the Russians, the Spanish, or the Japanese. In other cases, U.S. Americans created or interpreted new theories of racial affiliation, such as the theories of prehistoric migration that linked Native Americans to Asians, or they contemplated the future of racial mixtures and evolution in colonial settings. All of these racial theories were adaptable, contested, and contradictory, resulting in a situation where whiteness served as an object of great faith and great anxiety.

Since the eighteenth century, when Johann Friedrich Blumenbach inaugurated the study of ethnology in his doctoral thesis "On the Natural Variety of Mankind" (1775), scholars had struggled to reconcile faith in race's explanatory power with the lack of precise data revealing clear racial categories. As Blumenbach acknowledged, "Innumerable varieties of mankind run into each other by insensible degrees," and yet this acknowledgement did not prevent him from classifying mankind into the five categories of Caucasian, Mongolian, Ethiopian, American, and Malay.[6] Late-nineteenth-century anthropology still rested uneasily on this contradiction, at a time when, in the words of George Stocking Jr., heightened efforts to collect data on morphological characteristics of people around the world produced a "metric torrent" that eroded the underpinning of faith in race as a totalizing explanatory system. Stocking, writing in 1968, described this weakening as an "internal disciplinary crisis" that left the popular notion of race largely unaffected.[7] But since then, new models of critical race theory and historiography have found ways to acknowledge cultural contradictions and discontinuities, and scholars using these new models have begun describing race as simultaneously powerful and contested in the popular imagination.[8]

For this book I set out both to understand the era's conflicted ideological terrain, where faith in race as a totalizing system existed alongside anxieties and doubts about contradictory definitions of racial identity, and to explore the particular discursive strategies employed by writers who used literary forms to exploit this confusion. Kipling holds an important place in this book because, as I contend, the response to his poem in the United States both reflected and channeled anxieties about what it meant to be white and what that racial identity had to do with being American or with promoting civilization, democracy, or progress abroad. In other words, I show that the poem exacerbated uncertainty about what Etienne Balibar calls the "fictive ethnicity" around which modern nations were organized.[9]

I make this case in part I, arguing that when Kipling's readers formed interpretations of U.S. expansion as a white man's burden, they intentionally or unintentionally spotlighted conflicting and unstable conceptions of whiteness as a domestic and as a transnational racial construct. In this sense, these readers also "shadowed" the white man's burden by revealing the logical instability of whiteness—its indivisibility from its binary opposite and its continual swerving into darker opposites. In chapter 1, I examine the U.S. reception of Kipling's poem in a variety of forms such as newspaper opinions, scientific treatises, political speeches, and parodies. In chapter 2, I focus specifically on Thomas Dixon's novel *The Leopard's Spots: A Romance of the White Man's Burden* (1901) as an explicit response to Kipling.

However, "The White Man's Burden" is not the master text to which the multiethnic writers discussed in parts II and III merely react. Instead, the writers discussed in parts II and III seize on their culture's confusion about the racial meaning of empire, the same confusion that bubbled to the surface and found vent in public discussions of Kipling's poem. Nor are these writers cultural heroes who bravely evade their society's structures of race and empire. My account of Kipling's reception shows that skepticism about the notion of a racialized nation pursuing a white empire was a major feature of this period, and my study of these writers situates their thinking squarely within the very racial and nationalist structures that they challenge. As Robert S. Levine has written of this period, "Whiteness may well have been a constitutive component of American literary and cultural nationalism, but its terms were precarious and dependent upon fictions of blood that . . . sometimes were apprehended merely as fictions."[10] Thus while the authors I discuss in parts II and III don't specifically reference Kipling, they do amplify in various ways the troubling contradictions of positing whiteness as a basis for national and imperial identity.

Literature has proven a highly productive and valuable historical source for studying ideas about race and the social construction of racial categories, because in it we see ideas about personhood and social relations reflected, promoted, or challenged in literary forms. Cultural forms like novels and poems construct narratives that limit or expand readers' sense of social possibility, embodying abstract notions of similarity and difference and harnessing readers' desires to certain visions of group identity. Until the first decade of the twenty-first century, studies of racial formation through literature tended to isolate and privilege domestic contexts of U.S. ethnic formation, but recently scholars have begun looking outside of national borders to contemplate processes of U.S. racial formation that relate to contrasting, paralleling, or interconnecting processes in other places around the globe, particularly places that have had colonial and neocolonial relations with the United States. This book contributes to this scholarship, standing at the intersection of critical race theory and studies of the cultures of U.S. imperialism. As such, it extends and engages recent scholarship on comparative racialization and globalizing U.S. literary studies in several ways that I describe below.

I intend my arguments in this book to demonstrate the continued need for nuanced studies of U.S. imperial culture that more fully interrogate colonial dualisms and broaden the scope of analysis to consider global sites of imperial competition. I make this point in response to recent criticisms of the study of U.S. imperial cultures made by scholars pursuing transnational frames of knowledge. The study of U.S. empire—energized by Amy Kaplan and Donald Pease's 1993 anthology, *Cultures of United States Imperialism,* and including work by Andy Doolen, David Kazanjian, John Carlos Rowe, and Laura Wexler, among many others—seems according to these critics to have run its course and given way to new models that redress its blind spots and surpass its limitations.[11]

One of these limitations is the approach's attention to official forms of state power as its organizing framework for global relations. This privileging of state power leads studies of U.S. imperialism to ignore "forms of oppositional nationalism that take on pan-ethnic and transnational shapes and that are independent of the nation state."[12] Another limitation identified by scholars promoting a transnational turn is empire studies' unilateral attention to the United States as an actor, which renders the people and places affected by U.S. global power as "specters or victimized objects rather than actors, producers and sources within transnational circuitry."[13] And another objection targets the way that scholarship on U.S. empire can reify simple colonial binaries and dualisms by pitting "the United States as a fully formed, homogeneous entity against [a] myriad of peoples and nations."[14] Describing how reifying the United States in this way actually further isolates it, Paul Giles recommends that "rather than merely conflating America and empire and understanding U.S. power to be a 'colossus,' . . . there is an important sense in which we should read the United States itself as one of the objects of globalization, rather than as merely its malign agent, so that all of the insecurities associated with transnationalism are lived out experientially within the nation's own border as well."[15]

Motivated by these critiques, many scholars are currently seeking out new forms of transnational cultural interaction that more fully decenter and fracture the United States. Without devaluing scholarship taking these new directions, I hope in this book to demonstrate the possibility and importance of projects that maintain a focus on U.S. global power while heeding some of the above-mentioned critiques. In other words, instead of attempting to outpace or stake a claim in a series of scholarly trends rushing past—first postcolonial American studies in the early 1990s, then U.S. imperial studies in the late 1990s, and then transnational American studies in the new century—I want to draw on all of these movements to write a more nuanced study of the intersection of U.S. empire and transnational racial thinking. Through my focus on texts that portray both international and transnational identifications, my broadened geographical scope, and my critical method, in this study of empire I seek to more fully historicize postcolonial theory's insights into the dynamism of colonial power relations and the heterogeneity within generalized categories of "colonizer" and "colonized."

This goal explains why I approach my topic of race and empire through representations of nonwhite American figures circulating around the globe and "shadowing the white man's burden" in the wake of U.S. military, economic, and cultural expansion. These figures are the uprooted and mobile bodies that trouble romantic colonial assumptions about premodern indigenous or New World African populations rooted in local folk traditions. As Vijay Prashad writes, "The romance of the indigenous treats them as if they are trapped in the local while the rest of the world (us) is seen as footloose in the global."[16] The Native, African, and Asian American authors I discuss write against this romance of the indigenous, particularly engaging with white writers who sought to contain their stories in domestic, local contexts, hitched to familiar and seemingly more stable U.S. racial stereotypes. In this I follow Michelle Stephens's suggestion that we need "different and more mobile paradigms for thinking about the indigenous," revealing "the many and multiracial populations moving constantly throughout transatlantic history, . . . populations that are fully unable to be captured by the simple dualisms that have so structured our theorizing of intersubjective relations in the colonial world, the dualisms of self and other."[17]

For example, in chapter 3, I examine the fiction of Frank R. Steward, an African American captain who served in the U.S. Volunteer Army in the Philippines during the Filipino American War. His short stories, based loosely on his military experience, feature a formal experiment in literary perspective: an unraced narrator whom readers can choose to identify as black or white. I link this choice to Steward's interests both in detaching race from nation in representations of black military service and in opposing conventional representations of black soldiers structured by the forms of local color and plantation fiction; however, the effect of his stories is hardly to champion a raceless American self in opposition to a raced Filipino other. The stories, which feature a series of ambiguous interactions between the unraced narrator and Filipina women, graft a number of familiar colonial binaries onto the foundational dualism of self and other, such as civilized/savage, male/female, writing/speech, order/disorder, and yet, because of Steward's literary experimentation, they also fundamentally destabilize notions of white U.S. empire and create affiliations between Filipinos abroad and African Americans at home.

In this and other chapters I discuss strategic panracial and transnational affiliations such as those between blacks and Filipinos, or African Americans and Africans, or Pacific Northwest American Indians and Japanese, but my examination of these affiliations links them in important ways to the era's discourses of international relations and U.S. global power. Thus, I am less interested in finding representations of panethnic coalitions that radically reject the nation state than I am in exploring the strategic importance of narratives of international relations to multiethnic U.S. writers seeking to recast U.S. racial categories and prejudices at the turn of the twentieth century.[18] Ifeoma Kiddoe Nwankwo notes that when nineteenth-century African Americans developed transnational political articulations, they responded to preexisting structures of racism that would deny them access to other forms of identity such as nation or humanity, and they had to decide in these responses "whether and how to embrace both national/local and transnational/global affinities."[19] Such arguments—for racial unity, for national belonging, or for worldwide community—all had to be calibrated to different scales and sites of political struggle. For the writers discussed in this study, the affinity of national belonging and the scale of international relations and imperial competition were paramount. Rather than look beyond nation, my subject authors recast the fiction of a white nation embarking on a white man's burden by occupying positions of citizenship and imperial participation, and they project Afro-Asian and other racial coalitions from within these terms. Such strategies resemble Homi Bhabha's account of colonial mimicry, where "not quite/not white" subaltern subjects mimic the commonplaces of empire but render them incoherent through their difference.[20] Here incoherence arises from the nonwhite subject's presence within the fictive "white" nation and his or her literary recasting of its foundational racial binaries. If these authors do not point the way to sites of radical resistance to nation and empire, they do offer insight into the process of challenging hegemonic forms from within and the enduring potential and limitations of national forms in projects for global social transformation.[21]

Put another way, in this book I examine how transnational and nationalist fantasies collide when thinking about race and empire. The disconnect between supposedly transnational and global categories of races such as "black," "white," "Anglo-Saxon," "Celt," or "Asiatic," on the one hand, and the desire to view nation-states as bounded containers for racialized national identities that animate the action of a state and its citizens, on the other, provides the major tension that I set out to explore here. The tension comes from thinking globally about race on multiple levels. Telling the story of world politics often gives recourse to the clumsy, homogenizing logic that reifies nation states, so that one can imagine "the United States" or "China" appearing as a unified actor on a global stage. I ask how racial categories and racial meanings can both inform and destabilize this logic and the personified national entities that it creates. Global visions of race inform this process by narrating the racial characters and destiny of entities like "the United States" and "China," and yet at the same time they destabilize these entities by revealing a disorderly array of heterogeneities, mixtures, and migrations within and across national borders.

If spotlighting this heterogeneity is one way that these writers complicated simple colonial binaries, another way is by triangulating multiple and competing empires in these expressions of U.S. global power. It was not only representations of a heterogeneous United States that complicated racialized colonial scripts of self and other, but also the problem of competing colonial powers such as Great Britain, France, Spain, and Japan, whose diplomatic and military interactions were also racialized. Thus while this book is not a comparative study of empires, it does respond to Ann Laura Stoler's call to "historicize the *politics of comparison*" among empires rather than reinforcing isolated colonial dyads through scholarship that sequesters sites of U.S. expansion from the rest of the world.[22] Thus, instead of focusing only on the racialization of colonial sites such as the Philippines, I argue that visions of international alliances and geopolitical rivalries, such as those that imagined the United States and Russia facing off over Pacific expansion, were also battlegrounds for defining whiteness in the United States.

I make this argument most directly in part III, where a foreign war— the Russo-Japanese War of 1904—and a history of territorial competition between the United States and Great Britain in the Pacific Northwest create contexts in which multiple fictive transnational ethnicities (such as Anglo-Saxons, Slavs, Asiatics, and American Indians) and homogenized national or imperial interests (e.g., the United States, Great Britain, Canada, Russia, Japan, and the Chinook nation) form what Michelle Stephens calls "the various triangulations and quadrilateral human relations made possible, by force and by necessity, in colonial space."[23] Writers spinning narratives about U.S. expansion in the American West and in the Pacific could choose among these multiple, overlapping imagined racial and national agents to populate stories about global interaction, a condition that the authors I discuss use to shadow the white man's burden: to reveal the incoherence at the heart of fictions of race and nation.

Recent turns to transnational studies typically focus on expansive new geographical spaces for studying the circulation of cultural forms, such as the Atlantic or the hemisphere. In this study, in contrast, I avoid a specific geographic focus. Although Pacific expansion in the Philippines and economic and cultural influence in Asia are important contexts for all of the writers I discuss, my approach of examining literary engagement with discourses of international relations and colonial competition requires a broader geographic lens. Policy experts and popular commentators began describing their country as a "world power" during this period because of specific local incidents such as the Spanish American War, but what it meant to become a world power was tested and contested in ideas and fictions about U.S. influence in a variety of spaces around the world, including the Caribbean, the Pacific islands, Japan and China, Europe, the Middle East, and Africa. I have tried to demonstrate some of this breadth in this book by drawing on a wide variety of evidence that is not predetermined by geographic constructs such as the Pacific Rim, the Western Hemisphere, or the Atlantic world.

Although I am continuing the project of writing the cultures of U.S. imperialism by redressing some limitations pointed out by recent critics, one limitation that will not be redressed is my project's unquestionable centering of the United States. While I am concerned with global visions, those that I focus on in this book tend to be produced by writers who address U.S. audiences from the subject positions of "Americans," however contested their identities outside of the page may actually be. My interest in visions of state power leads me to explore how writers claiming the subject position of "American" constructed narratives of racialized global actors to imagine and contest notions of a white American global mission, as well as notions of whiteness itself. However, despite my intention to study a unilateral but fractured and contested vision of race and empire in the United States, national borders are continually crossed by texts and authors that I study. In the pages that follow I examine topics including the reception of Rudyard Kipling's poem "The White Man's Burden" in the United States, the claims to "negro cosmopolitanism" made in the pages of the *Colored American Magazine*, the efforts by Canadian-born Winnifred Eaton to access narratives of U.S. militarism in her attempt to whiten the Japanese, and the mixed-blood Chinook writer Ranald MacDonald's vacillating claims to agency within either a British Canadian or a U.S. American Pacific empire. In all of these efforts to reshape race in an era of global ambitions, we see bounded constructions of national identity and state power continually transected by authors whose writing and identities do not fit neatly inside of national borders. The authors I discuss seek to speak in national terms, but their identifications, references, and experiences often transcend national borders, and I see myself as furthering the transnational turn by acknowledging and finding meaning in such border crossings.

Another way that this study complicates current scholarship on race and empire is its argument with what Paul Kramer has called the "export" or "projection" model of racial formation and empire, in which "Americans simply applied racial formations drawn from the domestic United States, to the world beyond the United States."[24] Such theories contribute to the sense that a fully formed and coherent American colossus simply acted on the rest of the world. Instead, I contend that U.S. racial categories were adapted to fit with shifting transnational and international relationships in a process that was multidirectional and informed by new kinds of comparative thought. "Export" models have been influential in cultural studies of U.S. empire that seek to uncover broad historical continuities by linking the structures of thought underlying domestic racial hierarchy together with those underlying colonial and neocolonial U.S. expansion. John Carlos Rowe, for example, argues that U.S. Americans tended to find "isomorphic resemblance" between familiar constructs of racial others at home and the new peoples encountered abroad. Unidirectional and strategic, these analogies produced an "adaptable and yet surprisingly stable racist, sexist, and classist rhetoric that could be deployed for new foreign ventures even as it was required to maintain old systems of controlling familiar groups within the United States."[25] Perhaps the most influential formulation of the export model comes from Richard

Drinnon, who portrays U.S. colonial encounters as a series of chapters in a continuing mythic American encounter with "the West," accompanied by a pattern of racialization that projects a "metaphysics" of Indian hating from North American Indians and Mexicans to Chinese and Japanese immigrants in the United States and to Filipinos and Vietnamese in the twentieth century.[26]

In contrast, the examples of imperial comparison that I explore in this book reveal that U.S. Americans produced knowledge about race by both drawing from and revising domestic prejudices and identifications. These reproductions of racial knowledge worked multidirectionally across U.S. borders and for a variety of ends to generate new racial meanings abroad and to reshape racial identities at home. In this way my work augments new scholarly approaches that are examining transnational processes of racial formation, such as the construction of the U.S. notion of the mulatto in reaction to Latin American constructions of mestizo identity, by following different trajectories of multidirectional border crossings.[27] Demonstrating that we can assume neither that U.S. empire simply reproduced domestic racisms on a global scale nor, as recent historians have argued, that U.S. empire functioned discretely from if not antithetically to the racist politics of segregation and exclusion at home, I instead focus on discursive skirmishes where the fictive racial identity of the United States as a world power was being composed amid a tangle of conflicting global racial theories.[28]

One of the most famous theorists of race and colonialism during this period is W. E. B. Du Bois, whose "problem of the color line" has become a typical starting point in recent studies of race, nation, and transnational identities.[29] The particular dynamic that I see in Du Bois's formulation of the color line illustrates and shapes my distinct approach to global processes of racialization, providing a conceptual guide to the rest of this book. I turn to Du Bois here to explain and illustrate two key features grounding my study: attention to the era's shifting color lines and to the scale of the "world's stage" as a conceptual place for plotting their locations. My particular interest in Du Bois is in the role that narratives of geopolitical conflict and competing empires played in his categorization of world races. Comparing Du Bois's formulation of the color line with his earlier efforts to map race globally demonstrates the importance of international relations as a particular discourse and spatial scale influencing the construction of racial categories.

Du Bois repeated and revised his formulation of the color line through-out his career, creating what Eric Sundquist calls a "fluid metaphor" for the divisions that both segregate and align groups of people in relations of exploitation and imperialism.[30] His first formulation of the phrase ap-peared in a 1900 address to the American Negro Academy, "The Present Outlook for the Dark Races of Mankind." There Du Bois writes "[that] the color line belts the world and that the social problem of the twentieth cen-tury is to be the relation of the civilized world to the dark races of man-kind."[31] Organizing the world into two groups of light and dark, civilized and uncivilized, was Du Bois's strategic response to what Paul Kramer calls "Pan-European racial solidarities," imagined coalitions among "civi-lized" races and their competing imperial projects.[32] Du Bois uses this bi-furcation to call on American Negroes to assume an attitude of "deepest sympathy and strongest alliance" with Africans and Asians, all of whom belong together in a common racial grouping as dark or colored races. And he calls most especially for their identification with the "masses of dark men and women" in Puerto Rico, Cuba, and the Philippines. Ac-cording to Du Bois, their incorporation into the United States doubles "the colored population of our land" as "nearly twenty millions of brown and black people" fall under the protection of the American flag ("Present Outlook," 53). When Du Bois declares, "Negro and Filipino, Indian and Porto Rican, Cuban and Hawaiian, all must stand united under the stars and stripes for an America that knows no color line in the freedom of its opportunities" (53), his statement looks forward to the disappearance of the social color line dividing dark and light, but it also insists on the more immediate dissolution of color lines such as the one preventing unity be-tween Negro and Filipino.

That this mapping of color lines was a strategic move in response to world politics of empire becomes more evident when we compare it with the multiple color lines Du Bois plotted in an earlier address to the Amer-ican Negro Academy. A revealing counterpoint to his later conception of a world color line, "The Conservation of Races" (1897) has mostly attracted attention for its adoption of what Nancy Leys Stephen and Sander Gilman call a "strategy of reversal and transvaluation" in which black racial dif-ference is praised rather than denied as a response to white scientific rac-ism.[33] Du Bois declares that historically and sociologically, if not biologi-cally, race is "the animating force of human progress," one that adheres even as races mix and assimilate within different national borders. "The history of the world is the history, not of individuals, but of groups, not of nations, but of races," Du Bois writes, "and he who ignores or seeks to override the race idea in human history ignores and overrides the central thought of all history."[34] For my purposes here, I am less interested in how Du Bois complicates his seemingly deterministic conception of race with notions of historical contingency than I am in noting *which* historical contingencies influenced his racial schema. In "The Conservation of Races," Du Bois draws multiple color lines that form not a single belt bifurcating global light and dark but an eight-part set of races supposedly animating international relations.

Du Bois begins "The Conservation of Races" by quickly surveying ethnology's contradictory metric torrent of data on morphological criteria such as skin color, hair texture, skull size, and language, noting that "unfortunately for scientists," such criteria for race are "exasperatingly intermingled" and fail to reveal systematic groupings (39). And yet, race is the key to understanding world politics, leading Du Bois to identify eight races in a schema that he proposes should take the place of "the old five-race scheme of Blumenbach":

> We find upon the world's stage today eight distinctly differentiated races. . . . They are the Slavs of Eastern Europe, the Teutons of middle Europe, the English of Great Britain and America, the romance nations of Southern and Western Europe, the Negroes of Africa and America, the Semitic people of Western Asia and Northern Africa, the Hindoos of Central Asia and the Mongolians of Eastern Asia. (39–40)

From the contemporary viewpoint, Du Bois's categories seem odd and unfamiliar—far from "distinctly differentiated"—and I would argue that they seem so because they are founded on a historically specific understanding of colonial relations and imperial competition. This organizing principle emerges when we try to explain his classificatory schema.

Du Bois links these groups together by their "common history, common laws, and religion, similar habits of thought and a conscious striving together for certain ideals of life" (41), but surely the "English" and the "Hindoos," or the "English" and "the romance nations," share elements of history, language, law, and conscious striving in some areas, just as representatives of the "English" in Europe and the Americas diverge in some of these areas. As Anthony Appiah notes, history, language, law, and interest seem less compelling as criteria for categorizing this assortment of racial groups than does geography.[35] But I would add that an even more important criterion was the era's discourse of foreign policy and global politics. Du Bois chooses these groups at least in part for their perceived importance in geopolitical conflict. This is why the English are distinct from their colonial competitors—the Spanish and French romance nations, the German Teutons, and the Russian Slavs—and this is why "Hindoos" appear but American Indians do not. The latter are relegated by Du Bois to a list of "minor race groups," along with South Sea Islanders (41). These "minor race groups" include the American Indians and Filipinos whom Du Bois would only three years later position with the Negro on one side of the global color line as members of a racial grouping most crucial to world politics. But in 1897, before the Spanish American War, these "minor" race groups do not yet appear to Du Bois "upon the world's stage," a key phrase for specifying that his eight races are singled out as global actors functioning on the scale of international relations.

The notion of a world's stage invokes a political theater of colonial competition, international power relations, and anticolonial revolutionary movements. Saying that these races are viewed as distinct groups "upon the world's stage," Du Bois employs a conventional metaphor suggesting a global spectacle that is unified and made visible through journalistic and historical efforts to convey a single, worldwide narrative of civilized progress. Assuming a place on the world's stage means taking part in a dramatic contest for civilization or power, playing a role and assuming a kind of agency that is defined less by shared spiritual tendencies and more by opposing and antagonistic global interests. The phrase also suggests the performative, transient nature of these racial roles. This is why Du Bois's own sense of racial groups as global actors would shift over the next three years, as the Spanish American War and the rising mood of imperialism in the United States opened up new possibilities and necessities for coalitions among dark races.

By 1900, when Du Bois wrote that "the world problem of the 20th century is the Problem of the Color Line—the question of the relation of the advanced races of men who happen to be white to the great majority of the undeveloped or half developed nations of mankind who happen to be yellow, brown, or black" ("Present Outlook," 54), his choice of racial categories as actors on the world stage had changed radically. In 1900, black Americans' alliance to American Indians and South Sea Islanders (along with the previously unmentioned "Porto" Ricans and Cubans) was a major factor in world politics, while fractures among European imperial powers like Slavs and Teutons only "indirectly" touch "the question of color" (53). During those three years, the Spanish American and Filipino American Wars and the emergence of a widespread and intense public debate about racial capacity, benevolent assimilation, and the compatibility of democracy and empire in the United States had altered the configuration of global power and the actors in the drama that Du Bois saw taking place on the world's stage.

This process of strategically forming and re-forming color lines in light of shifting alliances, interests, and fantasies of world power during these years—here glimpsed in Du Bois's own developing racial theories—is the focus of this book. In the chapters that follow, I examine incidents of writers drawing or contesting a single color line or multiple color lines to explain and intervene in imperial and domestic politics of the early-twentieth-century United States. In some of these cases, color lines were drawn to narrate international conflicts between "civilized" imperial powers, such as wars between the United States and Spain or between Japan and Russia—conflicts in which the meaning of whiteness and the question of a color line provoked new reflection on the meaning of race in the domestic United States. In other cases, I examine how color lines were contested when African Americans and Native Americans explored what it meant to claim the imperial prerogatives of civilization by representing the United States on the world stage. And in all of the cases that I examine, the problem of the color line comes from recognizing contradictory racial narratives of world progress, with their various and internally heterogeneous groups cast as actors and unified subjects. What I take from Du Bois is thus an attention to the era's shifting color lines and an acknowledgment of the scale of the "world's stage" as a conceptual place for imagining and arguing their shapes.

Among the recent criticisms of U.S. empire studies as a project in American literary history, few make mention of its foundational assumption that literature and other cultural forms shaped popular ideologies and official policies of national expansion or international diplomacy. While some critics have complained that literary studies of U.S. empire have oversimplified texts by positioning them as either "for" or "against" a monolithic sense of expansionism, few have commented on the more basic argument for literature as an important historical force.[36] Indeed, movements toward comparative study of transnational cultural circuits have been so caught up in the daunting challenge of readjusting spatial and linguistic definitions of "culture" that older questions about literary method and the cultural work of literature in relation to other forms of knowledge tend for the moment to be bracketed. Amy Kaplan's influential essay "Left Alone with America: The Absence of Empire in the Study of American Culture" set out to redress not only the "absence of empire" in literary studies but also "the absence of culture from the history of U.S. imperialism," an argument that literary critics steeped in the era's historicist methodologies found readily convincing but that Kaplan aimed in important ways outside of the discipline.[37] While recent calls for transatlantic or transhemispheric studies include appeals to interdisciplinarity, these appeals rarely extend outside of humanities departments, and those that do tend to remain interdisciplinary at the level of the table of contents—in other words, bringing together multiple disciplinary perspectives without attempting to make them speak to one another.[38]

This effort to speak outside the discipline by arguing for fundamental assumptions about literature is another part of the project of imperial and transnational American studies that I seek to advance in this book. To do so, I employ a methodology that draws variously on reception and on discourse analysis of historically concurrent print culture as evidence for literature's perceived and actual potential to shape and contest popular notions of U.S. global power. Because I have been guided by the question of how to make this case convincing not only to literary critics, who share many of my disciplinary assumptions about cultural formation, but also to more skeptical readers outside the fold of U.S. cultural studies, I position my arguments in some chapters in relation to historical scholarship as well as literary criticism, and I aim to be explicit about where I am or am not suggesting causal relationships among literature, ideology, and state politics. My arguments in this book draw on racial narratives of empire gathered from a variety of kinds of cultural texts, including imaginative literary writing such as fiction and poetry but also essays, political speeches, social science, and law. Within this wide range of texts, I especially foreground moments when imaginative literature speaks to these other realms of knowledge about race and empire, and vice versa.

The fiction and poetry that I analyze vary in size of readership and extent of cultural influence; some literary works that I discuss have already been widely discussed across many spheres of U.S. culture, while others were published without much comment or were furiously revised in failed efforts to reach a wide readership. Thus, in some of these chapters, I argue for popular literature's influence on categories of race and on narratives of

U.S. expansion, but in others my interest is more in the particular ways that writers adapt conventional literary form and language to the task of reenvisioning race in light of newly imagined global relations. As I move from popular and influential formulations of race and empire in part I, on Rudyard Kipling's "The White Man's Burden" and Thomas Dixon's *The Leopard's Spots*, to less widely read or less-influential formulations of race and empire in parts II and III, my method shifts from tracing reception and influence to examining ways that individual literary texts adapt and reconfigure the ideological and cultural materials they have at hand in their efforts to revise global color lines. These materials are the literary tropes and techniques of the era, including fictional modes such as local color, conventional figures such as the "tragic mulatta," and formal elements such as narrative point of view. Where possible, I examine the rhetorical and narrative strategies of these texts in light of the author's inspirations, stated intentions, and intertexts, looking to archival materials such as manuscripts, letters, and interviews (where they exist) to understand the personal and political contexts that informed those literary strategies.

Because of the variety of texts examined, I do not argue here for a single role that literature played in representing race in the United States as part of a global phenomenon, but I do seek to explore some of the narrative and rhetorical moves that writers of imaginative literature crafted to make such representations. To the degree that I investigate the influence and reception of these writings, I also explore the possibilities and limitations of literary genres used as political devices. The literary forms employed by these writers were flexible, nuanced, and accessible but also slippery and often highly indeterminate in their openness to multiple and conflicting interpretations. As an exploration of the role of literature in constructing discourses of race and empire, I attend particularly to the work that literature can be made to perform in relation to state policy and cultural ideology.

This exploration begins in part I, "Reading Kipling in America," chapter 1, where I examine the U.S. reception of Kipling's poem to demonstrate that rather than intensifying Anglo-Saxonism or a racialized linkage between whiteness, U.S. nationalism, and overseas expansion, the poem instead exacerbated anxieties about the meaning and importance of whiteness for a U.S. global mission. In chapter 2, I extend this discussion by examining Thomas Dixon's response to Kipling in his novel, *The Leopard's Spots*. While numerous critics in Dixon's day and ours have observed that Dixon's popular novel weds Southern white supremacy with U.S. imperial mission, I focus on the way that Dixon does not merely invoke but actually adapts Kipling's poem to appeal to Southerners. Rather than binding the South to a hegemonic sense of the white man's burden, Dixon engaged with the uncertainties about race and empire channeled by the poem in an effort to reconcile racial segregation and imperial mission. In both of these chapters, I highlight moments when the image of an African American shouldering the white man's burden spotlights the inadequacy of racial narratives of empire, a key image that the writers in part II exploit.

In part II, "The Black Cosmopolite," I examine the construction of the figure of the black cosmopolitan in writings by two *Colored American Magazine (CAM)* authors, Frank R. Steward and Pauline Hopkins, between 1900 and 1904. Both Steward and Hopkins understood that their very participation in discussions and fantasies about military, scientific, or business ventures abroad had the power to recast racial narratives of U.S. empire. Exploiting this situation, their narrative devices and strategies highlight the contradictions of imagining a white U.S. world mission. In chapter 3, I examine Steward's short stories and essays based on his experience serving in the Philippines as a captain in a colored regiment of the U.S. Volunteer Army, arguing that his use of a racially nonidentified narrator attempts to deracialize African American military service but also reveals potential transnational identifications between blacks and Filipinos. An intriguing mix of Orientalism, local color storytelling, and multilingualism, Steward's stories complicate colonial binaries and conceptions of race, civilization, and authority in the Philippines.

Hopkins was Steward's editor, and I contend that in her 1903 novel *Of One Blood* she was actually responding to the ambivalently imperialist writings of Steward and others published in the *CAM*. Hopkins used her novel's protagonist Reuel Briggs to criticize and revise her contributors' constructions of black worldly expertise. With biographical evidence drawn from Hopkins's correspondence, I demonstrate that by parodying such constructions, Hopkins was also expressing the editorial conflict she experienced between her vision of a colored American "international policy" and the political pressure she received to steer clear of foreign interests. As a contribution to scholarly discussions about *Of One Blood*'s relationship to imperialism and civilizationist hierarchies, my discussion of Hopkins explores her treatment of the problematic concept of de-raced imperial authority in order to help us understand how the novel could fail to offer a radical critique of imperialism but still deliver a troubling challenge to the idea of the white man's burden.

In part III, "Pacific Expansion and Transnational Fictions of Race," chapters 5 and 6 shift attention to the context of competing global empires. In chapter 5, I argue that an important referent for U.S. racial formation was the popular discourse about a global showdown between so-called Saxons and Slavs over the Mongolian minds and markets of China. I examine the strategic use that Winnifred Eaton made of this discourse in her fiction, demonstrating that a foreign conflict, the 1904 Russo-Japanese War, was an important site for creating or destabilizing narratives about a white empire in the Philippines and coalescing notions of homogeneous European whiteness in law, ethnology, and science at home in the United States. In this chapter, I show that Eaton shadows the white man's burden by using an international racial discourse to fracture and oppose concepts of homogeneous European whiteness and homogeneous Asiatic otherness in U.S. law and culture. For Eaton, there may be an Anglo-Saxon U.S. imperial identity, but by including in it the Japanese and excluding from it questionable European ethnicities such as the Celts and Slavs, her writing exploits the contradictory racialized scripts of nation and empire.

In chapter 6, I examine Ranald MacDonald, a Scotch-Chinook descendent of the Northwest fur trade, whose liminal national identity was formed by competing British and American empires. Born in British Oregon, MacDonald's sense of national dislocation resulted from both his mixed blood and the 1846 movement of the U.S.–Canadian border. While MacDonald can be seen as a transnational figure, his efforts to write himself into the diplomatic histories of both the United States and Canadian Great Britain reveal his sustained effort to make his accomplishments legible to state power. I examine MacDonald and his coauthor Malcolm McLeod's revisions to *Japan Story of Adventure* (1893), a manuscript that tells the story of MacDonald's journey to Japan as a young man in 1849. In these revisions, MacDonald shadows the white man's burden both by introducing the narrative of a mixed-blood Indian leading the wave of U.S. or British colonization in Asia and by revealing the competing historical and geographical forms of racialization used to identify the mixed-blood people of the Pacific Northwest. I compare MacDonald's accounts of his own accomplishments with accounts by two U.S. writers who were more successful in publishing stories about MacDonald: Elizabeth Bacon Custer and Eva Emory Dye. In their versions, Bacon and Dye marshaled literary and anthropological tools to pin down MacDonald's disturbing mobility and indeterminacy. In the case of MacDonald, as with Steward, Hopkins, and Eaton, white writers provided countertexts that attempt to contain his story in domestic, local contexts. Reading Steward's, Hopkins's, Eaton's, and MacDonald's stories in relation to such countertexts and to the culture's confusion about race and empire, we understand that the power to rethink race on the global stage during this period was itself a rhetorically contested position of leverage.

PART I

Reading Kipling in America

"I move," said the legislator, "that we now take up the–"
"Mr. Chairman," interrupted a Senator, "hasn't that white man's
burden poetry been worked about enough?"
—A joke printed in the *North American,*
a Philadelphia newspaper, March 13, 1899

In the joke above, Kipling's poem has overstepped its bounds
when it enters the Senate halls, but as I demonstrate in this section, the
poem was indeed "worked about" in Congress and throughout the culture at large. On the reception of "The White Man's Burden" in the United
States, little has been written that goes beyond general assertions about its
influence on U.S imperialism.[1] This is an oversight of what was seen at the
time as the era's most important literary incursion into the realm of international politics. After its initial U.S. publication in the February 1899
issue of *McClure's Magazine,* the poem was extensively reprinted through
the McClure's newspaper syndicate; according to one estimate, it appeared
in at least six-hundred thousand copies of newspapers nationwide and
reached over one million American readers.[2] Its publication accompanied
an unprecedented surge in Kipling's popularity. In the following months,
newspapers produced supplements devoted to minutiae of Kipling's life
and career; a monthly journal entirely devoted to miscellaneous facts and
opinions about Kipling enjoyed a year-long run in New York; publishers
took advantage of the fashion by hastily rehashing and printing as free-
standing pamphlets brief articles on Kipling taken from monthlies; and all
sort of writers and politicians found ways to comment on Kipling's writing and on "The Kipling Boom."[3] One reviewer concluded, "Whatever be
the reasons for the popular appreciation of 'The White Man's Burden,' the
immensity of that appreciation is most remarkable. Sermons have been

preached about it, editorials written on it, jokes made of it, [and] parodies innumerable and cartoons have been inspired by it."[4] To satirize the fashion of banking on Kipling in the United States, the London *Academy* printed a false prospectus for "Kipling (Limited)," a U.S. corporation that would buy up and reproduce Kipling's childhood "attempts at pothooks and penmanship," as well as his current writings: "The Company will be vigilant that no imperial crisis shall pass without poetic comment from Mr. Kipling's pen. It trusts also that it will be successful in inducing Mr. Kipling to give these political poems a form which shall be easily parodied: thus providing for increased publicity."[5]

And, indeed, parodies abounded. Through references to "The White Man's Burden," something as vague as "U.S. imperialism"—as a set of policy choices, a philosophy, a popular mood, a logical rationale for certain actions—could be targeted and evaluated. Kipling's strident trimeter, repetition, and ordered, rhyming stanzas made an easy target for anti-imperialists interested in striking a satirical blow to expansion. E. S. Martin in *Harper's Weekly* wrote that the poem seemed to have a "red rag effect on the opponents of expansion," being "chiefly quoted by persons who find fault with its sentiments."[6] One 1899 parody mimicked the poem's emphatic meter while pointing out its self-serving rationale for wrongdoing:

> Take up the sword and rifle
> Still keep your conscience whole—
> So soon is found an unction
> To sooth a guilty soul"[7]

Other satirical treatments rendered the burden not as a trial but as stolen treasure; Robert Underwood Johnson's 1901 parody of the poem answers the question "What is the White Man's Burden?" in this final couplet: "Go bribe new ships to bring it—/ The White Man's Burden—loot!"[8] Or, as another parodist quipped, the "burden" was not to spread civilization but to teach the Philippines "what interest and taxes are / And what a mortgage means."[9] A favorite anti-imperialist tactic was pointing out the poem's obfuscating reversal, which diplomatic historian Albert K. Weinberg called in 1935 an example of onomantithesis, the figure wherein any unpleasant thing is designated not by its usual name but by the antithesis of its usual name. In Kipling's poem, Weinberg writes, "imperialism, connoting the burden of the race of color by military subjugation if not economic exploitation, was called in 'onomantithesis,' the white man's burden."[10] As one

THE WHITE (?) MAN'S BURDEN.

Figure 1. "The White (?) Man's Burden," by William H. Walker, *Life* 33 (March, 16 1899), 201.

critic of the day complained, "The trouble with the kind of White Man's Burden that Kipling talks about is that it really means the Brown Man's Burden. It means the white man taking his own burden and putting it upon the brown man's back and compelling the brown man to carry it."[11] Visual images pointing out this reversal frequently appeared in political cartoons depicting Uncle Sam carrying off bags of Filipino wealth or riding atop a Filipino over the title, "The White Man's Burden" (figures 1 and 2).

Figure 2. "Taking Up the First Installment of the White Man's Burden," by George Washington Rehse, *American Monthly Review of Reviews* 21, no. 4 (1900), 392.

In chapters 1 and 2, however, I aim to show that the poem was more than a jingoistic rallying cry or an easy mark for anti-imperialists. Readers of the poem expressed a surprising amount of confusion about its meaning, and at the root of this confusion, I argue, was their ambivalence about the idea of the United States taking up a "white" imperial mission. In chapter 1, I examine the poem's reception to argue that, rather than supporting the linkage between whiteness and American empire, the poem exacerbated anxieties about the meaning and importance of whiteness for a U.S. global mission. In other words, while some satirists demonstrated the poem's hypocrisy by pointing out the onomantithesis in Kipling's binary treatment of black beneficiaries and white servants, for some readers Kipling's binary was not deceptively reversed but troublingly collapsed in a context where the meaning and stability of whiteness was in question.

In chapter 2, I interpret Dixon's best-selling novel *The Leopard's Spots: A Romance of the White Man's Burden* as a response to the anxiety about white American empire that Kipling's poem provoked. Dixon's novel attempted to resolve the poem's contradictory meanings, especially for Southern Democrats who were invested in visions of racial homogeneity and domestic segregation and troubled by the poem's destabilizing conception of whiteness. I contend that in attempting to envision a white man's burden that would appeal to the South as well as the North, to Democrats as well as Republicans, Dixon sought to revise Kipling and extend the poem's appeal beyond the party of Theodore Roosevelt, the Republican imperialist to whom the poem was initially addressed. To create this appeal, Dixon tried to create a more stable sense of the white American imperial subject, and in doing so he had to address the questions that I argue were continually provoked by Kipling's poem: Who is the white man? What does the United States have to do with a white racial mission? And how does that mission coexist with internal racial heterogeneity? Ultimately, my purpose in chapter 2 goes beyond offering another example of Kipling's influence in provoking these questions, and, instead, examines Dixon's popular reinterpretation of Kipling as a sustained literary effort to reorganize U.S. racial categories and hierarchies in light of a global mission.

1

The Burden of Whiteness

In February 1899, a query was posed to "Chappy," the persona of a news columnist who served as resident expert for readers of the *Milwaukee Journal*:

> Dear Chappy,
>
> > Please state in your column what is the real meaning of the poem of Rudyard Kipling, entitled The White Man's Burden, published in McClure's Magazine for February, 1899.
> > Does it refer to expansion or to the ills of our present social system?
> > It may seem strange to you, but many people of intelligence are divided on this subject, and it has caused considerable discussion.
> > Please give us your idea as to which meaning is intended by the poet.
>
> *Yours very truly, T. F. H.*[1]

This particular question is one that literary critics today seldom puzzle over—when Kipling scholars write about this poem, they generally treat it as one of Kipling's simpler works, important as a reference point for comparison with the author's other works but not complex enough to merit its own analysis.[2] In short, literary critics seem inclined to agree with the interpretation given by Chappy, who answers T. F. H.'s question with a quick gloss of some of Kipling's lines and concludes with some chiding condescension: "It is clearly an 'expansion poem,'" which "seems to me to be quite clearly the meaning of the highly polished verses and I quite fail to understand how the other meaning in your letter could possibly be associated with them."[3]

Kipling's familiar and frequently cited poem is rarely the object of serious literary analysis, but the story of how "The White Man's Burden" was received in the United States demonstrates that the poem's meaning and effect are more complicated than often supposed. Historians have long held that Kipling's poem offered to the United States a key formulation of expansion as selfless duty, a moral justification based on idealism and racial mission for empire in the newly acquired Philippine islands.[4] More recently, scholars of U.S. imperialism have interpreted the poem, subtitled "The United States and the Philippines," as a representative articulation of transatlantic imperial identification.[5] But by taking seriously T. F. H.'s question about interpretation and looking for its echoes throughout U.S. political and literary discourse, we see much more. As I contend in this chapter, the reception of Kipling's poem in the United States reveals the poem's important role in channeling anxieties about the definition of whiteness and its relationship to U.S. empire and American "social ills." Following this trail of interpretive uncertainty, we see the productive confusion that arises when a poem enters into the public sphere as a political document, a confusion that points us back to some of the classic concerns of interpretive method: Where is the "real meaning" of a poem? What does a poem do in the world? For wondering what Kipling's poem in fact meant and did became one way that readers in the United States pondered some of their most pressing questions of national and racial identity.

As a reception study, this chapter suggests that the meaning of Kipling's poem derives not only from authorial intention or formal features but also from the interpretations made by readers of the poem in particular socio-historical contexts.[6] While I am primarily interested in using reader response as a window onto the turn-of-the-century U.S.'s vexed ideas about race and imperialism, "The White Man's Burden" also provides an interesting case study in literary reception, one in which readers' interpretations range widely, due in part to a conscious perception of the literary work as also a political document, a sort of mixed genre that readers experienced as unprecedented. During the three-year period of the Filipino American War following the poem's release, commentators often spoke of Kipling as a writer whose importance transcended "merely literary" concerns. Frederick Laurence Knowles published a *Kipling Primer*, a guidebook intended to help the common American reader understand the poet's importance; it introduces "The White Man's Burden" as "more widely read, discussed and parodied than any other poem of the time" and affirms another critic's claim that the poem is "an international document of the first order of importance." Walter L. Sheldon chose Kipling as his topic for an essay in the series "Ethical Addresses," stating the poet's reputation to be not "a problem for the literary critic or the man of letters, belonging only to the sphere of literature" but, rather, an issue of much broader political relevance. Kipling's reviewer in the *Outlook* similarly identified him as a writer who, although a private individual "detached from the world of affairs," has "won the place of a leader" among English speakers. And Paul Elmer More in the *Atlantic Monthly* contended that no other English or American poet has ever enjoyed popularity on par with Kipling, partly because others such as Tennyson, Browning, and Longfellow "remained more or less isolated in the realm of pure art," while Kipling used art to voice ideas that shaped world events.[7] We may wish to question the idea that other poets were more isolated in the "realm of pure art," but the *perception* that Kipling was special in escaping it evoked different reading practices.

Certainly Kipling intended the poem to influence U.S. foreign policy. Before its publication in *McClure's,* he sent an advance copy to Theodore Roosevelt, the recently elected governor of New York and hero of the Spanish American War. Kipling perhaps hoped that Roosevelt would find the poem relevant to questions gripping the United States: What did it mean to have beaten Spain, liberated Cuba, and taken possession of several Caribbean and Pacific islands, the most populous and distant of which were the Philippines? And, more urgently, what should be done with these new possessions? Roosevelt passed the poem along to fellow expansionist Henry Cabot Lodge, noting that it was "rather poor poetry, but good sense from the expansionist viewpoint." Lodge, the famously Anglophobic Massachusetts senator, appreciated sound but took issue with sense: "Thank you for the advance copy of Kipling's poem. I like it. I think it is better poetry than you say, apart from the sense of the verses."[8] Despite their different evaluations of the political message, both politicians take the poem's "sense" or meaning as something easily identified and separated from its form as poetry, an assumption challenged both by a close reading of the poem and by the story of the poem's broader reception.

Read as a poem and as a policy statement, "The White Man's Burden" resonated widely in a variety of cultural forms such as congressional debate and presidential policy, scientific writing, advertisements, sermons, newspaper and magazine editorials, personal letters, political satire, and literary criticism. Examining such a broad reception requires attention to divisions within the culture's politics and within its reading publics. Reception studies have explored the ways that interpretation can be motivated or primed in a number of ways: by political agendas, individual subjectivities, cultural assumptions, and literary expectation regarding genre and convention.[9] But when poetry is taken as policy, poetic ambiguity offers particular grounds for motivated interpretations by readers with varying interpretive skills. As a columnist with the Kansas *Atchison Daily Globe* wryly noted, "That is the trouble with poetry; people do not understand its meaning. We have read Kipling's poem, at the expense of a headache, and we say he advises the Filipinos to take up the white man's burden; that is, they should quit lying around in the shade like dogs, and go to work, die of dyspepsia, and go to hell, like the white man."[10] Here ideas about poetic indirectness create a satiric opportunity to rewrite the poem's meaning, expressing a sarcastic version of T. F. H's seemingly sincere sense that the poem might be critical of the nation's "present social system." And yet in doing so, the Kansas columnist only extends the poem's authority in turn-of-the-century debates about U.S imperialism. Instead of disqualifying poetry from serious discussion of foreign policy, poetic ambiguity in the case of Kipling's poem enabled a literary text to be marshaled in a number of debates. And one of the most important of these was about the importance of race for charting a global role for the United States.

With this ambiguity came a troubling anxiety about the meaning of whiteness. I argue that by celebrating whiteness as both an explanation and a goal of the civilizing mission, Kipling's poem invited reflection on the meaning and definition of whiteness that its fragile and shifting construct could not completely bear. This is not to say that this is the essential or ultimate meaning of the poem but that an interrogation of whiteness and empire was its most significant and presently unacknowledged social effect. The concept of race as a key tool for explaining world politics, history, and human potential reached its height at the turn of the twentieth century and was about to begin its decline as a legitimate scientific concept. In the interpretive controversy over Kipling's verse, we can see writers dwelling on and contending with the concept's fractures and contradictions, intentionally or unintentionally making its incoherence more visible, for widely different purposes. In other words, while the poem both harnessed and reinforced certain historical constructions of race such as "Anglo-Saxon" or "white," it also placed these groupings in a spotlight that cast critical attention on these strategic groupings and their attendant "social ills," as T. F. H puts it. As part of my inquiry into racialization and empire building, this chapter shows the importance of literature both in scripting and in interrogating fictions of racial identity.

What in the poem itself so confused and provoked American readers? I argue that two ambiguities in particular troubled them. One was the goal or endpoint of empire: Who, if anyone, becomes more civilized by the project of the white man's burden? And the second was the definition of whiteness itself. The first anxiety stems from the poem's famous emphasis on the hardship of imperial mission. Voiced as practical advice to the young imperialist United States, the poem exhorts:

> Take up the White Man's burden—
>   Send forth the best ye breed—
> Go, bind your sons to exile
>   To serve your captives' need;
> To wait, in heavy harness,
>   On fluttered folk and wild—
> Your new-caught sullen peoples,
>   Half devil and half child. (1–8)[11]

Here in a series of ironic reversals, he who carries the White Man's burden is a servant or a beast of burden, whose "heavy harness" binds him to the duty of a civilizing mission bereft of profit and self-interest. Instead of the "iron rule of kings" (26), the burden-carrier must endure the "toil of serf and sweeper" (26–27), building ports that he won't enter and roads he won't use, all for the benefit of "another's profit/ And . . . another's gain" (15–16). This civilizing mission is a "tale of common things," with few references to spreading enlightenment, democracy, or religion: instead, the White Man strives to provide more basic services: "To fill full the mouth of Famine/ And bid the sickness cease" (19–20). If the notion of a "burden" evoked the higher sacrifices of Protestant Christianity through its reference to Bunyan's *Pilgrim's Progress*, the actual substance of Kipling's burden was secular, not religious.

This form of self-sacrifice was an aspect of empire building that Kipling identified again and again in other forms. In August 1898, after the armistice with Spain was declared, Kipling returned to writing "The White Man's Burden," which he'd begun in the preceding year, before the outbreak of the Spanish American War. During the next few months, he wrote to a number of American friends with advice similar to that found in the poem he was completing. To George Cram Cook, professor of English literature at the University of Iowa and husband of playwright Susan Glaspell, then serving as corporal of the 50th Iowa Volunteers at Camp Cuba Libre, Kipling wrote:

I own I feel like Methusalah when I read your note—racially old beyond telling—a cave man as it were, listening to the chant of a new tribe. For you see, you are on the threshold of your work which, thank God, is the white man's work, the business of introducing a sane and orderly admin-istration into the dark places of the earth that lie to your hand. . . . The enthusiasm of your first conquest will die away: you will find yourselves brought horribly face to face with a vast amount of hard work; you will blunder horribly; you will fail, succeed, fail and succeed again. But in the long run you will come out all right and *then* you will be a nation indeed. Does this sound patronizing? Live another twenty years and you will see what I mean.[12]

It is crucial to note here that Kipling only promises that "*you* will come out all right" in the end, a qualification that leaves unspecified the destiny of the colonized: How will they come out? The poem is quite pessimis-tic about getting the colonized to embrace civilization. Despite all efforts, he who carries this burden will "watch sloth and heathen folly/ Bring all [his] hope to nought (23–24); he will watch his soldiers die and win as a "reward" only the blame and hate of inferiors (34–36). Like Moses leading the Israelites through the desert, he who guides the uncivilized toward the light must endure uncomprehending rebellion in the form of the question, "Why brought ye us from bondage,/ Our loved Egyptian night?" (39–40).

Indeed, the poem makes the service of the white man sound so debas-ing and its results so disappointing that one could conclude that the poem is a satire—that it criticizes the degrading cycle of imperialism and, in T. F. H.'s words, "the ills of our present social system." One becomes uncivilized himself—a harnessed beast of burden, a toiling servant, and a combatant in "savage wars of peace"—only to find that savages never change. In other words, instead of civilizing the savage, savagery undoes the civilized. This ironic reading of the pessimism in Kipling's poem, as I discuss below, was not an idiosyncratic response on the part of T. F. H. but, as he explained, one held by "many intelligent people." Along with Chappy, we could re-spond by demonstrating that both the words on the page and the author's stated intentions counter this reading, but, rather than isolating the cor-rect meaning, I propose a more interesting goal: to look further into what generates such interpretive differences and into the "ills of our present so-cial system" that the poem signified to readers in the U.S. context.

That the United States will "come out all right" while these "new caught sullen peoples" continue to reject the White Man's leadership raises what was in the United States a crucial question about territorial expansion: What if the inhabitants of new territories could never be made over in the image of the White Man? For Kipling, democratizing these territories is largely irrelevant to the purpose of administering them, but in the United States the idea of democratizing was so prevalent that it was and still is projected into the poem by readers. For example, literary critics Ashley Dawson and Malini Johar Schueller state that Kiping's poem fostered the United States' "obligation to liberate its 'new-caught, sullen peoples/ Half devil and half child.'"[13] How U.S. readers see a duty to *liberate* in Kipling's exhortation to *administer* is a result of both the centrality of democracy in justifications for U.S. empire and the poem's cryptic, troubling silence on the fate of the colonized. The poem mentions democratization only in the form of a contrived excuse that should not keep the listener from his task. The speaker warns not to "call too loud on Freedom/ To cloke your weariness" (43–44), a reference to anti-imperialist arguments for leaving Filipinos free to govern themselves. In "The White Man's Burden," such arguments for self-government merely conceal lazy unwillingness to carry out a difficult duty—an ignoble failure of courage and stamina. To Corporal Cook, Kipling warned that Americans must not "shirk and scuttle" by cheating "yourselves into the belief that written and paper Constitutions can help races who have never conceived of the western notion of liberty."[14]

If not democracy, another possible future for the colonized was recalled by Hamlin Garland, who describes a conversation with Kipling in which the British writer qualified his imperialist arguments "by reference to the 'white man's burden,' [stating that] the races who keep their dead out of their drinking water survive and those who don't—die. Which is as it should be. The white man's duty is to rule and sanitate." But why sanitate for others if it is "as it should be" that some races survive and others die? That the goal of the white man's burden is to successfully civilize— or even prolong the life of—the savage, or that such an outcome is even required in order for the United States to "come out all right," is hardly clear in Kipling's poem. Even the anti-imperialist Garland was struck by the problem that Kipling outlined of irremediable savagery; he comments that he left the discussion troubled by Kipling's question: "Why should so much of the earth be given over to pitiless, filthy, half-formed savage races?"[15] Garland's question begs an answer that was for many of the era's imperialist thinkers the proper goal of imperialism: things would "come out all right" not by civilizing or democratizing but by taking land from and eliminating or indefinitely controlling any incorrigible inhabitants.

In Kipling's poem, however, the true purpose and reward for imperialism is stated differently, and without reference at all to the fate of the colonized. His reward for bearing the White Man's burden comes neither from the successful propagation of civilized virtues nor from inheriting the earth from those unworthy to care for it. Rather, reward comes in the form of recognition from the community of imperialist nations who will celebrate America's manly valor for joining them in their struggle. The final stanza reads:

> Take up the White Man's burden!
>   Have done with childish days—
> The lightly-proffered laurel,
>   The easy ungrudged praise:
> Comes now, to search your manhood
>   Through all the thankless years,
> Cold, edged with dear-bought wisdom,
>   The judgment of your peers. (49–56)

In other words, the White Man must civilize the heathen "half child" (8) or remain himself in childhood, a vision of maturation that requires the United States to risk seemingly hopeless perils in order to prove its manhood among the powers of Europe. The savage's inability to rise above "sloth and heathen folly" (23) only makes the United States more beholden to prove to European peers its energetic and civilized determination.

The trope here is maturation, a gendered rite of passage from childhood to manhood, but it is also one of racial evolution. In his letter to Cook, Kipling speaks as the representative of an older, more-advanced tribe, addressing a new race that will somehow become more unquestionably white by picking up this burden:

> Don't you see that *now* the States have justified 'emselves as White Men. They are worth talking to: they are equals (which for all their wealth they were not before) they understand things. . . . Each year of administering alien races who have no rights, and for that reason must be dealt with an immense forbearance, will educate, stiffen and cleanse them.[16]

Kipling's language here is striking for the way that it describes empire building's benefits for the United States as a step toward their own civilization and racial maturation: administering the Philippines will educate, stiffen, and cleanse the *Americans,* not the Filipinos. What is more, it will "justify" them not only as grown men but also as *white* men, suggesting whiteness and manhood are not stable and presumed qualities but ones that must be proven, made official though acts and deeds. Existing more as ideals than as physical traits, Whiteness differs from whiteness, being of the male sex does not make one a Man, and all white men are not necessarily White Men. In terms of social Darwinism, carrying out the acts and deeds of the White Man affords the United States a chance to evolve toward a higher state of racial perfection and to distance itself further from those who still have not gained their racial maturity and perhaps never will.

Clearly evident here are some of the gendered ideologies that recent scholars have argued impelled the Spanish American War and the drive for overseas expansion at the turn of the twentieth century. Gail Bederman has shown that masculinization was a popular analog for the era's myth of racial maturation, in which a race mentally and physiologically "grows up" as it evolves from savagery to civilization.[17] And certainly Kipling's vision of manly self-sacrifice could reinforce the personification of the United States as a chivalrous hero that Kirsten Hogansen and Amy Kaplan show to be circulating in the era's political and literary discourse.[18] Readers in the United States readily likened Kipling's poem to Roosevelt's "Strenuous Life" and commented in general on the masculine virtues communicated in Kipling's poetry and prose. But in U.S. commentary on the poem, it was the meaning of whiteness as an ethnological phenomena that raised the most discussion.[19] After all, readers had numerous cultural and narrative forms to understand the concept of achieving manhood through behaviors and trials but few that would explain the concept of achieving or "justifying" whiteness. This was another of the productive ambiguities that Kipling's readers would seize on in their effort to articulate the U.S. world mission: Does the United States actually get "whiter," or more "racially old," or more evolved, by pursuing foreign empire? If so, that might imply a certain fragility of whiteness, both in Kipling's necessity of striving for it and in social Darwinist concepts of race suicide and racial degeneration. Whiteness seems more tenuous than stable when accidental racial regression was always a possibility, especially if the white man must become like a savage or a beast or a servant himself to justify his manhood and his whiteness.

This is a question about the diachronic stability of whiteness, its evolution over time, but the second controversy about the poem asks about the definition of whiteness synchronically, in a multiethnic national culture where the meaning of whiteness as a category was shifting and contested. In literary criticism of "The White Man's Burden," the meaning of whiteness as a category has caused some minor interpretive controversy. Some clarify that when Kipling wrote "White," he really meant "Anglo-Saxon," a racial grouping that would exclude imperial rivals like Spain and Russia.[20] And C. E. Carrington, one of Kipling's most famous biographers, contended in 1955 that Kipling uses the word "White" in the poem "colloquially" to invoke a "secondary symbolic meaning" of the non-racially specific quality of being *civilized,* an argument that more recent critics have repeated.[21] Other readers, perhaps in reaction to what appears as apologism in Carrington's sidestepping of race, have instead countered that the poem expresses racism pure and simple. For example, Peter Keating treats the poem as so unambiguous that it does not require analysis; it obviously "represents Kipling at his highest point of imperial faith and confidence" and is "profoundly racist in sentiment." My reading of the poem, in contrast, accepts that the meaning of White was unstable and ambiguous and that the poem's confident vision of empire was not entirely clear to readers.[22] In taking this position, I don't want to excuse the racism and imperialism in Kipling's poem but to situate them more effectively in the historical moment of reception in order to understand why the poem became a touchstone—and a stumbling block—for debates about the meaning of whiteness and its relationship to U.S. empire and democracy.

The Anglo-Saxon's Burden

In the spring of 1899, many speculated on the reason for Kipling's sudden popularity—what one dissatisfied critic in the *Dial* called "The Kipling Hysteria."[23] Some thought sympathy played a role, because the publication of "The White Man's Burden" was preceded a few days by Kipling's arrival with his family in New York, where he and his daughter suffered serious (and, in his daughter's case, fatal) bouts of pneumonia. The U.S. press covered their illnesses closely, prompting sympathy for Kipling in his illness and grief that caused, in one reporter's opinion, a "Kipling famine" at overrun book sellers in early 1899.[24] However, by far the most commonly discussed reason for Kipling's popularity was something more intangible than his personal crisis: a climate of Anglo-Saxonism.[25] The sudden and powerful emergence of this strong sense of Anglo-Saxon identity undoubtedly helped create both sympathy for Kipling in his illness and interest in his poem, although as I argue below, that Kipling's poem articulated Anglo-Saxon identity was a common but not universal interpretation. This climate is an important one for theorizing the transatlantic aspect of my analysis. In this climate, the topic of Kipling in America becomes not a matter of U.S. Americans enthusiastically reading a British poet but, rather, a matter of Anglo-Saxons enthusiastically reading an Anglo-Saxon poet. Observe how Kipling was racially identified by some U.S. writers. According to the *Living Age* in 1899, Kipling "has come to be a representative force, not only in English literature, but also in the more complex elements which make up a race."[26] John Jay Chapman called him "the Pindar of the Pan-Saxon movement," a poet with "the greatest immediate political influence that has ever been seen in literature."[27] His popularity was to another critic a "mental epidemic sweeping just now unaccountably over the Anglo-Saxon world," and his poem was "the organ-voice of the Anglo-Saxon race, drowning the shrill petulancy of some and the sullen petulancy of others, raising the minds of millions of people above the clamour for precedents, condensing into a single magazine page the whole philosophy of Anglo-Saxon progress toward manifest destiny!"[28]

Strictly speaking, Anglo-Saxonism held that the descendents of the Anglo-Saxon invaders of Britain carried a germ of racial superiority that caused and justified their imperial primacy. More broadly, it was a hazy notion of shared cultural, linguistic, political, and imperial superiority that rested uneasily on assumptions about racial kinship. Conjuring up Anglo-Saxonism as a justification for U.S. expansion had been common since the Mexican American War, but it reached new heights of confidence at the turn of the century, the era that Helen Knuth has called "the climax of American Anglo-Saxonism."[29] Along with it rose a strong sense of cultural identification with Great Britain and, for the first time, a diplomatic mood of transatlantic rapprochement in which Spain was a non-Anglo-Saxon enemy and England was an international partner.

The rapid emergence of this feeling of transatlantic kinship can be seen in a comparison of two commentaries on Kipling written by William Dean Howells: one published in 1897, the other in 1899. In the first, written before the Spanish American War, Howells feels that because of national differences, Americans don't quite appreciate Kipling:

> He is so intense in the English loyalty which always mystifies us poor Americans, that one has a little difficulty in taking him at his word in it. . . . [His patriotism extends to] the great England whose far-strewn

empire feels its mystical unity in every latitude and longitude on the globe. It has its sublimity, that emotion, and its reason, though we ourselves cannot share it; and it is only in asking ourselves why a man of any nation, any race, should so glory in its greatness of even its goodness, when he has the greatness, the goodness, of all of humanity to glory in, that we are sensible of limitations of this outborn Englishman."[30]

Here Kipling seems misguided to Americans, who according to Howells can't thrill to the English version of patriotism at the expense of a cosmopolitan love for humanity. In contrast, two years later, Howells writes about Kipling in America in entirely different terms. It is, he writes,

a prodigious thing to utter one's age, or one's day, as Mr. Kipling has uttered his, to sound the dominant of its scale so that it shall be felt in the nerves vibrating to the limits of our race, which is our world. The prodigy is none the less because this dominant is the note of race-patriotism, which is so much less pleasing to some fine ears than "the still, sad music of humanity." It is a mighty and a lusty note, full of faith and hope; and it is the note which makes Mr. Kipling famous wherever an Anglo-Saxon shot is fired; it stirs the blood both of Briton and American.[31]

Here Kipling appeals to all of "our race," which is "our world," a construction that could refer to either the human race or the world-spanning empire of the Anglo-Saxon race. Subsequent sentences affirm the latter interpretation: Howells characterizes Britons and Americans as Anglo-Saxons whose "blood" responds together to Kipling's race-patriotism. The cosmopolitan love of humanity that Howells previously felt motivated U.S. patriotism is now attributed only to "some fine ears," a reference to the marginalized place that Howells felt anti-imperialists like himself held in the United States. "Our world" changes, sadly in Howells's view, from all of humanity to the worldwide imperial territories marked by Anglo-Saxon bullets.

It was not unusual for commentators of the day to consider Anglo-Saxonism and transatlantic identification as the key conditions for Kipling's success. In 1900, W. J. Peddicord self-published a pamphlet describing this reciprocity between culture and politics: "[Kipling's popularity in the United States] will be found by future writers of literary history to coincide exactly with the period in which England and America were vieing [sic] with each other to bring about a strong Anglo-Saxon alliance . . . that promised to array England and America together against the Latin races and certain branches of the Teutonic race as least."[32] Rather than merely fulfilling Peddicord's prophecy about future writers of literary history, I want to understand the rise of Anglo-Saxonism as a conflicted process, one in which Kipling's poem provided an important site for rhetorical struggle and, ultimately, a watershed precipitating the decline of racial discourses of empire in the United States. My argument is neither that Kipling was popular because of Anglo-Saxonism nor that Anglo-Saxonism was reinforced by Kipling's poem, although both positions were held by commentators during this era, and both seem accurate upon first examining readers' responses to the poem. Instead, my argument hinges on recognizing that Anglo-Saxonism, built on a confused jumble of race, nation, and language, was not a static set of beliefs but an embattled and shifting strand of identification in this era's fundamental contests over defining whiteness, linking race and civilization, and narrating U.S. empire. Kipling's poem provided one highly visible argument that became, through interpretation, a window onto its contradictions. An examination of responses to the poem as a political argument reveals its influence not in political debates about whether or not the United States should seek a foreign empire but in intensifying a cultural confusion about the racial characterization of such a mission.

Parody, Irony, and the Misreading of Poetry

I'll return to reader's responses to the poem's construction of whiteness and Anglo-Saxonism below, but first I want to survey the surprising degree of interpretive confusion prompted by this seemingly simple poem. For a number of readers, parodying the poem to create an anti-imperialist response was unnecessary because the poem itself was an ironic indictment of empire. These were the "intelligent" readers that T. F. H. described in his letter to Chappy—the readers who contended the poem was about "the ills of our present social system." Perhaps the most prominent and immediate example of a reader taking this stance was South Carolina Senator "Pitchfork" Ben Tillman, who gave his interpretation of the poem on the floor of Congress on February 7, 1899, the day after Congress ratified U.S. control over the Philippines and two days after the poem appeared in U.S. publications. In a futile attempt to convince fellow senators to pass a resolution giving up control over the Philippines, Tillman read several stanzas of the poem, noting that its publication before the vote was "at the most opportune time possible," offering a "prophecy" of "our danger and our duty." After the first stanza, Tillman paused to remind his listeners why he and most other Southern senators voted against the treaty: "It was not because we are Democrats, but because we understand and realize what it is to have two races side by side that cannot mix without deterioration and injury to both and the ultimate destruction of the civilization of the higher. We of the South have borne this white man's burden of a colored race in our midst since their emancipation and before."[33] This experience, he argued, should teach white men not to seek out more racial responsibility but to recognize its danger.

For Tillman, one of many Southern Democrats who objected to U.S. empire on the grounds that annexing the Philippines would compound the nation's race problem, the poem is a warning in the form of an ironically illogical argument for an impossible and undesirable task.[34] Reading the poem's fourth stanza on toiling to build ports and roads only to "Go make them with your living, and mark them with your dead" (31–32), the senator warned that "if we go madly in the direction of crushing the Philippines into subjection and submission we will do so at the cost of many, many thousands of the flower of American youth." And, he noted, reading the fifth stanza, the poem reveals not only the fatal price paid by the soldiers of an imperialist nation but also their sacrifice's futility:

> Take up the White Man's burden—
>   And reap his old reward:
> The blame of those ye better,
>   The hate of those ye guard—
> The cry of hosts ye humor
>   (Ah, slowly!) towards the light:—
> "Why brought ye us from bondage,
>   Our loved Egyptian night?" (33–40)

Here Tillman finds support for his idea that Filipinos, like other non-whites, are "not suited to our institutions. They are not ready for liberty as we understand it. They do not want it. Why are we bent on forcing upon them a civilization not suited to them and which only means in their view degradation and a loss of self-respect, which is worse than the loss of life itself?"[35]

That a poem was read on the Senate floor is an interesting moment for cultural criticism, but is it even more interesting that a poem was misread on the Senate floor? Or can we even call this a misreading, if, as I have argued, the poem itself contains ambiguities that provoke this response? Contemporary Kipling scholars seem to have few disagreements about the poem's meaning, but it is not hard to find readers who do. Present the poem to a group of clever undergraduates who know little of Kipling and ask them to make sense of it: often one or two will convince the others that the poem is ironic, that it recommends all that is unpleasant about imperialism to dissuade readers from imperial ventures.[36] This experiment might seem to only demonstrate what teachers of literature already know: that unskilled readers struggle with grasping tone and like to extrapolate meaning from individual passages instead of reading an entire poem. But if one is interested in how a poem enters into a culture, surely one must consider interpretations by unskilled readers. What is more, it was not only unskilled readers who found irony in "The White Man's Burden." William Dean Howells said of Kipling's poem that, although it was "the most significant recent utterance of a literary man," "it has been taken rather differently from what was intended. To me it seems a note of warning. The idea that it is our destiny to assume the tremendous responsibility of governing several million savages, many thousand miles away, is not at all clear."[37] For Howells, Kipling's poetic account of empire was more insightful than its American readers were: the poem's real meaning "may not be plain to American senses, till we have trampled into the red mire of tropic morasses the faith in men which made us the hope of men."[38] As an editor for the *San Francisco Bulletin* similarly remarked, the poem's "blending of satire and irony . . . creates some doubts as to the spirit or purpose of the song."[39]

What we have here then is a fascinating moment when readers skilled and unskilled disagree or are unsure about tone and intention, an uncertainty that I would argue comes both from what is ambiguous in Kipling's poem itself—the synchronic meaning and diachronic stability of whiteness—and from the poem's entry into a context of national debate about imperialism marked by tensions that cast new lights on the poem. Of course, we must not overlook the possibility that any of these interpretations of Kipling could be themselves insincere rhetorical devices, as in the Kansas columnist's apparently glib statement that the poem advises Filipinos to die of dyspepsia and go to hell like the white man. One wonders if Tillman was really blind to the poem's other, and arguably more overt, pro-imperialist meaning: Did he really not realize that his interpretation of the poem ran against certain of the poem's lines or against authorial intention? It may be that the blustering South Carolinian was shrewdly appropriating the poem's ambiguity in order to demonstrate what seemed to him a source of incoherence in American racial attitudes, particularly around the question of whether racial uplift was possible or desirable at all. Demonstrating that even a poem by an ostensibly pro-imperialist British writer reveals the danger of empire could have been a theatrical tactic for Tillman to claim rhetorical advantage. Here, poetic ambiguity becomes a tool for a rhetorical attack on the coherence of imperialism itself.

In light of these considerations, I am proposing a view of Tillman's interpretation as a form of neither willful nor unintended misreading, but as an interpretive act that "shadows" the white man's burden as a paradigmatic story of racial world mission. This shadowing exacerbates the contradictory political and cultural tensions in the poem's language and in its subject. Readers such as Tillman, by exploiting or demonstrating poetry's openness of meaning, intentionally or unintentionally expressed the internal dissonance of American racial formations and U.S. narratives of racial progress.

In this way, my primary concern exceeds the question of whether Kipling's poem in fact promoted U.S. empire. That question is interestingly addressed by historian Eric T. Love, whose recent work *Race over Empire: Race and Imperialism, 1865–1900* challenges the assumption that the rhetoric of racism played a major role in the arguments made by imperialists at the turn of the twentieth century. According to Love, historians have given certain late-nineteenth-century racial ideologies too much of the credit for advancing empire, when, in fact, racial formulations like "The White Man's Burden" were too potentially divisive to be of much use in directing U.S. foreign policy and thus were put forward in arguments for expansion less often than we have assumed. Love argues that this historical error comes from assuming that the movement for empire abroad was inspired by, consistent with, and modeled after the domestic racial social order of the Southern United States: historians have too hastily concluded that "since the fierce resurgence of political and economic disenfranchisement and lynching based on race coincided with the United States extending its dominion over millions of people of color, the two must be connected—connected specifically in such a way that the former advanced the latter."[40] He argues that the reverse: that the former tended to operate as a counterweight or complication for the latter. In other words, the principal goal of the era's racial social order was the exclusion of all "nonwhite" racial and ethnic groups from equal participation in America's social and political mainstream, and this goal rested uneasily with talk of racial mission in the Philippines or Puerto Rico or Hawaii. For Love, the fact that it was an anti-imperialist and radical racist like Tillman who read Kipling's poem in front of Congress, instead of one of the Republican jingoes, would make perfect sense: the poem itself brings up racial ideologies that uncomfortably contrasted with the drives toward segregation and exclusion dominating domestic politics in this era.

On this point, my research on Kipling's reception inside and outside of policy circles supports Love's conclusion: while Kipling's poem was frequently cited in support of controlling the Philippines, even more common were responses that were critical of the poem or merely confused by it, and how the poem intersected with internal problems of racial heterogeneity was a major source of resistance and confusion. But beyond this point I disagree with Love, who moves from this argument to the assertion that therefore Kipling's poem specifically had *no* role in shaping U.S. foreign policy or diplomatic history. Part of Love's argument here is about historical method: he criticizes historians for placing weight on cultural sources such as poems and drifting too far from analysis of traditional sources like congressional debate, senate votes, and political correspondence—sources that he asserts exhibit the more direct causal relations between ideas and actions. Kipling's poem may have been discussed in the popular press, but, according to Love, it could not have influenced U.S. policy for two reasons: first, its time of publication in the February issue of *McClure's Magazine* was "after, not before, the U.S. seized its empire"; second, the poem's "churning irony and cynicism" was "hardly an appeal to the glories of empire."[41]

Here Love plainly oversimplifies both literary meaning and the question of causality in cultural history. His first point, about the poem's date of publication, would be slightly weakened if he noted Roosevelt's and Lodge's documented readings of the advance copy of the poem or the fact that, before its appearance in *McClure's Magazine,* the poem was printed in some of McClure's syndicate newspapers (including the *New York Sun*) on February 5, 1899—the day *before* the Senate voted by a narrow margin to ratify the treaty that stipulated that the U.S. government would take over the administration of the Philippines.[42] Although I agree with Love that the poem's influence on that particular vote is doubtful, his chronological error suggests a lack of interest in the very possibility of literary influence, a lack of interest also evident in the interpretive methods that he uses to back his second point. What evidence would show that a poem was too ironic and cynical to influence political thought or to be useful in persuasive rhetoric? Love offers only his reading of the poem in support of this statement. Doing so enacts a version of what he recommends against by prioritizing close reading over historical evidence, relying on a meaning drawn from formalist interpretive methods rather than more fully exploring the poem's reception in the interconnected worlds of public discourse and political action.[43]

If we take reception into consideration, we must accept that a sensitive reading that finds irony in Kipling's poem hardly disqualifies it as an important agent in debates about the status of race in imperial expansion in the Pacific. Poetic qualities ranging from easily parodied meter to irony and a perceived openness of meaning seem to have made "The White Man's Burden" all the more useful as a referent in imperialist debates, as a flexible rhetorical tool in supporting or questioning U.S. empire. Furthermore, analysis of reception suggests that, as a result of this widespread use, what was ambiguous and troubling about the poem's described racial mission exacerbated contradictions in racial ideologies themselves. For many readers, Kipling's words communicated a haunting mixed message that problematized rather than heralded the notion of whiteness as the primary motor of national progress and global civilization. Thus the poem became a continual referent in expressions that reveal the incoherence of racial narratives of human progress. In other words, if we do not learn why the United States took possession of the Philippines by reading Kipling in America, we do learn how and why the poem channeled and helped to articulate doubts about race as an explanation of imperial mission. In the remainder of this chapter, I'll do what Love neglects: explore exactly how "The White Man's Burden" exacerbated rather than abated doubt about racial identity and global mission. To understand this process, one must understand which "ills of our present social system" the poem was perceived by some readers to identify.

Weak Spots and Social Ills

Some readers who criticized the poem rejected its vision of racial maturity in favor of the era's powerful scientific discourses of racial difference and evolution. As mentioned earlier, the logic of "The White Man's Burden" begins to break down if it is, "as it should be," that some learn to sanitate and others die from dirty drinking water. When the poem entered into a culture humming with social Darwinism, the poem's vision of manly self-sacrifice was tested according to these terms. For example, the editor of the *San Francisco Bulletin* uses biological language of blood and racial degeneration to explain:

> When Mr. Kipling calls upon the white man to "send forth the best ye breed," he raises the question of whether "serving your captives' need" is compensation for the best blood of a nation. . . . Experience shows that the inferior races cannot be lifted out of their level. . . . The "best ye breed," if doomed to exile, will not reproduce themselves. The poison of the tropical climate will infuse itself in their blood.[44]

In short, how can it be that manly sacrifice earns racial maturity if at the same time it prevents the survival and procreation of the fittest members of the species? As a writer in the *New England Magazine* reasoned: "Suppose we kill off the fastest and best young horses in this country for series of years; how long a time will have passed before there will be a sensible degeneration of the horses of this land?. . . . Let us face the fact that 'sending forth the best we breed' to 'serve the new caught, sullen peoples' by fighting 'the savage wars of peace' in the tropics means and always must mean just this."[45]

Stanford president and biologist David Starr Jordan developed the most evidenced version of this evolutionist interpretation, arguing that "the real force of [Kipling's] verse is that there is no easy way to success" without racial decay and degeneration, resulting both from the death of the strongest members of the species in battle and the "personal degeneration" of those weaker U.S. soldiers who tend to vice and dissipation in the disease-, saloon-, and prostitute-ridden tropical climate. Like Tillman, Jordan views these scientifically "proven" facts as lessons that white Americans should have already learned from their contact with other races at home:

> Every alien race within our borders to-day is an element of danger. When the Anglo-Saxon meets the Negro, the Chinaman, the Indian, the Mexican as fellow citizens, equal before the law, we have a raw wound in our political organism. Democracy demands likeness of aims and purposes among its units. Each citizen must hold his own freedom in a republic. If men cannot hold their rights through our methods, our machinery runs over them. The Anglo-Saxon will not mix with the lower races. Neither

will he respect their rights if they are not strong enough to maintain them for themselves. If they can do this they cease to be lower races.[46]

For Jordan, subjugation and segregation of nonwhite Americans at home should be a clear sign that the Anglo-Saxon is unsuited to train any "inferior" race in the lessons of democracy, whether or not that race is capable of learning those lessons. Here social Darwinism and a theory of democracy based on racial homogeneity combine to contradict Kipling's moral argument for imperial mission. Like Tillman, Jordan sees the poem's pessimism about reforming the savage as a reflection on racial tensions at home—on the "ills of our present social system" in which democracy founders on racial heterogeneity and uneven evolutionary capability.

Thus, while the introduction to part I showed how satirists demonstrated the poem's hypocrisy by pointing out the false inversion in Kipling's binary treatment of black beneficiaries and white servants, Tillman, Jordan, and others argued against the poem's narrative of empire by complicating the binary itself. Instead of showing that it would be the Philippines rather than the United States that carries the burden, these writers call attention to the fact that the "United States" is not reducible simply to the "white man" but, rather, already is comprised of a dangerous amount of racial difference and conflict. This idea is also raised in Kipling's sense that Americans could become whiter, more racially evolved, and more manly by taking up the White Man's burden, a treatment of whiteness as something that could be lost or won, justified or compromised. In the era's ethnological sciences, this possibility correlates with a racial identity that is precarious and unstable because it is contingent on environment and breeding to prevent ever-threatening racial degeneracy. In this view, whiteness itself is always at risk of steering into its other.

Another method for casting doubt on the identity of the United States as white in responses to the poem was to call attention to the mere presence of nonwhites within the United States. Calling attention to such divisions brought to mind unresolved problems at home, such as displacing and battling American Indians and disenfranchising and lynching African Americans. A number of responses to Kipling written by whites and African Americans tried variations on this theme, challenging—or at least deferring and complicating—the notion of U.S. empire by calling attention to "burdens" or failures of civilization closer to home. An anonymous parody in *Harper's Weekly* asked white readers to

> Lift loads that lie beside you—
>   Try first your strength on these.
> Then seek the greater burdens
>   Beyond the western seas.[47]

Anna Manning Comfort's "Home Burdens of Uncle Sam" urged reader to take up the white man's burden, but

> Why seek other countries
>   Your burdens to renew?
> Great questions here confront you
>   Then too we have a past—
> Don't pose as a reformer!
>   Why, nations look aghast!"[48]

Alice Smith-Travers's parody, appearing in an African American publication, invited white readers to take up the burden of Southern lynching:

> Take up the white man's burden!
>   That causes the heart to quake
> As we read again with horror,
>   Of those burnings at the stake,
> Of white caps riding in the night
>   And burning black man's homes.

Recognizing these wrongs calls into question the supposedly civilized status of whites, because found in the South are

> Crimes that would outnumber
>   Those in the foreign isle,
> Committed by heathen people
>   "Half devil and half child."[49]

This point about the problem of heterogeneous histories and multiracial U.S. identities is made visually in an 1899 satirical political cartoon by Louis Dalrymple, which uses the trope of education to portray the relationship between the United States and its colonies (figure 3). Uncle Sam appears as a stern schoolmaster brandishing a stick at the students in the front row of his class, all racialized caricatures of the Philippines, Hawaii,

Puerto Rico, and Cuba. Behind this first row sits a group of well-behaved and mostly white children holding books labeled with the names of the states and territories (Alaska appears as a darker-skinned native, and California wears hair and earrings in a stylized Spanish mode). The caption has Uncle Sam speaking to his "new class on civilization": "Now children, you've got to learn these lessons whether you want to or not, but just take a look at the class ahead of you, and remember that, in a little while, you will feel as glad at heart as they are!" Whether these older children in the back rows feel glad (rather than merely docile and resigned) about their status as states and territories is unknown, as they are all absorbed in their books with eyes downcast, but the lessons written on chalkboards around the room suggest the latter. One says, "The consent of the governed is a good thing in theory, but very rare in fact," and others give examples of the many exceptions to the theory, including the South not giving its consent to be governed at the end of the Civil War and England governing its colonies without their consent. The value of the lessons is undercut further by a number of caricatured figures who appear on the fringes of the classroom: an American Indian sits in the back, huddled under a blanket with an upside-down primer in his hands, a Chinese boy stands outside the door, book under his arm, as though contemplating or wishing his entrance into the schoolhouse, and an African American boy looks over his shoulder at the class while washing the schoolroom windows. The cartoon satirically reminds readers of the exceptions to democratic theory and the theory's frequent clash with goals of "civilization," especially in its treatment of Native Americans, Chinese immigrants, and African Americans as domestic presences who are governed without the promise of joining the class as equal members.[50]

Beyond this explicit critique, however, a paradox of representation haunts this cartoon: a white, male Uncle Sam signifies the United States, but the United States as a figurative space—the schoolhouse—is inhabited by a number of darker races with differing claims to membership. How can the imaginary persona of the United States be white when the schoolroom is so racially diverse? Or, in other words, how can the United States, a nation-state consisting of a heterogeneous group of races, take up the White Man's burden when race and nation are not reducible to one another? In this cartoon, only the white male Uncle Sam engages in the task of civilizing nonwhite territories, but the contrasting message of racial heterogeneity within the "United States as classroom" is clearly suggested by the nonwhite figures in various states of marginalization and

Figure 3. "School Begins" by Louis Dalrymple, *Puck* (January 25, 1899), 8–9.

inclusion. Taken to its logical conclusion—something this cartoon stops well short of—one might ask what justifies representing Uncle Sam as a white man at all.

Some responses to Kipling's poem ask exactly this. While one form of satire raised the troubling idea that the United States was attempting to spread civilization and democracy abroad while such things were still lacking at home, just as problematic to racial justifications of empire would be the notion that African Americans, Asian Americans, and Native Americans were equal partners in *teaching* the lessons of empire. The latter notion is a haunting contradiction left unstated in Dalrymple's cartoon, but it was made more explicit in texts that portray the African American soldier helping to carry the white man's burden in the Spanish American and Filipino American Wars. As Susan Gillman has noted, "the figure of the black soldier became a flashpoint for both blacks and whites" during the Spanish American and Filipino American Wars.[51] Its force came not only from its suggestion of an armed, powerful, and disciplined black male but also from its inconsistency with visions of white military power as the metonym and medium of a racial civilizing mission. If the soldier is the figure who carries out the work represented by "Uncle

Sam" in the political cartoon, a black soldier begins to shadow an imperialist imaginary that identifies civilization with whiteness.

Peter MacQueen harnessed this destabilizing force to conclude an 1899 essay in the *Arena* questioning the ability of the United States to win the bloody and morally uncertain fight against the Filipinos. Describing his own visit to the Philippines, MacQueen tells the story of conversing with members of the first colored regiment to land in Manila: "One young man told me of his firm determination not to kill or wound any Filipinos that he could help. He said: 'Dese shyar folks is jes' der same as our kullud folks was befo' de war. I doan believe in fightin' dese poor critters.'" The conversation ends when the soldier is called to fall in, and MacQueen describes the colored soldier lifting his heavy knapsack and remarking to a comrade, "Dis shyar white man's burden ain't all its cracked up to be."[52] MacQueen makes no comment on the anecdote, which concludes his essay, leaving the reader to ponder the problems it suggests. By linking Filipinos and African Americans before the Civil War as groups wrongly oppressed, the anecdote reminds the reader of failures to live up to democratic ideals at home. More subtly, by reminding readers that this comic, dialect-speaking representation of a colored soldier skeptically shares the White Man's burden, the anecdote de-romanticizes any sense of imperial mission resting on simple but emotionally charged ideas of racial progress.

For African Americans themselves, the title of Willard Gatewood's classic 1975 history of these soldiers, *Black Americans and the White Man's Burden,* clearly identifies the paradox they experienced participating in a war that was narrated and perceived as an example of a white civilizing mission.[53] Poetry celebrating African American soldiers was common during the Spanish American War (both James Weldon Johnson and Paul Lawrence Dunbar wrote poems on the subject), and references to these soldiers appear frequently in parodies of Kipling. These poems implicitly or implicitly ask what sense the notion of a white man's burden makes if it is partly carried out by African American soldiers. This is the question posed by Bruce Grit in the *Colored American* newspaper in February 1899:

> Why talk of the white man's burden;
>   What burdens hath he borne
> That have not been shared by the black man
>   From the day creation dawned?[54]

Rather than questioning the morality of empire and expansionism themselves, such works celebrate the victory against the Spanish as an endeavor jointly achieved by whites and blacks. Yet in doing so, these verses problematize any narrative of imperial progress based on whiteness and race and pry apart the assumed link between race and civilization that formed some part of the emotional motivation for empire building. An imperial burden may be valorous and necessary, these poems acknowledge, but its relationship to whiteness is exaggerated at best.

We see some of the effects of this sort of parody in the case of the popular humorist Peter Finley Dunne, who commented on the reception of Kipling's poem through his canny Irish American character, Mr. Dooley. In a piece called "The Decline of National Feeling," Mr. Dooley and his interlocutor Mr. Hennessy discuss the rise of pro-British (and the decline of pro-Irish) sentiment in the United States after the Spanish American War. Dooley marvels that even Henry Cabot Lodge, previously a staunch Anglophobe, has "changed his chune, an' 'tis 'Strangers wanst, but brothers now,' with him, an' 'Hands across th' sea an' into some wan's pocket,' an 'Take up the white man's burden an' hand it to the coons.'"[55] Dooley's revision of the notion of a White Man's burden especially caught the attention of Theodore Roosevelt, who wrote a note to Dunne explaining his reaction: "As you know, I am an expansionist, but your delicious phrase about 'take up the white man's burden and put it on the coons' exactly hit off the weak spot in my own theory; though, mind you, I am by no means willing to give up the theory yet."[56]

What was the weak spot that this parody so precisely struck? Dunne's formulation could be another example of satirizing the poem by pointing out its self-serving inversion of white beneficiaries and nonwhite sufferers. In this reading, the "coons" are Filipinos, who were often identified by racial slurs like "nigger" during the conflict. That Roosevelt changed the verb phrasing from "hand it to" to "put it on" might emphasize the perceived problem that the Filipinos would be saddled with a new burden under U.S. control. But this interpretation seems unlikely, considering Roosevelt's faith in expansionism: here he would be admitting the rather large "weak spot" of Filipino oppression as the result of the white man's burden. Another interpretation seems more likely: that the "coons" are the African American soldiers who fought against the Filipinos. Here the "weak spot" identified in expansionist theory is not that Filipinos rather than Americans will bear the burden of war but that racial theories of progress defining the role of the white man are undercut when African

Americans represent and carry out the civilizing mission. The white man's burden is shadowed here not by challenging the mission itself but by challenging the racial logic underlying the mission that confuses race and nation. When the burden of civilizing Filipinos is "put on" African Americans as agents of progress, the phenomenon of civilization must be theorized as separable from race.

Roosevelt's interest in the relationship between race, citizenship, and nation in addresses such as "True Americanism" and his notorious representation of loyal but submissive African American soldiers fighting in Cuba in *The Rough Riders* adds weight to this latter interpretation, as does a reading of Dunne's entire "Mr. Dooley" article, which goes on to satirize the newly claimed familial bond between England and the United States by pointing out the political opportunism of such racial realignments.[57] That Roosevelt himself, the first recipient of Kipling's poem and apparently one of its sympathetic readers, felt the force of its parodists' and critics' examination of whiteness suggests the success of these critical responses in using the poem to cast doubt on the idea of a white U.S. imperial mission.

A less widely read jab at this same "weak spot" in racial narratives of empire came from J. D. O'Connell in the *New York Irish World and American Industrial Liberator,* who points to African American soldiers taking up the white man's burden in order to question both the "Anglo-Saxon humbug" and invented ideas of race justifying expansion. Responding to the unconvincing defense that Anglo-Saxonism in America refers to a shared language or colonial history, not a shared race, O'Connell pointedly asks, "How do you class our colored brethren? They speak the English language; therefore, are they also Anglo-Saxons? If so, must the black Anglo-Saxon also 'take up the white man's burden?' And what would be the sense of making any distinction of color in respect to the 'burden'?"[58] Far more explicitly than the schoolroom cartoon, Mr. Dooley's satire and J. D. O'Connell's criticisms challenge the illogical but rhetorically powerful assumption that the United States can represent or champion the racial progress of a group unified under the name of *either* Anglo-Saxon or white.

If Anglo-Saxonism was on the rise in the United States at this time, it was also a deeply contested and confusing notion of cultural identity. As these Irish American responses suggest, Anglo-Saxonism often clashed with the process of redrawing lines of racial inclusion and exclusion inside the United States to produce a monolithic sense of "Caucasian" European whiteness.[59] These tensions between Anglo-Saxonism and Caucasian whiteness were another form of racial controversy for which Kipling's poem provided a vehicle and highly visible referent. Deciding which Europeans inside or outside the United States could share in the white man's burden required a judgment about the meaning of whiteness, either as Kipling intended it or as it existed in the minds of readers as a fact of life. Either way, Kipling's poem offered readers an opportunity to claim for themselves the imaginary content of whiteness.

A reviewer in *The Living Age* flatly explains: Kipling "bids America 'take up the white man's burden'; but it must be well understood that only Britain and America and our colonial kinsman are appointed for this labor. We are the chosen people; let strange nations beware how they interfere with our mission."[60] These "strange nations" were competing European powers unfit for a specifically Anglo-Saxon imperial project.[61] Yet not all of the poem's readers agreed that "white" meant "Anglo-Saxon." When another political commentator cited the poem in the *North American Review* to comment on colonialism in the Pacific, he stressed a broader meaning for whiteness: "The white man's burden in Samoa rests as heavily upon German shoulders as upon those of England and America."[62]

The very existence of such contradictory arguments and discrepancies had the potential to highlight what was illogical and absurd about stories of racial affiliation and mission, producing an uneasy sense of the fluidity of race and its non-equivalence with national identity. Kipling's poem was not only an important rhetorical tool for interrogating linkages between race, nation, and empire; it was also more specifically a highly visible referent and vehicle for the demise of Anglo-Saxonism. Historian Stuart Anderson has argued that Anglo-Saxonism met its demise shortly after its peak at the turn of the twentieth century largely because its absurdities became too illogical to bear. As Anderson writes, Britons and Americans could not

> hide themselves forever from the unpleasant fact that no such thing as "the Anglo-Saxon" race had ever existed. The British people, like all the other peoples of Europe, were descended from a multitude of tribes and nations: not Angles and Saxons only, but Scots, Welshmen, Irishmen, Danes, Normans, Flemings, Walloons, French Huguenots and others. And if the ancestry of the British was complex, how much more complex was the ethnic heritage of the United States? Of course it was absurd to speak of the British and Americans as comprising a distinct racial group.[63]

But how at one point in time does a popular theory and discourse begin to seem illogical and absurd? My speculative answer is that this comes about partly as a result of satire, parody, and criticism in public debate, and my effort in this chapter is to show the importance of Kipling's poem as a highly visible referent that writers used in creating these forms. What better way to point out a commonplace absurdity than by referencing the poem on everyone's lips? Paul A. Kramer argues that one factor precipitating this decline of Anglo-Saxonism was the "de-Saxonization of colonialism in the Philippines" through the undeniable colonial participation of European immigrants and Filipinos themselves as soldiers, entrepreneurs, or colonial officials under U.S. administration in the Philippines.[64] Even more troubling was the participation of African American soldiers. Responses to Kipling's poem, by harping again and again on the problem of racial heterogeneity in the United States, enacted this de-Saxonization by parody and criticism of the culture's most visible colonial referent.

What "The White Man's Burden" provides in all of these responses is a conduit for conversations already taking place in the United States about the racial character that supposedly motivates or identifies the nation as a world power. But by making the linkage of whiteness and U.S. empire tangible and visible, and by providing a sufficiently vague referent for that linkage, the poem also pressures such concepts. Declaring whiteness vaguely as both an explanation and a goal of the civilizing mission, Kipling's poem invited reflection on the racial construct's definition and status, attention that highlighted its strains and contradictions. Intentionally or unintentionally, writers with a variety of agendas—racist and antiracist, imperialist and anti-imperialist—exposed this fragility in their responses to and adaptations of "The White Man's Burden," precipitating the decline of racial identity, whether Anglo-Saxon or white, as the theoretical motor of U.S. foreign policy. Discussion of Kipling's poem provided a major site for revealing the inconsistencies that riddled competing racial narratives for describing U.S. foreign policy, and, as such, that very visible and widespread discussion exposed the seams of those racial narratives. If this is correct, Kipling's poem not only generated or rode the wave of Anglo-Saxonism and racial theories of empire, it also began to still the waters.

For histories of whiteness in the United States, my argument emphasizes the way that racialization in the United States took on new meanings in the discourse surrounding imperial expansion. Empire was not, for example, merely a discursive occasion for enacting the assimilation of Irish Americans into a homogeneous category of whiteness opposed to "nonwhite" Filipinos and African Americans. Rather, it was a discursive occasion for claiming the content of whiteness, according to contradictory standards and definitions. As a famous and ambiguous formulation of a racial narrative of empire, Kipling's poem became a medium for interpreting whiteness domestically and internationally—as the colloquial expression of a supposed Anglo-Saxon kinship with Great Britain, as the fragile product of new theories of evolution and racial degeneration, or as a prerequisite for democratic self-government inside and outside the United States. Rather than geographic extensions of familiar racial prejudices and identities, racial narratives of empire evoked and tested conflicting formulations of U.S. whiteness.

My argument claims the importance of literature and literary interpretation in this historical process. I offer evidence that a discursive object like a poem, because of its particular formal qualities and cultural associations, could occasion cultural debates channeling the skepticism that drove the decline of Anglo-Saxonism's diplomatic and nationalist appeal. This poem's impact has been long overlooked, not only because historians and literary critics have tended to perceive it as obvious and explicit in its racism and imperialism but also because the interpretation of a British poem in the United States seemed like a less-pressing topic before the transnational turn in literary studies. Reading the transatlantic crossing of Kipling in America reveals some of the era's efforts and failures at using race to narrate global relations and conflicts, and it spotlights a literary work that made a remarkable stir in U.S. culture. Freely adapting Kipling seemed witty and profitable at this time, as we see from the many insurance, overcoat, and soap companies that borrowed slogans from the poem (e.g., "Insurance takes up the white man's burden. . . . If he isn't insured, he isn't white).[65] But beyond catchy verse, Kipling's poem called to mind discrepancies in racial narratives of empire and the tenuousness of whiteness as empire's justification and goal. As familiar and recognizable verse, the poem became a powerful conduit for channeling and broadcasting those discrepancies.

2

The White Man's Burden or the Leopard's Spots?

Dixon's Political Conundrum

Thomas Dixon's first novel, *The Leopard's Spots: A Romance of the White Man's Burden—1865–1900*, surprised publishers by becoming an instant success. Published late in 1901, it topped *Bookman's* monthly bestseller lists for over a year, leading to a rapid depletion of its first printing of fifteen thousand copies.[1] Reprinted every year for the next half decade, Dixon's first novel was followed by two more top-selling sequels. In its day, *The Leopard's Spots* was thus one of the most widely read responses to Kipling's poem in the United States. A current approach to interpreting Dixon's novel is to look for and describe gaps, contradictions, and instabilities in Dixon's definition of whiteness. Scott Romine calls this "a dominant pattern in recent criticism of Dixon's work that seeks to expose or deconstruct his contradictory, illogical, and fragile construction of whiteness."[2] This trend in Dixon criticism resembles my approach to Kipling, although Dixon's critics tend to rely on close reading alone rather than reception to make their case. For example, Sandra Gunning convincingly argues that *The Leopard's Spots* expresses "a profound anxiety over the maintenance of a stable white identity" and registers "both the complexity and internal contradictions of radical white supremacist thought."[3] For Gunning, this anxiety comes from Dixon's suppressed knowledge that whites possess the very traits that they have projected onto the black other: the text depicts examples of white male savagery and sexual violence even while it attempts to systemize a racial hierarchy assigning these traits only to inferior blacks.

Kim Magowan similarly claims that "in spite of himself, Dixon unravels the very notion of difference upon which his white supremacy is so crucially based. Racist ideology is predicated upon a notion of fixed, stable identity. In Dixon, the white man's identity, as white, as male, and this as superior, breaks down."[4] Susan Gillman goes further to speculate that Dixon's failure to maintain in his novel a unified category of whiteness in contradistinction to blackness was an inevitable feature of late-nine-teenth-century racial discourse. According to Gillman, the novel functions like other popular racial rhetorics, including Anglo-Saxonism and Kipling's influential notion of a white man's burden. Such "central tropes and figures of American racial-national discourse" attempt to systematize difference into clear binaries and oppositions, but in operation they only "reveal the many fissures, shifting alignments, and cross- and countercurrents that form the polarized racial realities of the turn of the century."[5]

Refining Gillman's argument, I see "the white man's burden" not as one more unstable trope that Dixon couldn't control but as a central grounding concept that Dixon aimed to reconcile with and anchor a network of other racial and nationalist ideas. In addition to trying to shore up the porous racial categories of whiteness in a culture that was beside itself with contradictory definitions and usages for that concept, Dixon also sought to adapt for his own purposes Kipling's powerful linkage between unchangeable racial hierarchy and heroic civilizing mission. In this linkage Dixon saw a chance to revise the political landscape and challenge what was for him a troubling opposition in U.S. party politics—the perceived opposition between, on the one hand, the Republicans' idealistic global mission to spread civilization to the person sitting in darkness and, on the other, the Southern Democrats' Jim Crow policies of racial segregation and control.[6] While Harilaos Stecopoulos has argued that *The Leopard's Spots* is Dixon's attempt to convince Northerners that the experiences of the white South were "an important source of wisdom for white Americans eager to take up 'the white man's burden,'"[7] I argue that the novel also adapts the highly charged poem to appeal to white Southerners. In other words, Dixon's goal was nothing less than resolving the political opposition in rhetorics of U.S. imperialism between "the leopard's spots" and "the white man's burden."

As a consideration of rhetoric, this chapter focuses less on literary elements of the novel such as plot, characterization, and narrative and, instead, analyzes the racial arguments found in the sermons and speeches of Dixon's characters and of Dixon himself, placing them in relation to political and racial rhetoric of the day. To begin, I propose that to understand the political opposition between "the leopard's spots" and "the white man's burden," we must first identify the role of biblical allusions to "the leopard's spots," both in the novel and in these political debates over U.S. imperialism. The other half of Dixon's title, "The Leopard's Spots" seems on first analysis to be a statement of the novel's central argument. Dixon's title is an allusion to Jeremiah 13:23: "Can the Ethiopian change his skin, or the leopard his spots? Then may ye also do good, That are accustomed to doing evil." The leopard's spots, like the Ethiopian's color, are the signs of a visible difference that cannot be altered, analogous with invisible but unchanging moral character and custom.

Dixon's citation of this passage, like others in nineteenth-century U.S. racial politics, turned analogy into metonymy, so that unchanging skin pigmentation was no longer merely comparable with unchanging inferior character but, rather, another indicator of that inferiority. The implication is that so-called racial inferiors cannot be educated or civilized but must be controlled or excluded. The novel's romantic hero Charlie Gaston and his uncle the Reverend John Durham make this point quite explicitly, re-peatedly arguing in didactic (and often emphatically italicized) speeches that *"the future American must be either an Anglo-Saxon or a Mulatto."*[8] Dixon's Southern heroes struggle to convince Northern meddlers that Ne-gro education and uplift is more than a lost cause; it is a form of race sui-cide. As Durham tells one Northerner, "the Ethiopian cannot change his skin, nor the leopard his spots. . . . Your scheme of education is humbug. You don't believe that any amount of education can fit a Negro to rule an Anglo-Saxon, or to marry his daughter" (463–64). Domestic segrega-tion is the only answer for these men, because it preserves white racial purity from mixture and thus prevents the United States from becoming, in the words of one character, a "new 'Mulatto' nation" (81). Accordingly, at times the genocidal goal envisioned by Dixon's characters looks beyond total racial subjugation to the actual "elimination of the Negro from na-tional life" and from the North American continent (443).

As in Kipling's poem, Dixon's racial differences are insurmountable, but unlike Kipling, Dixon uses a hazy Darwinist theory to support this point. Anglo-Saxons are superior because of the "priceless heritage of two thousand years of struggle" (35), during which time they became "the proudest and strongest race of men evolved in two thousand years of human history" (98). African Americans cannot be uplifted to partici-pate in American economic, political, and social life because, in contrast, they are "but fifty years removed from the savagery of African jungles" (46) and thus hopelessly unable to catch up with the Anglo-Saxons. Yet this theory, intended to give scientific grounding to racist policies, also admits the *possibility* of future African evolution and white devolution: if natural selection controls evolution and races evolve over time, then, of course, the leopard *can*, over time, change its spots.[9] By appealing to social Darwinism, Dixon admits one of the most troubling implications of Darwin's ideas: the lack of an identifiable and fixed direction in evolutionary processes.

So can the leopard change its spots, or can't it? The phrase was usually invoked to suggest everlasting difference, and thus it appeared frequently in political discourse that opposed an imperialist program of benevolent assimilation. For example, we see Senator John Daniel, a Virginia Democrat, citing the biblical passage in his February 1899 address to Congress about the dangers of annexing the Philippines:

> Mr. President, there is one thing that neither time nor education can change. You may change the leopard's spots, but you will never change the different qualities of races which God has created in order that they may fulfill separate and distinct missions in the cultivation and civilization of this world. The Indian of one hundred and twenty-five years ago is the Indian of to-day—ameliorated, to a certain extent civilized, and yet the wisdom of our forefathers, when, in the Constitution, they set them apart as one people, separate and distinct from the great dominant race which had come to take this land and inhabit it, is indicated in what we are still doing and must forever do with them so long as they maintain their tribal relations and so long as they are Indians.[10]

In this circular argument, Daniel argues that the biblical impossibility of changing leopard's spots is more feasible than altering racial qualities, leaving "the great dominant race" to seek only the wisdom of racial separation and segregation, something that can be considered wise because it is ongoing. In this address to the Senate, Daniel reasons from Indian tribal relations to his primary topic, overseas expansion: he insists that a similar policy of segregation should be followed in the future by rejecting "benevolent assimilation" in the Philippines. While Kipling, whose poem was published a few days after Daniel's speech, represents such an impossible task as a source of romantic, manly maturity, Daniel joined other Southern Democrats like Senator "Pitchfork" Ben Tillman in advising the practical refusal of doomed imperial responsibilities. According to Daniel, annexing the Philippines was a huge mistake, similar to the one made when the first slave ship carried Africans to the New World: "The interjection of a race nonassimilable with the American people has been the fly in the ointment of American institutions, of American peace, of American history."[11] For Democratic spokesmen like Tillman and Daniel, domestic segregation forms an instructive metaphor for global segregation; they argue that what could not be prevented domestically should absolutely be prevented internationally.

For Dixon, however, the fixity of the leopard's spots should not prevent the white man's burden, and, accordingly, *The Leopard's Spots* represents segregation in the South as one crucial component of a worldwide mission to promote and protect civilization. Domestic segregation and the white man's duty to uplift other races, concepts that Tillman and Daniel placed in conflict with one another, achieve a precarious balance in Dixon's efforts to chart the relationship between color lines at home and abroad. The two parts of Dixon's title, held tenuously together by the colon, indicate a central purpose of the novel: to alert Americans to the peculiar place of African Americans in this mission. Instead of countering with optimism about the possibility of civilizing the Filipinos, Dixon employs Kipling to amplify the poem's pessimism about the fate of the colonized and the need to shore up and prove whiteness. His adaptation of Kipling thus countered both anti-imperial Democrats and those who would use Kipling's poem as a reminder of duties to uplift African Americans. For example, the editor of the *American Missionary* wrote in 1899 that U.S. Americans must shoulder the white man's burden at home and abroad: "The white man has a burden to bear. . . . It is the white man's duty to educate and elevate those whom he has in the past robbed of natural privileges."[12] Dixon, in contrast, invokes Kipling to argue that the white man's burden abroad is instead contingent on *not* carrying out this duty for African Americans at home.

Reconciling domestic racism and world mission was for Dixon an important goal because the tension between segregation and expansion that he balanced in his title and attempted to resolve in his narrative was one that politically separated him from his white supremacist allies during the Spanish American War. Consider a forum published in the *Arena* in January 1900 titled "The White Man's Problem." Featuring articles responding to this theme by Varina Davis and Charles Minor Blackford, among others, the forum reveals the strong tendency for Southern democrats like Davis and Blackford to describe administering the Philippines as another race problem compounding the one at home and to use Kipling's poem for support and rhetorical flourish on this point. Varina Davis, wife of the deceased confederate president, titled her piece "The White Man's Problem: Why We Do Not Want the Philippines" and offered as her reason the irremediable savagery of the Negro: "The question is, What are we going to do with these additional millions of Negroes? Civilize them?"[13] Charles Minor Blackford, a physician from Lynchburg, Virginia, raises similar doubts: "The United States has attempted to educate, according to our standards, the Indian and the negro; and it cannot be said that brilliant success has attended the efforts put forth. A system of mental training that may be eminently suited to an intelligence fitted to receive it by the heritage of generations of culture is not necessarily the best to apply to a barbarian 'half devil and half child.'"[14]

This was the skeptical view of Kipling and of the U.S. racial mission that Dixon contested in *The Leopard's Spots*. That Dixon instead celebrated an expansive, aggressive role for the United States as a colonizer and world power put him at odds with many in his party on the key issue of U.S. empire after the outbreak of the Spanish American War. Expansionism was Dixon's passion and mission in the years before he became a novelist, and his vision of the United States as a world power defined his career as a radical minister to the nondenominational New York People's Church in 1898–99. During these years his sermons followed the pattern of the Social Gospel movement and the influential imperialist Reverend Josiah Strong, combining theology and politics to outline a divinely ordained world mission.[15] Dixon gave his sermons secular titles such as "The Anglo-Saxon Alliance," "The Battle of Manila," and "The Mightiest Navy in the World," and he delivered them in a hall draped with Cuban and American flags.[16] He claimed that through these meetings, his People's Church turned the hall into a sort of revolutionary headquarters for the cause of liberating Cuba from Spain. Calling his congregation "our little revolutionary Junta," he proudly admitted that his work "prepared the minds of the people [for the war] in a wide propaganda."[17]

Despite this political fervor, departing from his party's anti-imperialist politics troubled Dixon's sense of loyalty. He tells in his autobiography about the times that he broke with the Democrats to vote for Theodore Roosevelt for governor of New York in 1898, and then again for vice president (along with McKinley for president) in the heated presidential race of 1900: "I broke with the faith of my fathers (I didn't let my father know about it). . . . I confess that when I saw the word 'Republican' in big black letters across the top of my ticket and remembered that its radical leaders had defeated the South to torture, I hesitated a moment. But I gritted my teeth and voted it."[18] Dixon's conflict at the ballot box between his expansionist leanings and his Democratic loyalty was one that he attempted to resolve in his novel. Charlie Gaston, Dixon's protagonist in *The Leopard's Spots,* shares his creator's frustration with the parochialism of the "old Fogies" of the Democratic Party (198), but he responds not by covertly voting Republican but by heroically rejuvenating the party with a new political faction aimed at awakening the Democrats and the nation to interconnected racial missions at home and abroad. We might say that at the ballot box Dixon faced an Oedipal conflict that he worked to resolve in the story of Charlie Gaston.

That Dixon's novel assumes this interconnection between race relations at home and U.S. expansion abroad is not a new observation; his readers have long recognized that his novel unites Southern white supremacy with the global spread of Anglo-Saxon civilization. In fact, some of his earliest critics saw this convergence as the reason for his popularity. W. H. Johnson, in his 1903 and 1905 reviews of Dixon's novels, claims that Dixon shrewdly decided to publish his ideas at a time when "our unfortunate experiment in the Philippines has so generally deadened the public conscience toward any appeal to that finer regard for the rights of man simply as man, which was such an inspiration to the masses of the North in the initial years of our experiment with Negro freedom."[19] Republican ideals about the rights of man were supposedly extinguished in the experience of enthusiastically accepting colonial power over the Caribbean and Pacific possessions, and this loss explains why, according to Johnson, "so many Northern readers are so ready to accept today a line of argument which would have met with instant rejection, throughout the entire North, only a few years ago."[20]

According to Johnson, the strong acceptance of Dixon's novels in the North proves that W. E. B. Du Bois understood more accurately than Booker T. Washington the effect of 1898 on U.S. racial politics: "Mr. Washington thought that he saw great hope in the fact that white and black fought bravely together in the battles of the Spanish American War," but Du Bois showed "far truer insight" when he identified "the silently growing assumption in this age that the probation of races is past, and that the backward races of today are of proven inefficiency and not worth the saving."[21] In his 1905 discussion of Dixon's novels, Sutton Griggs agrees that the historical conditions surrounding the Spanish American War aided the reception of Dixon's novel, and he adds his own analysis of the role of Anglo-Saxonism in this new racial assumption of the age. According to

Griggs, Anglo-Saxonism was generated by Queen Victoria's death and by Rudyard Kipling, the "poet [who] had arisen with the voice to reach, for the time being, at least, the whole English speaking world." This newly felt Anglo-Saxonism, compounded with the Northerners' new colonial relation to overseas possessions won during the war, made them even more receptive to Dixon's message. Compelled "to force an unaccepted relation on an alien race," Northerners felt more sympathy with Southerners' race problems.[22]

More recent critics have gone further to argue that expansionism and Anglo-Saxonism influenced both Dixon's receptive audience and Dixon himself. According to Maxwell Bloomfield and Michael Rogin, the Spanish American and Filipino American Wars transformed Dixon's thinking, or at least his rhetoric, about race. As a Social Gospel preacher in Boston and New York before the war, Dixon concerned himself more with Northern social issues such as immigration and the plight of the urban poor than with the so-called Negro Question. (He was so vocal on these urban issues that Stephen Crane selected Dixon as one of the readers to receive an early, self-published version of *Maggie: A Girl of the Streets,* likely seeing in the outspoken minister a sympathetic and influential audience member.[23]) On the issue of African American rights, Dixon's writings before 1898 are surprisingly moderate. For example, in *The Failure of Protestantism in New York and Its Causes* (1896), Dixon writes that although slavery "lifted the African from the bondage of savagery into the light and strength of true Christian civilization" and carried him "across the chasm of centuries," still, Dixon "thank[s] God that there is not to-day the clang of a single slave's chain on this continent. Slavery may have had its beneficent aspects, but democracy is the destiny of the race, because all men are bound together in the bonds of fraternal equality with one common Father above."[24] Here Dixon himself uses the rhetoric of the republican rights of man that Johnson claims was extinguished with the Spanish American War to claim that African Americans are already a "chasm of centuries" removed from savagery and destined for democratic participation as brother citizens.

Dixon's more radically racist notion that African Americans remained evolutionarily unfit for American democracy emerged only after the last of his several career changes, when the law school graduate turned minister retired from the pulpit in 1899 and returned south to publish his first novel. By this time, Rogin argues, Dixon's relationship to U.S. race relations had been transformed by U.S. expansion. According to Rogin, it was the "subjugation of the Philippines" that "reconnected this transplanted Southerner to his past," allowing him a unifying vision that "tied the racial question at home to America's world mission abroad."[25] Bloomfield identifies this rhetorical shift in one of Dixon's final sermons, which depicts a kind of rebirth occurring among Anglo-Saxon Americans due to their newfound racial mission abroad. Titled "A Friendly Warning to the Negro," the sermon claims that, because of the Spanish American War, Americans were recognizing a "new world-destiny" that changed the position of the Negro: "Before us looms up in the dawning century a mighty Republic of three hundred millions of people—Anglo-Saxon people, with Anglo-Saxon government and Anglo-Saxon rulers. The negro is a vanishing quantity in our national life. As we move toward our great future he becomes less and less important." While not yet casting African Americans as a threat whose very presence jeopardizes the racial purity of the nation, Dixon advises in his sermon that they "get out of politics in the South and go into business" because "the mission of the African is not to govern the Anglo-Saxon," a direct contradiction to his earlier rhetoric about democratic fraternal equality.[26]

All of these accounts of the change in Dixon's rhetoric identify a growing tendency at the turn of the century to replace Enlightenment ideas about "the rights of men as men" with racialist thought about Anglo-Saxon domination and Spencerian survival of the fittest. But the dualism that Dixon's critics propose is too easy, for it oversimplifies the flexibility of U.S. racial and imperialist discourse. In Rogin's and Bloomfield's formulations, taking control of the Philippines shares with Jim Crow racism a fundamental and baldly expressed will to subjugate and exploit those deemed racially inferior, and this similarity allowed foreign war to bring Dixon home to white supremacy. Similarly, Johnson and Griggs depict the growing willingness of U.S. Americans to govern the Philippines and to become a world power as resting together on the overt goal of subjugating or eliminating so-called inferior races. Yet examination of the language of U.S. imperialism reveals that concepts like "the rights of man" and imperial expansion do not always exist autochthonously, in total separation from and opposition to one another. For example, the concept of a triumphant "empire for liberty," one that expands benevolently as part of a democratizing mission, powerfully combines these two positions, championing aggressive expansion as part of the mission to civilize and lead people toward their currently deferred democratic destinies. Ubiquitous during debates about governing overseas possessions after the Spanish

American War, the concept of the empire for liberty was also a mainstay in Dixon's earlier expansionist sermons. But in *The Leopard's Spots,* it is not an empire for liberty but a white man's burden that Dixon invokes to soften and blur the Manichean opposition between republican rights of man and colonial power.

This substitution serves an important purpose: to maintain the concept of a philanthropic mission while denying a democratic destiny for all men. Dixon took from Kipling's poem a way to complicate the stark opposition between republic and empire that Rogin, Bloomfield, Johnson, and Griggs identified in his thinking. His imperialist mission, as Dixon depicts it, does not trample on the rights of man; it calls for an administrative duty *because* of, not in spite of, the impossibility of racial uplift and future racial equality. Dixon's ideological homecoming to white supremacy after the Spanish American War was more circuitous and nuanced than Rogin allows, and it was marked by his struggle to bridge regionalist, nationalist, and imperialist fantasies and rhetorics in a new interpretation of "The White Man's Burden."

The White Man's Burden Is the Anglo-Saxon's Trust

As I argue, one of the key problems for adapting Kipling's concept of the White Man's Burden in the United States was defining whiteness. Dixon mostly refers to non–African Americans as inheriting the two thousand-year-old "Anglo-Saxon" racial character, but he occasionally departs from this terminology, as when Gaston calls on "the manhood of the Aryan race, with its four thousand years of authentic history" (*Leopard's Spots,* 440), and when he refers to one character as a model physical example of the "Caucasian" type (63). The variation in terms perhaps helps prepare readers for the more pronounced slippage between "Anglo-Saxon" and "white," Dixon's two most frequent and seemingly interchangeable terms for non–African Americans. All of these racial terms designate a capacious racial category approximating Mathew Frye Jacobson's homogenous Caucasian whiteness, making no important distinctions among European racial groups. In Dixon, the line between "black" and "white/ Anglo-Saxon" is the only one that matters, with African Americans standing as the primary examples of blacks. (Filipinos get brief mention in *The Leopard's Spots* as another race standing on the side of blackness, as I discuss later in this chapter.) As usual, however, the vague concept of the Anglo-Saxon raises it own questions, especially when Dixon's use of the term seems to confuse matters by making it both one ethnic component among the many that comprise U.S. whiteness and the single most important ancestral source of racial superiority.

At times Dixon includes Anglo-Saxon as one among many European white ethnicities, as when Gaston, the constant champion of the Anglo-Saxon, counts among "the men of [his] race," sharing his "martyr blood" the "Norman and Celt, Angle and Saxon, Dane and Frank, Huguenot and German" (441). Yet Dixon simultaneously grounds his scientific basis for white superiority directly in Anglo-Saxon blood by calling it, as we have seen, a "priceless heritage of two thousand years of struggle" (35) that cannot be passed on by mere learning. One might be disposed to dismiss this as another example of Dixon's characteristically hazy and nonsensical racist thought, but it deserves closer attention for revealing a key aspect of his struggle to adapt Kipling's "White Man's Burden." "Anglo-Saxon" in *The Leopard's Spots* is both a racial grouping and a title for a political project uniting nation-states in shared imperial power. To be Anglo-Saxon is, quite illogically, both to inherit something racially through one's ancestry and to share voluntarily in a worldwide political project through one's national citizenship.

This is why the Spanish American War functions so importantly in *The Leopard's Spots* to awaken all sorts of whites to their Anglo-Saxon world mission. As Amy Kaplan and Susan Gillman have argued, the novel uses the explosion of the *Maine* in Havana and the subsequent attack on Spain in Cuba and the Philippines as plot devices to bind together a variety of non–African Americans: rich and poor, North and South, Catholic and Protestant.[27] Like Dixon's "Friendly Warning to the Negro" sermon, their newfound unity as a "world conquering race" (416) makes apparent the necessary exclusion of the Negro; Dixon's narrator observes that, at that moment, "it was seen by thoughtful men that the Negro was an impossibility in the new-born unity of national life. When the Anglo-Saxon race was united into one homogeneous mass in the fire of this crisis, the Negro ceased that moment to be a ward of the nation" (413). Here, as in Dixon's sermons, using the term "Anglo-Saxon" rather than "white" actually helps to subsume ethnic differences through the formation of a specifically geopolitical—rather then ethnic—formation of Anglo-Saxon alliance. These Americans cohere as part of a "sudden union of the English speaking people in friendly alliance that disturbed the equilibrium of the world, and confirmed the Anglo-Saxon in his title to the primacy of racial sway" (412). Being "confirmed" as the dominant Anglo-Saxon guarantees

biological superiority, but confirmation occurs only through a political response to military conflicts and international alliances, *not* through what
certain Americans thought they already had: a pure Anglo-Saxon blood-
line. As in Kipling's formulation, where all white men are not already
White Men, all ethnic Anglo-Saxons do not already hold a confirmed title
to racial primacy, and that title is instead earned through domestic and
international alliances advancing civilization. In chapter 1, I argue that
Anglo-Saxonism had at this time reached its peak and was beginning its
decline, but in *The Leopard's Spots*, Kipling is determined to prop it up as
a useful tool for reconciling imperial mission and domestic segregation.

Dixon most explicitly outlines the imperial mission of this Anglo-
Saxon alliance in Gaston's final speech to the North Carolina Democratic
Convention. The speech is the climax of the novel, in which Gaston convinces the state party of their interconnected domestic and international
racial missions, changing "the current of history and fix[ing] the status
of life for millions of people" (450). A public and personal victory, the
speech fuses the Anglo-Saxon race (or at least the Anglo-Saxon Democrats) into "a solid mass" (450) determined to overthrow Republican control of the state, winning for Charlie Gaston the destiny earlier predicted
for him: nomination for the position of governor of North Carolina. Most
important, the speech sways General Worth, the novel's representative of
the parochial and conservative Democratic old guard, who is also the pro-
tective father of Gaston's beloved Sallie Worth, thus reunifying the Southern Democratic family. Gaston's message invigorates the general: "the audacity of [Gaston's] resolutions had swept him for a moment off his feet
and back into the years of his own daring young manhood. He could not
help admiring this challenge of the modern world to stand at the bar
of elemental manhood and make good its right to existence" (438). The
hero's words return General Worth and the North Carolina Democrats
to youthful ardor by drawing them out of isolation and into the modern
world, with its strenuous new demands and challenges. Seen as a response
to Dixon's conflict about breaking with his father's Democratic Party in
the voting booth, General Worth becomes a father figure willing to learn
from his son.

In a novel that frequently repeats certain central phrases and patterns
of character interaction, Gaston's speech has appeared to some critics to
be only another articulation of the text's unitary and pervasive message of
white supremacy. For Walter Benn Michaels, Gaston's speech merely reit-
erates as the only plank of the Democratic Party—the need to disestablish

the Negro—and it succeeds in convincing his listeners because they have finally come to realize the importance of their racial identities.[28] For Gillman, the speech is one in a repetitive series of climaxes that temporarily "paper over" intraracial differences among whites: along with the outbreak of the Spanish American War, the rapes of two white women, and a lynching, Gaston's stirring speech functions to dramatically but only provisionally produce the illusion of white solidarity.[29] I contend, however, that these scenes are not exact iterations of the same dynamic but, instead, reach their climax with Gaston's speech, which not only forges white solidarity but also articulates it as part of an Anglo-Saxon world mission. That the speech's real purpose is to connect the novel's racism to imperialism was remarked on by one of the book's contemporary reviewers, B. O. Flower, who commented that Gaston's "spread eagle stump speech . . . doubtless voices the sentiments of the reverend author. It is filled with the poison virus of imperialism and reflects the pitiful spirit of pride and vainglory that exalts one race, nation, or State to the plane of superiority over all others, and that paves the way for the justification of wars of subjugation."[30]

Importantly, then, the speech does not only repeat the call for white supremacy: Gaston makes it clear that this has already been the one-note tune of the Democratic Party for too long. Earlier in the novel, Gaston meets with his opponent, Allan McLeod, an opportunist who defected from the Democrats to support the populist "Negro-Farmer" political party. McLeod argues that the Democrats are caught in the past, and Gaston can't help but agree. When Gaston speaks of white supremacy and the Negro's threat to white civilization, McLeod counters by accusing him of "talking a dead language. We are living a new world" (196). Because the Democrats have not yet entered this new world, McLeod complains, they have no real principles—only memories of old Civil War and Reconstruction humiliations no longer relevant in the modern age (196). As Gaston thinks over McLeod's offer, he can't help but agree that the "old fogies" of the party had "kept down the younger men with their war cries and old soldier candidates" (198). They deliberately alienated the Farmer's Alliance by adhering to outdated class distinctions and standing for only one isolated issue: the Negro problem. Tempted by McLeod's offer, Gaston thinks, "His own party stood for no principle except the supremacy of the Anglo-Saxon. On the issue of the party platforms he was in accord with the modern Republican utterances at almost every issue, and so were his associates in the Southern Democracy. The Negro was the point. What was the use now in persisting in the stupid reiteration of the old slogan of white supremacy?" (199). Gaston, faced with a choice between the tired old plank of white supremacy and the new "modern Republican utterances," learns over the course of the novel that he does not have to choose between them, and his speech is the grand articulation of this realization. Its intent is not another "stupid iteration" of the same but a radical updating of the old.

He updates the old plank by reframing it with modern expansionist principles, making local prejudices part of a national and global mission He tells the Democrats:

> The Old South fought against the stars in their courses—the resistless tide of the rising consciousness of Nationality and World-Mission. The young South greets this new era and glories in its manhood. He joins his voice in the cheers of triumph which are ushering in this all-conquering Saxon. Our old men dreamed of local supremacy. We dream of the conquest of the globe. (439)

The Old South must no longer fight the inevitable but, instead, join the rising consciousness of Nationality and World Mission that Republicans like Theodore Roosevelt were championing. Changes in economy and technology brought about a global era, binding the region into the nation and the nation into the rest of the world: "Threads of steel have knit state to state. Steam and electricity have silently transformed the face of the earth, annihilated time and space, and swept the ocean barriers from the path of man. The steam shuttles of commerce have woven continent to continent" (439). These new conditions require a new mission. "We believe," Gaston continues, "that God has raised up our race, as he ordained Israel of old, in this world-crisis to establish and maintain for weaker races, as a trust for civilization, the principles of civil and religious Liberty and forms of Constitutional Government" (439).

In this new world crisis, Anglo-Saxons have a new divine charge, but their burden is not bringing civilization to the hopelessly inferior races; rather, they aim to keep it away from them. Gaston describes a sort of liberty trust fund, wherein civilization becomes not a source of light that the Anglo-Saxon man must painstakingly reveal to the savage but a "trust" or inheritance to be hoarded—a precious torch that must be kept burning by shielding it *from* savagery. Anglo-Saxon racial identity becomes the source of U.S. power to carry that torch—and thus its most guarded quality. That the torch is merely safeguarded, not used to illuminate or uplift or civilize, is how Dixon reconciles the unchanging racial inferiority of the leopard's spots with a heroic conception of the White Man's Burden.

This liberty "trust" solves an important ideological problem by bridging the altruism of formulations like an empire for liberty or White Man's Burden to the radical racism of segregation and removal. Dixon clearly borrowed from the popular British theorist of empire, Benjamin Kidd, whose 1898 book *Control of the Tropics* was widely read in the United States. Kidd explains the trust for civilization in these terms:

> If we have to meet the fact that by force of circumstances the tropics *must* be developed, and if the evidence is equally emphatic that such a development can only take place under the white man, we are confronted with a larger issue than any mere question of commercial policy or national selfishness. The tropics in such circumstances can only be governed as a trust for civilization, and with a full sense of the responsibility which such a trust involves.

Here Kidd calls on higher responsibility to meet counterarguments that imperialism is mere selfishness. It is the solemn responsibility of this trust that makes it necessary to reexamine "the doctrine of the native equality of men" as white men "scrutinize more closely the existing differences between ourselves and the coloured races, as regards the qualities contributing to social efficiency."[31]

Dixon's gradual adoption of these ideas or this language is apparent in a shift that occurred in his expansionist sermons during 1898–99. While his earlier sermons invoke the more typical ideal of the empire for liberty aimed at a spreading civilization and democracy to all, later sermons show Kidd's civilized trust idea developing. One sermon delivered early in the Spanish American War claims that "the soldier who follows our flag into Cuba, the Philippines, and Porta Rico [*sic*] carries more than a musket on his shoulder and cartridges in his belt. He carries bread for the poor, healing for the sick, knowledge for the ignorant, and freedom for the oppressed." Here the global mission of the United States is to civilize and offer freedom to all races: "We conquer no territory and hold it subject, but we proclaim that all men—Anglo-Saxon, Mongolian, African, Celt and Slav— all men are born free and equal. What we claim for ourselves we give to them and to the humblest child—the possibilities of becoming the supreme ruler of the great republic. Such an empire the world never saw before."[32]

For this reason, the earlier Dixon writes, "it is the decree of nature, and therefore the voice of God that America in the twentieth century becomes the most powerful and influential nation in the world." This overblown rhetoric claims that Africans share with Mongolians and Slavs equal political opportunities to become president of the United States, and it contrasts strongly with Dixon's later speech, "Friendly Warning to the Negro," in which "the mission of the African is not to govern the Anglo-Saxon."

In his return to Jim Crow racism, Dixon needed to replace the popular and affirmative understanding of U.S. expansion as a magnanimous effort to uplift, civilize, and, above all, liberate all men in accord with an Enlightenment belief in their equality. Kipling, his inspiration, does so by making the white man's burden more a matter of reinforcing white masculinity than of successfully bringing the savage to the light. Dixon, adapting Kipling and Kidd, does so by replacing the pretense of an empire for democracy with a selfless mission to preserve and strengthen a civilized trust. This language dominates Dixon's later sermons, which in places practically plagiarize Kidd in stating, "it is the duty of the English speaking race to hold these garden spots of nature [the tropics] as a solemn trust for civilization and progress."[33]

In this way, Dixon represented the local supremacy of Southern whites as something other than an outdated issue; instead, it is a key to accomplishing the modern Anglo-Saxon's world mission. This idea draws on the thought of Gaston's adopted guardian, the Reverend Durham, who repeatedly and emphatically reminds the young man that *the future American must be an Anglo-Saxon or a Mulatto. We are now deciding which it shall be. The future of the world depends on the future of this Republic* (200; italics in the original). In other words, white supremacy will still be needed, not only to protect the South but also to protect the nation and its global mission, because a mulatto nation cannot achieve world conquest or safeguard a civilized trust. Thus Southern power and independence from Yankee and Negro domination becomes in this speech not a parochial issue of the past but a global issue bound up in modern visions of world mission, and Gaston's powerful delivery of this idea in front of the convention signifies the moment when it meets the right conditions to take hold and transform state, national, and world politics. The "trust" to be cherished is not so much a political system like democracy or a cultural or technical accomplishment like the English language, Protestantism, or water sanitation: it is whiteness itself that must be protected for the good of the nation and the world.

Tracing these changes in the way Dixon promoted U.S. empire and represented race and democracy from his early sermons to his later ones and then to his first novel, we cannot tell if these are actual shifts in Dixon's thought or whether he was, as Griggs and Johnson suspected, craftily selecting the appropriate time to reveal his true colors of radical instead of merely moderate racism. It may be that, unlike his idealized character Reverend Durham, Dixon was willing to hide his feelings about race in front of more liberal Northern parishioners. But either way, the racist vision that prevailed in his later sermons and in *The Leopard's Spots* did more than replace the rights of man with racial hierarchy. Rather, Dixon adapted Kipling and Kidd to promote a U.S. racial hierarchy that is grounded both in a program of Southern segregation and in concert with a newly conceived world mission to safeguard republicanism, civilization, and whiteness itself.

Because notions of racial hierarchy and imperialism are inextricable, critics have been quick to notice that Dixon aligned the two in his novels, but this observation conceals the tensions found in party politics, in emerging evolutionary theories, and in conceptions of whiteness that made the two seem opposed for many in Dixon's intended audience. Dixon revised Kipling to soften that opposition, creating a new narrative of racial mission in which the inherent racial difference of the leopard's spots and Dixon's genocidal vision does not bar administering colonies altruistically, as vaguely conceived "trusts" in preserving whiteness and civilization. That Dixon looked to Kipling as a key text for his efforts offers more evidence for the widespread circulation of Kipling's poem in discursive debates on the importance of whiteness in processes of U.S. global expansion. Beyond this, however, Dixon's adaptation also provides an example of a writer of popular fiction attempting to refigure local race prejudices and ethnographic categories in light of new transnational formulations of race and imperial mission. Drawing on several transnational elements and ideas, Dixon reformulated whiteness at home before building a global mission on it. These transnational elements were formulations and theories of Kidd and Kipling that portrayed whiteness as a prize to be won or protected and the new conception of Anglo-Saxonism as a political coalition rather than racial essence or specific lineage. Dixon used these two concepts to draw a global color line that linked, as Du Bois warned, the fates of Filipinos to those of Negroes, while replacing the idealistic discourse of benevolent assimilation and uplift with the New South's imperatives of segregation and control.

Coda: Shadowing Dixon's White Man's Burden

I have described a textual strategy that attempts to create a unifying vision by realigning racial segregation at home and Pacific expansion abroad, but many critics have pointed out that Dixon's visions of race often show straining seams. A telling moment of tension occurs in a curious passage in Gaston's speech to the North Carolina State Democratic Convention. As discussed, Gaston intended to awaken his audience to their duty of guarding civilization, but in this strangely pessimistic passage he admits a frank uncertainty about the ultimate result of their efforts:

> The historian tells us that all things pass in time. Wolves whelp and stable in the palaces of dead kings and forgotten civilization. Memphis, Thebes and Babylon are but names to-day. So New Orleans and New York may perish. African antiquarians may explore their ruins and speculate upon their life, but we may safely fix upon a thousand years of intervening time. On your shoulders rests the burden of civilization. We must face its responsibilities. (*Leopard's Spots,* 200)

In a novel that repeats like a mantra the idea that blacks will forever be unfit for democracy and equality with whites, this apocalyptic vision of learned African scholars poring over the ruins of fallen American cities admits a strange lack of confidence about the result of bearing the burden of civilization. For the passage does not say that such events will come about only if Gaston's listeners do not heed his warning and rise to the challenge of asserting white supremacy. Rather, it implies a cyclical law of history in which civilizations inevitably rise and fall, some following after others. The only reassurance that Gaston offers to his audience is that the inevitable decline of western civilization—and its substitution by Africa—is a long way off, and that, in the meantime, responsibilities must be faced.

If the leopard cannot change his spots, how will these future African scholars someday execute one of the nineteenth century's fondest imperial fantasies: exploring lost worlds and seeking histories of fallen civilizations? How will they inherit the imperial roles that Dixon has associated with whiteness and the safeguarding of civilization? These African antiquarians offer a key image for my book: they shadow the white man's burden both by following after it and by darkening it, creating the paradox and the problem of the nonwhite figure imagined as an agent rather than the object of an imperial mission. In Dixon's novel, this incongruous image seems like a brief slip, possibly provoking a quick moment of anxiety, questioning, or confusion. But for the writers whom I discuss in the remaining chapters of this book, the idea of the potentially nonwhite figure playing the role of the civilized imperial agent is a central concern and ideological strategy. In the writing of Frank Steward, Pauline Hopkins, Winnifred Eaton, and Ranald MacDonald, ambiguously raced figures play the roles and invoke the imperial discourses of explorers, soldiers, geographers, ethnologists, translators, cosmopolitans, and diplomats, and in doing so they provoke readers to question the role of race in narratives of imperial mission. In different ways, these writers make shadowing the white man's burden a tactic to manipulate the various terms of racialization that were at odds in narratives of U.S. empire.

These writers do not explicitly reference Kipling's poem, but they do speak to the sense of confusion about race and empire that was evident in its reception and that made the poem a touchstone for debates about whiteness and empire. It is tempting to say that these writers seek to undo the linkages between whiteness and U.S. empire that Dixon's novel seeks to support, but Dixon's novels' contradictory slips and Kipling's multiple interpretations prepare us for the complicated discursive formation that these writers engage without always subverting. In other words, it would be too simple to suggest that Kipling and Dixon promote a unified vision of U.S. white empire while Steward, Hopkins, Eaton, and MacDonald challenge it. Instead, I argue that all of these writers weigh on the "weak spot" that so troubled Roosevelt when he read Mr. Dooley's joke about handing the white man's burden to the "coons." That weak spot is the relationship of whiteness to U.S. national identity, as refracted through competing understandings of the country's global role and competing claims to whiteness.

PART II

The Black Cosmopolite

In William Huntington Wilson's short story "The Return of the Sergeant" (1900), inhabitants of the South Carolina village Possum Hollow inflate with pride only to be crushed by disappointment. Their downfall is rendered comic with minstrel-style humor: Possum Hollow's solely African American inhabitants glory in one of their young men returning wounded from military service in Cuba, then learn that they are being deceived. It turns out that "de Sargent" has not been to Cuba at all but invented the story after stealing a white officer's uniform at a Charleston hotel where he worked as a bellboy. Stock characters like the earnest, simple Uncle Mose and the refined mulatto Lincoln Carter plan festivities in honor of the Sergeant, declaring that "de 'casion may go vibratin' down in hist'ry ez de granduss an' proudess an' biguss 'casion which de Holler has ebber knowed!" They learn the truth during the celebration and chase the Sergeant from the church hall, only to have their banquet feast stolen by sneaky "country niggers" while the Sergeant escapes. The story concludes with Uncle Mose collapsing into loud sobs and an angry cry: "'Oh, Gawd: Gawd!'" he sobbed, "hab pity on me! Ma heart is full ob murder fur de Sargent an' dem country niggers, an' ma stummick's emptier'n a dry well! An' dat *roas' peeg!* An dat *possum!* An dat *jelly cake!* Oh *Gawd! Gawd!* I cyan stan' it *no-how!*"[1]

Wilson's story, published in the widely circulating *Harper's Weekly,* offers clumsy reassurance to white readers anxious about the "weak spot" that troubled Theodore Roosevelt in Mr. Dooley's quip, "Take up the white man's burden an' hand it to the coons." Heroic black masculinity is revealed as a pose underneath which a comic minstrel always lurks, so that the deceived patriarch Uncle Mose regrets the loss of his dinner more than the loss of a community hero, holding murder in his heart but lacking the manly will to get justice or revenge. For Wilson, African American patriotism is the opportunity for a devastating, clichéd joke invoking the local types of the black South: the simple, ignorant village elders, the uppity mulattos in ostentatious dress clothes, the lazy "country niggers," and the cunning but cowardly trickster who almost pulls a fast one. While Amy Kaplan has shown that whites responded to black heroism on the battlefield in Cuba by writing accounts that "reestablished the reassuring order of the domestic color line in a foreign terrain," Wilson's story goes one step further in denying black heroism by mocking the very idea that blacks could even *leave* home, replacing them spatially and temporally back into the South—in Possum Hollow, a mythical village untouched by modernity.[2]

The chapters in the next section demonstrate that this emphatic placement of African Americans in local, domestic, and vernacular spaces rather than on "foreign terrain" was a rhetorical strategy for configuring race and empire in the turn-of-the-century United States, and that African American writers both adapted and inverted this strategy. At stake in these relocations is an important symbolic battle. Since the Civil War, African American military service had provided an important argument and representational field for claiming or limiting black manhood and national belonging, but participation in a world mission at the turn of the century signified more than a means to prove equal citizenship within the United States.[3] Such participation was also a claim to civilization and cosmopolitanism, forms of authority won by claiming a dominant position in global contests and hierarchies. Wilson's story laughingly demonstrates the impossibility of an African American military hero by insisting on his immobility outside South Carolina and the generic local space of Possum Hollow, a strategy of shoring up Roosevelt's "weak spot" that I return to in the chapters in part II. In contrast, representations of black cosmopolitanism countered such moves by making global mission a route to progressing beyond outmoded and local racial hierarchies at home and abroad.

These chapters examine the *Colored American Magazine* (hereafter *CAM*) as one source of this construction of the black cosmopolitan. I chose this periodical based on its relatively wide circulation, its emphasis on fiction as an element in racial politics, and its editorial conflicts surrounding internationalism, a topic I say more about in chapter 4.[4] The years I have selected follow from the magazine's inception in 1900 to its sale in 1904 to new owners, who moved the *CAM* from Boston to New York, changed its format to exclude fiction as a regular feature, and fired Pauline Hopkins as literary editor.[5] My purpose in examining this magazine during this period is to describe a historically specific, heterogeneous, and contested discourse of black cosmopolitanism as it was produced in nonfictional and fictional writing that negotiates claims to African American power in the field of global politics.

A topic of much recent philosophical and social interest, cosmopolitanism raises key questions about its racial character. If a cosmopolitan seeks worldly identifications beyond race and nation, is the figure of the cosmopolitan necessarily a de-raced and deracinated one? In other words, is "black cosmopolitanism" an oxymoron, insofar as insisting on a racial identity contradicts the wider commitment to raceless and nationless humanity implied by the latter term?[6] Ifeoma Kiddoe Nwankwo's use of the term in her 2005 study *Black Cosmopolitanism* denies this seeming dichotomy between authentic or essentialized "blackness" and raceless, libratory cosmopolitanism, arguing that both are "the master's tools" and that both were grasped by nineteenth-century people of African descent in the Americas to define self and community. Nwankwo describes these efforts at definition and affiliation as a struggle borne out of efforts of whites to deny people of African descent access to prevalent categories of identity, such as nation and humanity, leaving only race as the sole determinant for indexing the self. In response to this limitation, African-descended people of the Americas had to "decide where to position themselves, particularly in print, and decide how to embrace both national/local and transnational/global affinities," and decide "whether and how to express their connection both to their country of residence and to the world of people of African descent beyond their country."[7] Such arguments—for racial unity, for national belonging, and for worldwide community—all had to be calibrated to exigencies of political struggle on a number of scales.

I seek to extend Nwankwo's argument by discussing a historically specific set of articulations of black cosmopolitanism in the *CAM* at the turn of the century. During this period, the struggles over identity that Nwankwo writes about were still in effect, despite emancipation and formal enfranchisement. But one important historical change was the influence of new articulations of global thinking emerging in the United States at this time. While Nwankwo's writers looked to the Americas and to transnational events like the Haitian Revolution as containers and catalysts for identity formation, African American writers at the turn of the century reckoned with different global forces, such as the era's widespread claims for relocating the United States as a world power with formal and informal imperial responsibilities in the Pacific, Asia, and the Caribbean, as well as the era's concomitant scientific and literary discourses of race and civilization. At the turn of the century, African Americans were pressed to negotiate not only between national belonging and transnational identifications with an Atlantic black diaspora but also between identifications with "civilized" cosmopolitan worldliness and identifications with people defined as nonwhite in Asia and the Pacific, Africa, and the Caribbean.

While my work examines fiction primarily for its formal methods of figuring this conflict, historians Willard Gatewood and George Marks have identified manifestations of these tensions in nonfictional African American responses to the Spanish American, Filipino American, and Boer Wars. In *Black Americans and the White Man's Burden*, Gatewood emphasizes a major division within the African American community over whether a world mission for the United States meant increased opportunities for proving the manly patriotism of black soldiers and citizens or a frightening turn toward racialist arguments about fitness for self-government that could only further disenfranchise African Americans. Within this debate, Gatewood suggests that individuals themselves were divided, reluctant to settle on either position, and uncomfortably forced to conceive of foreign policy through their own deteriorating status in the United States. He characterizes this divide using the words of W. E. B. Du Bois in "The Conservation of Races" as "a time of vacillation and contradiction for the American Negro," compelled to ask "Am I an American or am I a Negro? Can I be both? Or is it my duty to cease to be a Negro as soon as possible and be an American? If I strive as a Negro, am I not perpetuating the very cleft that threatens and separates Black and White America?"[8] Where Gatewood sees vacillation, however, Marks sees more strategic concealment; he contends that anti-imperialism in the black community was squelched by forced loyalty to the national Republican Party leading up to and following the highly contested 1900 presidential election, the same electoral contest that so tested Dixon's loyalties to the South.[9] As Howard University sociologist Kelly Miller wrote in 1900, the election placed African Americans "politically between the devil and the deep blue sea," faced by a choice between the traditionally hostile Democratic Party and a new form of Republicanism marching to the poetry of Rudyard Kipling, whom Miller called "the mouthpiece" of the rising imperialist disregard of the rights of man.[10]

In this historical context, assuming a cosmopolitan identity meant more, or perhaps we should say less, than striving for intellectual commitment to humanity or universalism. It meant reckoning with narratives of global interconnection as they ranged from visions of a worldwide liberation movement with oppressed peoples of color to more commonplace stories of civilizing the primitive, Americanizing the oppressed, and converting the heathen. In this way, my use of the phrase "black cosmopolitanism" builds from Gatewood's and Marks's observations about vacillation and political strategy to create a category that is slippery and capacious enough to include the variety of ways that the *CAM* figured and related national and global engagement. With this term, I mean to include a variety of global visions, acknowledging that historically cosmopolitanism and imperialism are not always opposed terms or impulses.[11] If, as Walter Mignolo contends, cosmopolitanism is a "set of projects for planetary conviviality," such global projects could include religious and military expansion.[12] Drawing the line between what Mignolo calls "critical cosmopolitanism" and its hegemonic forms is not always easy—and not always critically advantageous—in instances of black cosmopolitanism found in the *CAM*. The expressions studied in part II echo and adapt ethnocentric and imperialist rhetoric, even while expressing discomfort with their terms. They strain between the goal of carrying an equal part in the white man's burden and redefining that burden as a different kind of global authority more akin to Du Bois's anticolonial "burden [of] manhood/ Be it yellow or black or white."[13]

Caught between claims to citizenship and claims to civilization, this strand of divided black cosmopolitanism found in the *CAM* lacks much of the self-conscious, radical force of Marxist anticolonial identifications that black intellectuals would develop in later decades. Pauline Hopkins, who served as literary editor for the *CAM* in 1903 and 1904, and who, as I discuss in chapter 4, was a key player in the magazine's conflicts about internationalism, describes this ambivalent, divided figure of the "negro cosmopolite" in a piece that she wrote under one of her pen names, J. Shirley Shadrach. This description comes at the end of a biographical sketch titled "Charles Winter Woods: From Bootblack to Professor," which begins in the Horatio Algeresque mode suggested by the subtitle, describing its subject's rise from shining shoes to teaching English at Booker T. Washington's Tuskegee Institute. The end of the article breaks out of this biographical mode with a series of fragmented reflections separated by section breaks and only obliquely related to the initial biography. One of these segments reads:

> Since the settlement of America a new and virile type of man whom we call "cosmopolite," for want of a more explicit name, has given impetus to civilization in every part of the globe. Nowhere do we find a corner of

the earth that one or many citizens of this republic are not coloring the social and civil life of the community in which they happen to have cast their lot for the time being. The parent stock from which these "cosmopolitans" have sprung is of every known nationality.

Like the old Negro who claimed to have had every known disease, "Bless de Lord, we've got this replaint, too." There is Lawyer T. McCants Stewart, late of New York, now of Hawaii, figuring conspicuously in the politics of the islands, doing all that he can to break the growing inclination there to disenfranchise the Hawaiians after the style of the South towards that section.[14]

This curious passage follows from the article's theme of racial uplift by suggesting that through their own merits, African Americans are ascending to new levels of achievement. The position of the explicitly masculine ("virile") cosmopolite is cast as yet another of these self-made achievements. This figure is at once national—described as a new development specifically in the United States—and open in its national affiliations: able to temporarily cast its lot with any people. However, its fluid identifications are directed by spatial movement and location, not by a philosophical commitment to humanity or universalism; one becomes a cosmopolite by physically traveling to new "corners" of the earth and "coloring" them with civilization. There is no indication that the Afro-American cosmopolite will do this any differently from the Anglo-American one; until we read Hopkins's example of Thomas McCants Stewart working to prevent disenfranchisement of the Hawaiians, it seems that the word "cosmopolite" could as well be replaced with "imperialist" or "missionary" or "businessman"—any successful man with worldwide vision and ambitions. This ambition is what the intentionally humorous reference to the "old Negro" and his dialect speech seems to emphasize: the marked difference between the new cosmopolite and the outdated, supposedly placebound, vernacular figure of Southern folk culture.

Hopkins's passage exhibits four sites of contestation found more broadly in the *CAM*'s representations of black cosmopolitanism, all of which are explored in chapters 3 and 4. First, we see a tension between the *vernacular* and the *global*. Here Hopkins privileges the accomplished, learned cosmopolitan world traveler over the old-fashioned, dialect-speaking Negro stereotype of regional literatures. This tension will be familiar to readers of Jennifer C. James's study of African American war literature, which argues that pro-imperialist black writers of this era resisted discursive strategies of "domestic immobilization" in their accounts of the Spanish

American and Filipino American Wars. James borrows the phrase from Houston Baker to name symbolic containment of African Americans in nostalgic, agrarian, and domestic settings, an effort that tales of African American martial valor attempted to contest by insisting on modern imperial mobility beyond vernacular settings and portrayals.[15]

A second tension is found in this passage's uncomfortable conflation of *civilizing* and *enfranchising* native peoples, indicating the blending of these goals in imperialist discourse more generally and the conflicted impulse to separate and oppose them in black cosmopolitan writing. Third, the black cosmopolitan is explicitly gendered male in this passage and linked to narratives of manly, individualist accomplishment within the United States. Fourth, his travels are routed by preexisting circuits of trade and state power, and thus they extend across the Atlantic and the Pacific along nationalist and transnationalist lines of capitalist and cultural exchange and military conflict. Hopkins's example of Thomas McCants Stewart reveals this routing: a lawyer whose legal career took him to Liberia in 1888, to Hawaii in 1898, and to the Virgin Islands in 1921, Stewart was a virtual shadow of U.S. state power as it created new routes for its citizens' travel and employment, offering him access to places where he could establish temporary forms of cosmopolitan identification and partial coalitions with those disenfranchised there.

This routing is one of the ways that this figure of the black cosmopolitan shadows the white man's burden, following the routes of military, commercial, and scientific interests, with modes of linguistic and narrative representation that both echo and contest those interests. That linguistic echo appears vividly in a 1902 *CAM* editorial, reprinted from the *Freeman*, which begins by opposing African American repatriation to Africa but ends by inserting the African American male into fantasies of Anglo-Saxon imperial adventure around the world:

> We are opposed to any wholesale movement to Africa since it has its problem, the same as America, but on a more gigantic scale, which will someday cause the universe to tremble as on the resurrection morn. But the call should be heeded as if it were issued to the Anglo-Saxon that acknowledged no impediment as master buffeting the wave following the slanting keel—Greenland's icy mountains, India's coral strand—on the grottoes of the sea or on the Himalaya's aspiring peak the eternal abode of light. Colored men must learn to follow the dipping prow, scale mountains and brave the red-hot sun as the Saxons.[16]

This paragraph gets so caught up in rhetorical flourish that its syntax loses coherence, a sign of discomfort in situating the colored American globally as an imperial competitor to the Anglo-Saxon. Colored men may rival, not follow, Anglo-Saxons in this effort, but their actions remain structured by conventional imperialist rhetoric of strenuous manhood and domination of the landscape. What they will do with their dramatic global mastery is left unstated, another sign of uncertainty and vacillation in this vision of black cosmopolitanism. Oppression in Africa and the U.S. South are cast as biblical crimes waiting for divine correction, but left unstated is how that divine reckoning relates to the ambitious black cosmopolitan turning outward to global adventure.

Along with Homi Bhabha, we might call this rhetoric a kind of colonial mimicry, where "not quite / not white" subaltern subjects mimic imperial commonplaces but render them incoherent through their difference.[17] Linguistically, this incoherence arises from the nonwhite subject's presence within the imperial project and his effect on its foundational racial binaries. This is one of the implications, sometimes unintended, of representations of the black cosmopolite. The effect is similar to that described by Amy Kaplan, writing about the figure of the black military officer during the Spanish American War: "The challenge of black officers to white authority lay in their capacity to represent American nationhood abroad, when society required that their blackness be subsumed into a white nation. Black officers would challenge the coherence of imperialist boundaries that align masculinity, whiteness and nationhood against the anarchy of black misrule." Perhaps even more troubling than the idea that African Americans would ally with Africans and Asians against white colonial power was their "challenge to the internal coherence of . . . empire by demanding participation and representation as equals."[18] This is the same "weak spot" that Roosevelt admitted in his response to Mr. Dooley's parody of Kipling: If a black man carries the white man's burden, how can that burden manifest and establish white masculinity?

In the following two chapters, I describe how two writers for the *CAM*, Frank R. Steward and Pauline E. Hopkins, raise this question in their fiction. Steward and Hopkins sound out the vacillating figure of the black cosmopolitan, both as an emblem of the potential and the limitations of shadowing the white man's burden and as a tool for revising from within racial narratives of empire and civilization. In chapter 3, I examine the fiction of Frank Steward, which appeared in the *CAM* alongside reports of his manly accomplishment as an officer in the U.S. Volunteer Army serving in the Philippines. Steward's fiction both replicates and attempts to evade the narrative of racial uplift referenced above, in which an accomplished black cosmopolite proves domestic inclusion and worldwide mastery through strenuous adventure abroad. In chapter 4, I examine the character of Reuel Briggs in Hopkins's magazine novel *Of One Blood* as an intertextual commentary on the construction of black global expertise that appeared in Steward's fiction and elsewhere in the *CAM*.

3

The Plain Citizen of
Black Orientalism

*Frank R. Steward's Filipino
American War Fiction*

In 1903, the *Colored American Magazine (CAM)* featured a story about Micaela Flores of Manila, a Filipina who had recently taken second place in the "Popular School Teacher Contest" conducted by her city's newspaper. The brief profile tells Flores's story as an example of Filipino nationalism under the U.S. occupation. By winning second place, the article explains, Flores ranked ahead of many U.S. candidates and behind only the U.S. "military contingent's candidate." The piece ends by noting that, despite Flores's employment by the colonial government, "the young lady's motto, apparently, is "Peace, good will to all, but the Philippines and Filipinas for Filipinos only." Figuring both land and women as the possessions solely of male Filipinos, this nationalist piece raises the question of what interest readers of the *CAM* should take in Flores's story.[1]

The article neither draws an explicit parallel between the situation of African Americans and Filipinos nor suggests that the two groups are bound by a common cause. But an implicit parallel is drawn by the article's appearance in the "Here and There" segment of the *CAM*. Usually devoted to biographical sketches of prominent African Americans, the "Here and There" feature is introduced in each issue as covering "social movements of the colored race, not only throughout the country but the world," a global frame that appears to identify Filipinos as fellow members of the "colored race" struggling for self-determination "there" while African Americans do it "here."[2]

Two years earlier, the "Here and There" section included another profile that was more typical of the magazine's representation of the war in the

Figure 4. Photograph of
Frank R. Steward, LC-
USZ62-132219, Library of
Congress, Prints and Pho-
tographs Division, Wash-
ington D.C. Misidentified
at the Library of Congress
as "2nd Lt. Frank Newland
(i.e. Stewart)," the image is
the same one that appears
in *CAM*'s 1901 profile of
Steward. The picture was
taken sometime during the
Spanish American War,
when Steward was serving
with the 8th U.S. Volunteer
Infantry.

Philippines. This piece does not mention Filipinos or Filipinas at all and, instead, tells a story of African American uplift. It profiles Captain Frank R. Steward, an African American officer in the U.S. Volunteer Army, who had recently received a judicial post in the province of Laguna, where his troop, the 49th infantry, was stationed (figure 4).

Steward was appointed provost judge for the town of San Pablo, a position holding "exclusive jurisdiction over its forty thousand inhabitants, and empowered to impose a fine as heavy as $1,000 or to imprison for as long a term as two years." On this impressive authority the *CAM* comments, "It is particularly gratifying that in this instance honor has followed merit," because Steward, a Harvard graduate, is "the product of the best education that America can afford" and had previously served with honor as a lieutenant in the 8th U.S. Volunteers in the Spanish American War.[3] In Steward's profile, the story of individual accomplishment replaces any link between African Americans and Filipinos as members of a globally unified colored race struggling for self-determination and, instead, stresses the captain's authority over Filipinos as a sign of merited African American achievement within the frame of U.S. citizenship.

One way to relate these two articles is to view them as two aspects of the heterogeneous discourse that Helen J. Jun calls "black Orientalism," the discursive mode in which African Americans represent the Orient to engage with the limitations of their own citizenship and belonging in the United States.[4] Jun defines this field of black Orientalism as flexible enough to encompass stories both of Afro-Asian anticolonial sympathy and black racial uplift via imperial mission. As Jun acknowledges, however, the latter form was common in the nineteenth century, when demands on African Americans to constitute humanity and citizenship through hegemonic ideas about race, gender, and nation required them to negotiate their exclusion in relation to excluded others such as Chinese immigrants or, in this case, colonized Filipinos. Caught in this bind, the *CAM*'s representations of Filipinos and of the conflict in the Philippines are Orientalist forms that, in the terms of Edward Said, convert the Orient into an image necessary for figuring the westerner's own identity.

Here I examine the fictional and nonfictional writing of Captain Frank Rudolph Steward (1872–1931), the subject of the above-described profile, as he himself explored and attempted to expand this field of black Orientalism. How to imagine the racial meaning of his military service was Steward's motivating question. Not satisfied with the frame of individual accomplishment and black racial uplift, Steward sought other meanings that still strained within the narrow confines of popular literary form and national narrative. Studies of African American letters and editorials have described what Susan Gillman has called the "Negro Question of the Spanish American War," and recent scholarship on the cultures of U.S. imperialism has examined the complicated investment of African Americans in civilizationist discourse and the Spanish American and Filipino American Wars.[5] But we have few examples of African Americans addressing this conflict through fictional narratives, with the formal effects, imaginative license, and modes of identification attendant to storytelling.[6]

Frank Steward is practically unknown by scholars of late-nineteenth-century African American literature.[7] Slightly more familiar is Steward's father, Theophilus Gould (T. G.) Steward (1843–1925), a major figure in the African Methodist Church (AME). The subject of several recent biographies, T. G. Steward wrote seven nonfiction books and one novel (*A Charleston Love Story*, 1899), taught on the faculty at Wilberforce University, and became one of the first African Americans to serve as chaplain in the regular U.S. Army. Like his son, he also served in the Philippines, as chaplain of the 25th Infantry, where he was assigned to superintend a series of schools around Manila taught by U.S. soldiers.[8] (A frequent contributor to the *CAM*, he was probably the magazine's source for the story about Micaela Flores.) T. G's influence undoubtedly helped Frank and his brothers attend Harvard University, where they were contemporaries, but apparently not close friends or correspondents, with W. E. B. Du Bois and William Monroe Trotter.

Unlike his father, Frank Steward has never been the subject of an academic study devoted to his life or writing. After being mustered out of the 49th, Frank moved to Pittsburgh where he married, opened a law practice, and pursued a career in politics. He ran unsuccessfully for the state legislature, was appointed to the Electoral College of Pennsylvania, and applied to the U.S. State Department for diplomatic posts in Brazil in 1906 and Haiti in 1911.[9] With all of these attempts to advance his political career, he apparently discontinued his literary efforts. Currently I am aware of only a handful of published pieces by Steward: three fictional stories published in the *CAM* during 1902–3, an essay published as an appendix to one of his father's books a year later, and a 1906 review in the *Voice of the Negro* of a book written in French by Haitian scholar and statesman Anténor Firmin: *M. Roosevelt, President des Estats-unis et la Republique D'Haiti*.[10]

Despite Steward's short literary career, at stake in recovering his writing is our understanding of how African American writers experimented formally to represent through fiction their relationship with a racialized imperialist project. Steward's enigmatic short stories, although few in number, use a complicated literary method to destabilize the linkages between whiteness, authority, and imperial mission. They also offer a complex rendering of the gendered and sexual intimacies of empire. A key narrative element for Steward's literary effort to evade the narrow choice between civilized soldier and colonized subaltern is the feminized figure of the Asiatic. In his use of this element, Steward genders colonial relations between east and west, creating in his stories an ambivalent version of Micaela Flores's motto, "the Philippines and Filipinas for Filipinos only."

Local Color and the Colored Officer

An issue central to both Steward's military and literary careers was the question of whether or not African Americans should serve as military officers. Both Steward's commission as an officer and his judicial appointment as part of the temporary colonial government in Laguna were possible because he served in the Volunteer Army, where troops were mustered for the specific purpose of short-term service in a particular campaign. Among the career soldiers in the Army Regulars, African Americans were prevented from serving as officers during the period between the Civil War and the Spanish American War, after which two highly contested commissions were awarded in 1901. In contrast, in the Volunteer Army, African American soldiers could serve at ranks as high as lieutenant in the Spanish American War and as captain in the Filipino American War. Steward thus served at the highest rank open to him, a status that he found even more significant than his judicial appointment. In his essay on "Colored Officers," Steward wrote that while judges, legislators, governors, and mayors are still "our 'fellow citizens'" enjoying only an honorary dignity, an officer in the Army holds a special kind of authority: "Fifty thousand soldiers must stand attention to the merest second lieutenant! His rank is a *fact*."[11]

Steward's essay "Colored Officers," printed as an appendix to his father's *The Colored Regulars in the United States Army* (1904), argues that, although whites are reluctant to invest such authority in Negroes, they hide their prejudice behind a "formula" that took hold in the "popular mind" through a "secure setting of type on the printed page"—the formula that "Negroes cannot command."[12] His essay then proceeds to debunk this formula by listing many instances of honorable leadership, demanding that representation conform to reality. In his short stories, however, Steward attempts not to replace fiction with fact but to compete more directly with the literary and cultural modes that made this formula, "Negroes cannot command," a compelling one. Minstrel shows, dialect stories, and sentimental appeals to Negro devotion were the tools adopted by whites to manage the place of African Americans in the U.S. military and in the new U.S. empire, and, to counter them, Steward experimented with new literary forms.

One of these was the fashionable literary mode of local color, which Steward adapted to invent a new fictional characterization of black Orientalist imperial authority. If the formula that "Negroes cannot command" took hold in the popular mind by its "secure setting" in print, one of its most compelling forms in the post–Reconstruction era was the new fictional mode called "local color," aimed at portraying real life and fixing regional "types" in local spaces. Steward adapted the power of local color to map national hierarchies, and he contested its geographical and temporal marginalizing of African Americans as humble "folk." By considering Steward's intervention in the literary form most aimed at capturing the local, I extend Jennifer C. James's argument that, during this era, black writers (including T. G. Steward) resisted "domestic immobilization" of agrarian settings and images by figuring African American soldiers as mobile and modern members of an expansive imperialist project.[13]

For an example of local color's domestic immobilization of African Americans, consider John Fox Jr.'s *Crittenden: A Kentucky Story of Love and War* (1900), which assuages fear of empowered black soldiers by affixing Negro character locally, as a plantation "type." In a plot that, like Dixon's *The Leopard's Spots,* figures the Spanish American War as a "purgative final battle" or a "romance of reunion" healing the wounds and divisiveness of the Civil War, *Crittenden* reunites North and South as a nation without regional divides by resituating African Americans in the regional past.[14] The novel tells the story of Clay Crittenden, a white Southerner initially tormented by memories of Civil War and Reconstruction. At first, Crittenden, who is convinced that black citizenship will end in a race war, finds the sight of colored troops on their way to Cuba both repugnant and threatening. But after serving in Cuba alongside Northerners and accompanied by his family's servant, the ex-slave "faithful Bob," Crittenden aspires to be "an American now, not a Southerner" and to look beyond regional and racial prejudices. After his return, he delivers a rousing speech affirming the national unity generated by the war, which "brought together every social element in our national life . . . into a solid front against a common foe. . . . In the interest of humanity, it had freed twelve million people of an alien race and another land, and it had given us a better hope for the alien race in our own."[15] But instead of deriving this "better hope" from the experience of seeing African American soldiers fight as equals or as leaders, it comes from the figure of Bob, who reassuringly shows that wherever they go, blacks will stay true to nostalgic images of plantation-era loyalty.

Crittenden's Bob serves in Cuba not by enlisting but by secretly stowing away aboard the ship that takes Crittenden and the colored soldiers of the 10th Calvary to Cuba. Arriving at the front unattached to any unit, Bob wants only to stay with his employer and father's young master: "I wish you'd jes show me how to wuk this gun. I'se gwine to fight right side o' you—you heah me. . . . I tol' you in Kentucky that I gwine to fight wid the niggers ef you don't lemme fight wid you. I don't like disgracin' the family dis way, but 'tain't my fault, an' s'pose you git shot." While the colored regulars are portrayed as comic minstrel buffoons, Bob proves himself by saving Crittenden's injured younger brother in a battle, and black and white seem to unite at the sound of a trumpet calling them to battle: "It was the call of America to the American, white and black: and race and colour forgotten, the American answered with the grit of the Saxon, the Celt's pure love of fight, and all the dash of the passionate Gaul."[16] This curious passage encapsulates the confusion of the white man's burden in the United States: the summoned Americans are white and black, but combined in their answer are only the qualities of the European ethnic groups securing a stronger claim to whiteness through imperial service. Blacks in *Crittenden* answer that call not by assuming the position of the modern, nonregionalized American, as the white hero does, but by a spatial and temporal return to Kentucky plantation life.

This return to folk tradition is emphasized in the final chapter, which takes place at Christmas and features a prolonged scene in which the Negroes of Crittenden's estate seek a slow-burning Yule log in the woods, because "as long as the log burned, just that long lasted the holiday for every darky on the place." Bob, "as ex-warrior," leads the search, but the improvised songs and frolics carefully detailed in the scene reveal that the power of the African American soldier can be reharnessed to a nostalgic vision of slavery alive in the present. Black masculinity is manifested in the service of folk tradition as the Yule log is lifted with "a tightening of big, black biceps, a swelling of powerful thighs, and straightening of mighty backs."[17]

Such fictional relocalizations of African American soldiers as regional types merged with and upheld factual iterations of Steward's formula, "Negroes cannot command." John T. Bramhall appealed to such regional "knowledge" in support of his 1901 argument that black soldiers should be invited to enlist for service in the Philippines; he assures readers that obedient black soldiers will "go singing to their work, as though it were a raccoon hunt or a barbeque in Georgia or Carolina."[18] War correspondent Poultney Bigelow also takes local color fiction for authority while describing "The Negro as an Element in Colonial Expansion," when he cites support for the truism that Negroes make loyal soldiers with "knowledge of the African . . . from the earliest historical times to this day, from Herodotus to Uncle Remus."[19] Here Joel Chandler Harris's fictional "Uncle Remus" becomes historical evidence fixing the Negro in space and time. Similarly, Major General Joseph Wheeler grounds the praise that he offers to black soldiers in Cuba with another explicit reference to regional fiction:

The men of the South know that the prominent characteristic of the old Negro slave was loyalty—a loyalty touching in its beauty and simplicity. How few examples we have of treachery compared with the many instances of unselfish devotion exhibited by the slave in his loyalty to a loved master or mistress. Who has not seen a thousand times the true counterpart of Sam in "Mars[e] Chan," a story so touchingly true to life that one can scarcely read it with dry eyes. Is it any wonder or any matter of surprise that the colored troops true to their inborn spirit of loyalty, went forth full of martial enthusiasm to battle with a foreign foe, and returned from Cuba's bloodstained fields covered with glory?[20]

Wheeler sees African American soldiers directly through the lens of Thomas Nelson Page's nostalgic 1887 plantation tale "Marse Chan," authorized as real, regional knowledge of the South. Page's story features Sam, an earlier version of *Crittenden*'s Bob: an ex-slave living out his days in the Reconstruction era, longing for the intimacy and carelessness of the Old South. Sam recalls with pride accompanying his young "Marse Chan" to fight for the Confederacy during the Civil War, but as a slave his only duties at the front were to care for his beloved master and ultimately to bring Marse Chan's corpse home. Encouraging readers to accept African Americans as military subordinates by appealing to the "reality" of Page's "Marse Chan," General Wheeler uses local color fiction as an authoritative device for managing racial hierarchies.

Frank Steward mocked such condescending praise in "Colored Officers," claiming that it only reinforced the "formula" that Negroes couldn't lead:

In the fullness of his manhood [the colored soldier] has no rejoicing in the patronizing paean, "the colored troops fought nobly," nor does he glow at all when told of his "faithfulness and devotion" to his white officers, qualities accentuated to the point where they might well fit an affectionate dog. He lays claim to no prerogative other than that of a plain citizen of the Republic trained to the profession of arms. The measure of his demand . . . is that the full manhood privileges of a soldier be accorded him.[21]

To argue for these "full manhood privileges" in his fiction, Steward adapted two popular representational forms of turn-of-the-century American literature. One was the local color genre that established the "reality" of the

Negro character for Major General Wheeler and other whites. The other was the set of gendered Orientalist narrative devices found in transpacific romances such as John Luther Long's 1898 novella *Madame Butterfly* that helped produce the "reality" of the U.S. expansion into the Pacific.[22] By combining and adapting these forms, Steward relocated African Americans as cosmopolitans positioned to direct a military mission against and produce knowledge about Filipino locals. His fiction constructs this position of power by developing two key points from his "Colored Officers" essay quoted above: fully entitled masculinity and the deracialized authority of the "plain citizen." Yet as I demonstrate, Steward's Orientalist and local color formulas also raise questions about imperial intimacies in the Philippines that reinsert into his narratives criticism of the racial color line at home and abroad. His short stories argue for dissolving provincial U.S. prejudices against African Americans on the wider field of imperial mission, but at the same time they reveal those local prejudices to be reinscribed wherever the white man's burden travels.

Steward's first two published stories, "Pepe's Anting Anting" and "Starlik," share some major characteristics of the local color genre. Both bear the subtitle "A Tale of Laguna," announcing themselves as stories of a particular place in the tradition of local color subtitles such as "Creole Life," "the recent west," or "A Tale of Wisconsin." Both are narrated in the first person by a visitor to the Philippines whose cosmopolitan perspective contrasts with the superstitious and garrulous simplicity of the Laguna province's inhabitants, a narrative point of view that several critics identify as a major formal feature of local color writing, common to Page's "Marse Chan," Sarah Orne Jewett's *Country of the Pointed Firs,* and Charles Chesnutt's *Conjure Tales.*[23] Steward's visitor seldom takes part in the action but listens to and reflects on dialect stories, folk beliefs, and local prejudices, creating a metropolitan perspective with seeming authority to translate the Philippines for readers at home.

Of course, Steward's version of local color describes not a peripheral region but a new territorial possession whose political and cultural relationship to the United States was a subject of intense debate. A major aim of local color as it was discussed by its promoters of the day, including Hamlin Garland and William Dean Howells, was to "nationalize" and unify the United States. But if regional writing's expressed purpose was to "glue fragments together to form a vessel of national consciousness,"[24] its unexpressed meanings tended to simultaneously divide these fragments along lines of economic and cultural power as a function of the global processes of modernity. It described "not just the 'place' where certain people lived but also the 'place' they inhabited in a social hierarchy."[25] Steward's geographic expansion of regional writing to the Philippines literalizes the imperializing process that Amy Kaplan describes wherein regionalism represents the "island communities outside urban centers" as "exotically other" and "painted with the luster of empire." In Kaplan's analysis, local color—a form she compares with travel writing and ethnography—takes on some of the exoticizing and othering effects of Orientalist romance and shares with the imperialist imagination the goal of mapping spaces and peoples into new networks of power and capital. Both discourses organize culturally "foreign" people, cultures, and places into modes of knowledge that are reassuring to the identity of the knower.[26]

This is not to say that the two forms are irreducible to one another but to explain their combination in Steward's writing. Unlike turn-of-the-century Orientalist romances, local color manages difference within the national horizon of identification, where the boundaries between self and other must remain permeable to national desires for imagined fraternal bonds. Steward's Philippines are plotted at the intersection of these forms, raising the question of the islands' relationship to national and imperial imaginings and rendering them as a space to map the color line as it traversed the domestic and the foreign.

In critically aligning local color with U.S. Orientalism, my goal is not to overemphasize the former's hegemonic effects. Postcolonial theorists have shown that Orientalist discourse never fully succeeds in reassuring the west's stable and homogenous identity vis-à-vis the east, demonstrating the variable effects of individual Orientalist texts, and this caveat about ideological diversity and linguistic instability applies to the relatively small set of novels that use gender and romance to figure transpacific relations at the turn of the century.[27] Americanists have found similar variability and instability in the genre of turn-of-the-century U.S. local color writing. Many do see local color as effacing the conflicts of race, class, and gender experienced "at home" in urban centers through a variety of tactics: by representing a nostalgic, premodern space free of conflict, by projecting familiar urban heterogeneity onto discrete regions that are anchored and bound as internally homogenous separate spaces, or by reaffirming the stable authority of the cosmopolitan traveler over the peripheral, rural object of knowledge.[28] But many of these same critics emphasize the potential of local color to push readers beyond such evasions, whether by dissolving fantasies of rural escape with traces of expansive capitalism, by troubling readerly identification with the presumptuous cosmopolitan visitor-narrator, or by revealing the exploitative consequences that certain national policies had for rural Americans.[29] Steward's local color tales exhibit the former colonizing tendency when they subordinate domestic black/white racial conflicts to a more spatially and culturally dramatic binary of Filipino/American. Yet, at times, his "Tales of Laguna" push against this tendency in ways that undo this symbolic effort, allowing us to consider Steward among the writers who Nancy Glazener claims appropriated dominant modes of realism to engage readers in a dialogue about literary realism and national belonging.[30]

Deracialized Empire and the Prerogatives of Plain Citizenship

Steward engages this dialogue about national belonging by not specifying his unnamed first-person narrator's race. All that readers know about Steward's narrator is that he is a Harvard-educated American captain of a regiment garrisoned in a small town in the province of Laguna. Readers of the *CAM* may have assumed that the narrator was white, especially because the magazine occasionally included fictional stories told from the point of view of white characters or even stories in which all the primary characters were white. Here we might read Steward as authorizing himself, as Paul Lawrence Dunbar did in *The Uncalled* (1898) and *The Love of Landry* (1900), to assume artistic freedom to tell a story in which a black perspective simply does not matter.[31] As J. Saunders Redding wrote about Dunbar's authorship of his so-called white novels: "He drew white characters in a typical white environment and sought to inspire the whole thing with the breath of living truth. . . . Fundamentally, he said, there is no difference between Negro and white: the artist is free to work in whatever material he wishes." Or readers might have assumed that the narrator was black or mulatto, especially if they identified the narrator with the author, who as we know had been profiled two years earlier in the *CAM*'s "Here and There" and whose father was a moderately well known race man.[32] This tendency to identify the racially indeterminate narrator with the colored American author would be particularly encouraged if readers took note that the author of the "Tales of Laguna" was given with his title, "Captain Frank R. Steward," the same rank that the fictional narrator holds.

If they read the fictional captain as black or white, however, readers were also prompted to see the character as "de-raced," a third term that demands theoretical and historical attention, for it simultaneously marks the captain with a race even as it refuses any social meaning to the category. As I use these terms, the "de-raced" captain is not *raceless*, because the latter implies a character presumed to lack a race worth remembering, while a de-raced character has one that must be deliberately left unspoken and negated, only seemingly forgotten. The former is prevalent in writing by whites that leaves whiteness unmarked and assumed, as though to be white were to be raceless, while the latter is a rarity in the African American literary tradition. Toni Morrison's "Recitatif," published in 1983, still seems experimental for its choice not to disclose the race of the narrator while making race a central theme of the story. Like the choice to write about markedly white characters, the choice to create a "de-raced" character could be linked, in Steward's case, to the endeavor that Ross Posnock has claimed engaged the era's black intellectuals: to construct a black intellectual identity with a "cosmopolitan" perspective, one not bound by racial essentialism.[33]

In what follows here, I explore the possibilities and limitations of such a strategy in the case of Steward's writing, where cosmopolitan vision is predicated on not only an escape from racialized self-definition but also a geographic voyage away from domestic racial hierarchies. Steward's fiction may be an "escape from race" insofar as the narrator's masculine authority denies a black/white binary and illustrates that race does not matter when identifying the American officer. But the story of U.S. military authority in the Philippines invites race back into the story in ways that trouble the "antirace" impulses seen in the construction of the de-raced narrator.

One of the most significant critical discussions about de-raced characterization as a literary device in Steward's era has followed from the Schomburg Library of Black Women Writers series' now-admitted mistake of classifying Emma Dunham Kelly—author of *Megda* (1891) and *Four Girls at Cottage City* (1898)—as a black woman. Trusting that Kelly was indeed black, critics reading the Schomburg edition frequently took Kelly's production of raceless characters for de-raced characters; in other words, they interpreted the novels' general silence on the middle-class characters' race as a subversive rather than a conventional move and assumed that the characters shared a black or mulatto racial identity with the author. As Ann duCille warned before she learned about this mistake, "to query too intensely the characters racial identity . . . may be to place undue emphasis on the very subjectivity Kelly has chosen to place under erasure."[34] DuCille's observation seems less persuasive now that Kelly's works have been deleted from the Schomburg's series and Kelly herself, as well as her characters, are assumed to be white (or, to be exact, to be as white as any persons who claim that they and all their ancestors are white). This contingency of interpretation suggests the extent to which presumed authorial identity and racial perspective play crucial roles distinguishing the intentionally de-raced character from the unconsciously raceless.[35]

If a character is de-raced, the reader must interpret racial silence as self-conscious forgetting, thus bringing race back into view through a more critical lens as it begs the question of its importance. For Steward, it seems likely that this was at least part of the point: the captain's race doesn't matter, but his rank and ability do. As in his essay "Colored Officers," Steward demands in the "Tales of Laguna" that his fictional officer has no identity other than that of "a plain citizen of the Republic trained to the profession of arms."[36] Steward's narrator asserts "plain citizenship" by differentiating himself from his Filipino interlocutors, a superiority materialized through three intersecting modes of differentiation: race, gender, and language. Before moving on to support this claim with a close reading of Steward's Filipino American encounters, this third term of "language" demands more explanation, because while linked binaries of male/female and white/nonwhite are no doubt familiar to critical readers of imperialist and Orientalist texts, that of linguistic fluency/nonfluency or standard/vernacular may be less so.

Language cannot be fully separated from its intersections with gender or race, insofar as femininity is conventionally associated with either volubility or with silence, and race is often produced textually with marked accents and dialects. In addition, at Steward's historical moment, language is important for producing the simultaneous unifying and dividing meanings that local color writing conveyed. Representing a variety of accents, dialects, and pidgin languages provided one means by which U.S. writers of this era explored the possibilities for democratic communication and marked the limitations, dangers, and ideals of racial and cultural heterogeneity within the United States. Dialect writing was also a conventional form that, as the varying reception of Dunbar's dialect and nondialect poetry by literary critics attests, could both celebrate a black vernacular voice and cage black expression within an "authentic" local mode.[37] Extending this convention to the Philippines, Steward uses language as a trope for the possibilities of cultural and political assimilation.

Both of the "Tales of Laguna" hinge on scenes where the captain listens to the speech of the camp's laundress, Flora. The captain takes interest in Flora's gossip yet is repulsed by her language and her feminine volubility.

"Starlik: A Tale of Laguna" begins with Flora delivering the captain's laundry and aimlessly waiting around his residence: "It was plain the hag was purposely staying," the narrator observes, so he "continued indolently scratching away on a blank sheet of paper on the table in front of me, and bided events." [38] He knows "that she had something to tell," a verbosity that he marks as disgusting: when she opens her mouth to speak with him, he comments that "her buyo-stained lips parted to show a hideous mouthful of ill-formed reddened teeth" ("Starlik," 387). She only gets two words out—"Capitan dicen"—before the narrator pauses to criticize: she begins with "the inevitable 'they say,' . . . the gossip's unvarying language in every clime." (Steward's stories are peppered with both Spanish and words intended to be Tagalog, only some of which are translated for the reader.) As she continues, he struggles to control his impatience with her long-winded story: "remembering her past services to us, I resolved to resign myself as good-naturedly as I could to her womanish prattle" (387).

Here gender and speech differentiate American from Filipina: he writes and she talks; he is silent and she verbose. Flora's dialect similarly disgusts the captain, who deems himself linguistically and logically masterful for even understanding her: "Grown accustomed by this time to Flora's lingo, a polyglot of English, Spanish and Tagalog, I succeeded in detaching her slender story out of the mass of meaningless matter which her halting and stumbling speech wove into the narrative, and mentally reduced it as follows" (387). The narrator performs such acts of translation throughout the story; he makes known from a passing comment that he learned Spanish at Harvard and represents himself as more at home in the language than the Filipino Spanish speakers, who seem mere mimics in comparison with his metropolitan bilingualism. In one scene he exchanges formal pleasantries with Filipino gentlemen and comments on their use of Spanish: "their polite phrases, which I faintly remembered to have thumbed out of the pages of Knapp and Galdos, when I was in for it at Harvard, sound[ed] strangely out of tune in the mouths of these little brown-faced, white pantalooned courtiers of the bosky" (388). Here language and color intersect to stress the civilized agency of the captain, whose up-to-date college slang ("in for it") and rusty Ivy League Spanish is somehow more "in tune" than the speech of these Asian colonial Spanish speakers. The captain's face, although never described, is symbolically whitened by comparing his speech with that of "brown-faced" Filipinos. If the story deraces the narrator by rendering him a "plain citizen," that neutral citizenship is implicitly marked as *whiter* than the Filipino noncitizens.

As an element of the paradigmatic local color scenario, Steward's narrator exhibits not the condescendingly bemused or earnestly sympathetic interest of Page's or Jewett's narrator-visitors, instead showing a more marked sense of superiority toward these local Filipino speakers. But how is the reader encouraged to relate to this narrator? Compare Steward's "Tales of Laguna" with Chesnutt's "Conjure Tales," which critics recognize as a complex parodic response to local color's ethnographic collection of authentic regional voices and beliefs. Chesnutt mirrors plantation tales like Page's "Marse Chan" by creating a dialogic situation in which a white Northern narrator assumes rational superiority over his African American folk interlocutor, but Chesnutt undercuts his white narrator's limited perspective with a powerful portrayal of conjure, tricksterism, and African American speech that offers to the reader more insight into slavery and its aftermath than the white narrator gleans from listening.[39] In contrast, the "Tales of Laguna" give no obvious cues to readers that they should question the captain's view of the Philippines or appreciate the power or insight of Filipino voice and folk belief, leaving the reader with the possible implication that the "de-raced" captain's story is another iteration of the narratives of racial uplift that commonly appeared in the *CAM*'s coverage of the Filipino American War—one propped up on Orientalist binaries of east/west and female/male.

A central question in both of the "Tales of Laguna" is whether a beautiful young Filipina can learn English, a skill represented as a form of Americanization. This question even further emphasizes the linguistic authority of the narrator and invokes a central question about the Philippines in the United States: Can the Philippines be "Americanized"? The scenario of Filipinas learning English is sexualized in both stories, investing the story of imperial expansion with the erotics that fueled both desires for imperial intimacies and fears of racial contamination. "Pepe's Anting-Anting," the first tale Steward published in the *CAM,* begins with the narrator agreeing to exchange English lessons for Tagalog with a fascinating Filipina maiden named Chata. The lessons begin immediately, but just as they turn to subtle flirtation, Chata's Filipino admirer Pepe passes by and casts his jealous eye on the narrator. At the very moment that this suggestion of a love triangle arises, the action breaks off to describe Pepe at length, including both his devoted and polite courtship of Chata and his work as an official for the Americans: Pepe is a "scribiente," a minor official working for the U.S. government who receives and writes requests for passes from Filipinos wishing to travel from the city. Yet, despite the

Americans' trust, Pepe is found to be a covert insurrectionist, a fact that the narrator learns from his laundress, Flora, who reports that Chata and Pepe have been observed holding whispered conversations about "Independencia . . . combatte . . . los Americanos" and that Chata was known to have made a charm for Pepe called an Anting-Anting, intended to protect Filipino warriors in battle.[40] Flora, a devout Catholic, becomes hysterical telling the story, certain that Chata and Pepe have cursed themselves with their sacrilegious behavior: Chata was seen bringing the Anting Anting into church and holding up the fetish before the image of the Virgin, an affront certain to result in calamity.

Upon hearing this incriminating story, the narrator is immediately called off by the officer's bell, alerting him of a briefing where he hears a report confirming Flora's gossip. Pepe has disappeared, leaving a note explaining his purpose: to join the insurrectos, who have overnight attacked and taken over the barrio of San Antonio, cutting its telegraph lines and imprisoning its commander. The officers are called to attack the insurrectos and retake San Antonio, which they do successfully. But instead of reporting the battle, the story jumps to a brief scene afterward in which the narrator looks down on Pepe's dead body among the fallen Filipinos and notices that the charm is still around his neck. When his body is returned home, a sympathetic American sergeant permits Chata to remove the charm before Pepe is buried next to an image of the Virgin Mary, a proximity that troubles old Flora. A week later, the narrator reports seeing another funeral pass by. Peering behind the shrouds of the funeral bier, he and Flora see Chata's body with the Anting Anting around her neck. The mourners at her funeral apparently believe that she has been killed by malaria, but, as the story ends, "old Flora, the buyo-chewing hag of Calle Concepcion knew better. / So did I" ("Pepe's Anting Anting," 362).

The story invests the narrator with what Steward claims African Americans deserve in his essay "Colored Officers": "the full manhood privileges of a soldier." The captain interacts only with Filipina women in the story—besides Pepe, with whom we never see the narrator speaking, no other characters are named. These gendered interactions emphasize both the captain's sexual power and his rationality. In the opening scene's language lessons, which take place in the canteen where Chata works, her dark sexuality is elaborately described: "In the bestowal of her favors, Nature had been more than generous with this humble daughter of the 'bosky'—an oval face of unmatched olive tint—the despair of the West; a wealth of lustrous black hair, and the deep, dark, elusive eyes of the Malay ever in furtive glow" ("Pepe's Anting Anting," 358). Here it is uncertain whether her face's beauty or its color is the despair of the west, hinting at the fear of miscegenation that accompanied the taking of colonial possessions. The narrator says that because of her appealing form, he had to "struggle" to look away, mesmerized by "her corsetless bosom" barely concealed by a "thin, low cut jusi waist," her "plump, round neck and shoulders," and her bare ankles (358). Responding to her receptive gestures during the language lesson, the narrator says that he "took the lead" by attempting to teach her the English word "sweetheart," a move that suggests to the reader some budding romance between Chata and the narrator.

This expectation is not only unfulfilled but replaced with treachery and gruesome death, a substitution that deromanticizes the U.S. occupation and thwarts the expectation that Filipinas, as the colonial symbols of feminized subalterns, are eager to become Americanized. Indeed, the clearest statement of the story's meaning comes as the narrator recalls some wise advice, shedding light on Pepe and Chata's treachery:

> I could not help feeling the truth of the statement of the blunt old soldier lately come to command the division, who had declared that the entire Filipino population was at heart hostile to the Americans and that no people surpassed the Filipinos in dissembling. For no Filipino in all the pueblo professed greater friendship for the Americans, or had denounced more fervently the foolhardiness of the "locos" campaigning in the bosky, than Pepe. As for Chata, her zeal to learn everything American had earned her in the pueblo the contemptuous epithet of "Americanista." (361)

For all Chata's apparent interest in Americanization, linked in this story with her desire to learn English and her sexual receptivity toward the captain, she conceals treachery: she expresses her real loyalty to the revolution and her Filipino solider through her wearing of his Anting Anting, the sign and talismanic source of a Filipino warrior's power. The Filipina's dark beauty is the despair of the west because it conceals the heart and mind of the other.

Chata's treachery and apparent rejection of the captain and his American colonial influence in favor of Pepe and his Anting Anting might seem more like the captain's emasculation than the exercise of his "full manhood privileges," but this implication is countered in the text by the narrator's lack of emotional expression about Chata's betrayal and by reestablishing his rational superiority in opposition to old Flora. The quotation above aligns the narrator with masculine experience: taking refuge in the blunt and cynical old soldier's distrust of the Filipinos draws him closer to American male authority. Furthermore, as this information comes from Flora, her hysteria and fervent Catholicism—she mumbles prayers and falls to her knees, quaking as she worries about Chata's idolatry—further distances the captain from the superstitious locals. At the story's end, the final comment that both Flora and the narrator "knew better" than to believe that malaria killed Chata only ironically unites them. Flora's "better" knowledge is represented as merely more superstition of the Catholic rather than the indigenous variety: she thinks the Virgin Mary has cursed Chata for her religious affronts. The narrator, readers are prompted to assume, draws a more logical conclusion that Chata's death was from sorrow and remorse, and was perhaps self-inflicted, because of her still-forbidden loyalty to Pepe and the lost insurrectionist cause.

In "Pepe's Anting Anting," the colloquial interests of the local color narrator give way to the distancing judgment of Orientalist expert, opposing east and west through a string of typical binaries such as male/female, rational/irrational, and transparent/hidden. The Philippines cannot be romanced into the American nation as a new region of quaint folk customs and dialects, despite outward appearances. Instead, the de-raced, "plain citizen" harnesses Orientalist binaries to further project conflicts of racial difference away from the United States: it simply does not matter to the story of U.S. empire if the observant, rational, and articulate captain is black or white.

In this way, Steward's stories denied the suspicion, occasionally voiced in the white press, that a disproportionate number of colored soldiers turned traitor on the Philippine islands by joining the rebels.[41] In one well-known instance, white military historian Stephen Bonsal claimed in the *North American Review* that African American soldiers in the Philippines "got on much too well" with their "little brown sisters," to whom "they became united by the tenderest of ties," until by 1901 "the color line had been drawn again to our [white American] disadvantage, and . . . the negro soldiers were in closer sympathy with the aims of the native population than they were with those of their white leaders and the policy of the United States."[42] Notable in Bonsal's formulation is the agent who "draws again" the color line in the Philippines: it is redrawn not by racialized white imperialist mission but by Afro-Asian anticolonial sympathy and sexual intimacy. In "Pepe's Anting Anting," Steward's narrator dramatically refuses to extend the color line dividing black from white, maintaining instead only a sharp contrast between foreign and American, east and west.

Starlik *Mulattas and Tragic Filipinas*

Such neat contrasts come undone in "Starlik: A Tale of Laguna," the story published next in the *CAM*, in which the specter of U.S. domestic racial hierarchy threatens the de-raced subject position of "plain citizen." This threat reveals a color line in the Philippines drawn not by the romantic ties of Afro-Asian anticolonialism, as Bonsal accused, but by civilized hierarchies of color and purity that bridge Spanish and U.S. American colonial influence.

The captain's ambivalent relationships with Flora and with the Americanization of sexually available young Filipinas continue in "Starlik," which features the same characters and takes place some time after Chata's death. "Starlik" begins with the captain listening to Flora's news that an English-speaking Filipina is visiting the pueblo, prompting him to express doubt that "among these Tagals, was one who had learned our Western tongue and could speak it." Recalling "poor Chata's efforts to speak English," he skeptically asks the name of this "young, English-speaking prodigy" ("Starlik," 388). Here, remembering Chata recalls the link between language, female sexuality, and Americanization in the previous story. If Chata's flirtatious English lessons treacherously concealed rejection of the American occupation in favor of Filipino male potency, is it possible this other young Filipina has truly learned English—and truly embraced American influence and masculine power? An affirmative answer might mean that the captain could renew his previous flirtation uninterrupted by Filipino men and their insurgent nationalism.

Flora says that the young woman's name is "Enriqueta . . . pero (but), capitan, esta Enriqueta es (is) mucho starlik" (388; translations in original). The captain is unfamiliar with the "native vernacular term" *starlik* and requires Flora to pantomime its meaning, from which he guesses that it means "airish"—the laundress puts on a performance reminding the captain of "how children in their play often deck themselves out in the clothes of their grown-up sisters, and set about aping the manners and carriage of their elders" (388). This mimicry provides the story's central enigma: Is Enriqueta really capable of acting like her "grown-up" sisters, or is she only pretending to take on manners for which she is unprepared?

Figured here is the basic question of the debate about Filipino independence in the United States, mapped onto female social behavior and language: Are the Filipinos mature enough to govern themselves, or are they
still children who can only play at democracy? And left unstated is the
given assumption that authorizes the narrator to judge this *starlik* behavior: white or black, the American captain himself is supremely qualified
for democracy and citizenship.

Flora and the other Filipinas in the town ostracize Enriqueta for dress-
ing and talking like an American instead of in the native fashion, but after
meeting her the captain finds her fascinating, especially for her "nearly
perfect" pronunciation of English, which he discovers that she learned
from the daughter of a British engineer who established an electric light
works in her city of Lipa and from an American prisoner held captive
there during the early days of the Filipino insurrection. Even her Spanish
accent pleases the captain: when she addresses him as "sir," he comments
that he "liked the way she lisped out 'sair'" (389), a word that reinforces his
authority and rank with an appealing but nonthreatening accent of difference. Linguistically she is clearly superior to Chata, but while conversing
with her, the captain guesses another potential similarity between the two
Filipinas: that Enriqueta's father is an insurrectionist. He asks if she has
been reticent on the topic of her father to conceal his revolutionary ac-
tivities, but her answer reveals otherwise: "My father ees no insurrecto . . .
if her were only *that*, I would not care. Eet ees much worse, capitan, he
was—." Too distraught to continue, she leaves him with another enigma
to solve, one that he "resolve[s] to penetrate" as he lies awake wondering
about her at night (389).

There are hints of a detective narrative here, as in "Pepe's Anting
Anting"—the captain enacts his masculine agency in solving the myster-
ies of these dark women—but this agency is partly countered by his de-
pendence on Flora and her network of feminine gossip for the answers,
a form of narrative passivity consistent with the local color form, where
the narrator more often hears about local intrigue than participates in it.
Flora clears up the mystery later on when she explains why the towns-
women disdained Enriqueta: "Esta Starlik, capitan, no like Filipinos. Esta
mucho like be alle-same Spanish. Esta pickaninny de frailes!" The captain
quickly translates for the reader: "Enriqueta was the daughter of a hated
friar!" ("Starlik," 390). This realization provokes a long digression about
the corruption of the Catholic Church, which remained in the Philippines
after the Spanish government was forced out. The narrator breaks out of

the narrative past tense to address the reader directly on the topic: "Now, stark and bare before us lies the real question of the Philippines. . . . The vast estates which these begowned men of God have amassed in these isles, show the dimensions of their avarice quite as strikingly as here and there the whitened faces among the populace have revealed the trail of their lust" (390). How the United States should deal with the Catholic Church in the Philippines after Spain's defeat was a current policy question that the narrator pauses to editorialize upon, urging William Howard Taft as colonial governor not to compromise in upcoming negotiations with the Vatican about control of the friars' property and power on the islands.

The narrator cites the Filipino nationalist José Rizal (misspelling or misprinting his novel's title, *Noli Me Tangere*) as an authority on this matter: "A cause which made a martyr of the lofty soul of the gifted author of "Noline Tangere," will not be defeated by a calculating compromise, be it dictated by the claims of expedience, however insistent." Citing Rizal indicates that Steward realized his plot echoed that of Rizal's famous 1896 novel in which the heroine Maria Clara is revealed at the end to be the illegitimate daughter of Father Damaso, a corrupt friar—except in Steward's version, there are no heroic Filipino nationalists to fall in love with this tragic heroine, leaving her in the hands of ambiguously portrayed American soldiers. Steward's political message, in which the narrator remasters Flora's trifling town gossip by reducing it to the "stark and bare" essential issue, takes the place of any personal reaction from the narrator about what this revelation of Enriqueta's mixed-race identity means to him. Returning to the narrative frame, he merely explains that social ostracism caused Enriqueta to move on later that year to Manila. This explanation's brevity implies that with Enriqueta's mysterious identity and its significance laid bare, the narrator retains not even enough interest to keep up her acquaintance.

This sense of disinterest is belied by the suppressed emotion straining through in the final scene. The story ends with the captain catching sight of Enriqueta one day in Manila, where he learns she has become a prostitute, a revelation that is presented quite dramatically but without any comment from the narrator. He tells of accidentally being lost in Manila's "domain of the half world" and stuck on a congested street, where he sees a woman leaning out of a brightly lit house and bantering with a drunken soldier, saying "in tones insistent,—'Come in, sair.'" The story ends tersely and enigmatically, as in "Pepe's Anting-Anting," with the narrator only confirming that "the eyes had grown a bit steely and the face a trifle bleary; for all that I knew Starlik." Immediately after this line, the story ends with a one-sentence paragraph: "In a moment the blockade opened, and my quilez went whirling on its way toward the Escolta" (391).

Regarding the story's most overt purpose (to show the corruption of the Catholic Church in the Philippines and to recommend a hard line in negotiations with the Vatican), this final scene illustrates the ultimate results of the friars' sexual wrongdoings. But the strange position of the narrator and his deliberate lack of comment at the end, combined with his alternating expressions of deep interest and neutral distance from Enriqueta, suggest other meanings. At times, Steward's narrative point of view and theme could be described as Hemingwayesque—we see hints of emotion from a tight-lipped, world-wearied narrator who tells about more-expressive but unreliable female characters. Whirling away in his quilez at the end of the story, the narrator's silence makes him seem speechless in the wake of Enriqueta's sexual degradation and her own apparent complicity with her degradation: she is using the very linguistic abilities that so pleased him and so differentiated her from Chata to summon a client, and even calling this stranger "sair," the same word that earlier evoked the captain's pleasure and affirmed his authority. These hints make it possible that, underneath his pose of objective neutrality, Steward's captain is made a cuckold in this final scene as successful westernization and racial uplift give way to colonial and sexual exploitation. In this way, the firm hierarchy of power relations placing American/colonizer/male over Filipino/colonized/female seen in "Pepe's Anting Anting" becomes more unstable as the narrator is left silenced and again potentially jilted.

That binary is even more disrupted because the enigmatic ending subtly implicates the U.S. occupation in the Catholic Church's abuse of power. While on the surface the story criticizes the corruption of the friars as a remnant of imperial Spain, the United States and possibly the narrator himself share in the guilt for ravishing, ruining, and miscegenating the Philippines, figured as a female subaltern. The fact that it is an American soldier whom Enriqueta invites to enter the brothel implicates the United States in the cycle of colonial sexual exploitation begun with the Spanish friars, making this story, like "Pepe's Anting-Anting," rather pessimistic about the mission to Americanize the Philippines. Sexual impurity is a by-product of imperial intimacies, whether Spanish or American, and even the cool-headed narrator is confronted by, if not implicated in, the sordid situation.

Ann Laura Stoler has shown the fears surrounding racial mixture in imperial contexts to be a powerful trope for challenges to imperial rule: "conceived of as a source of subversion, *métissage* was seen as a threat to white prestige, an embodiment of European degeneration and moral decay." With the appearance of this trope in Steward's fiction, the story of de-raced military service in the Philippines by "plain citizens," not besieged upon or divided by what Stoler calls "interior frontiers," begins to break down.[43] In the ambiguous portrayal of the narrator's interest in Enriqueta, "Starlik" offers enough obvious contradiction to make the narrator's claims to rational distance from and superiority to his subjects seem unreliable. As in Chesnutt's "Conjure Tales," the authoritative, cosmopolitan narrator loses credibility with the reader when gaps in his powers of perception and interpretation are revealed. Once this possibility for critical distance is evoked, the idea of de-raced American power itself becomes an object of scrutiny, especially as its colonial incarnation in the Philippines seems to re-create the color line dividing the post-Reconstruction United States. Enriqueta appears as a new version of the tragic mulatta, that standard African American fictional character of the era.[44] Because of her "starlik" aspirations to rise socially above the people of her mother, apparent in her English language and western dress, she is at home nowhere and driven to the tragic fate of prostitution. Flora calls her the "pickaninny" of the friars, an intentionally comic appropriation of an American term that in this context draws an unmistakable parallel between African Americans and Filipinos.

Steward's father, T. G. Steward, drew such a parallel in one of his 1901 drafts for an essay on "The Color Problem World Wide," where he writes, "We are accustomed to think the color question an American question, and to regard the Negro race as the only race affected by it, but it is a world-wide question, and establishes the most important cleavage among men." T. G. Steward's essay recounts instances of Filipinos placing their hands beside those of black soldiers, saying "we are the same," and he gives a mixed-race character from Rizal's *Noli Me Tangere,* the model for Frank Steward's story, as another parallel between American Negro and Filipino: "Entering the literature [of the Philippines] I found the same color question which prevails in the United States. . . . I found a historical class of servile mestizoes, few and far between, which were like the mulattoes of Hayti, and like that poor remnant of mulattoes in Charleston, entitled to be classed as mascots and monkeys of the race that sired and scorned them. Rizal pictures one such in his Dona Victorina in his great novel

'Noli me Tangere.'"[45] Here naming Rizal's comic Tagalog-Spanish mixed-race character, a bourgeois lady with elite pretensions, T. G. Steward draws an explicit connection between this instance of the color line at home and abroad, a connection that his son draws far more subtly in his portrayal of Enriqueta as a tragic mulatta modeled after Rizal's heroine Maria Clara. Whether Frank Steward read his father's drafts or discussed such parallels with his father is unknown (no correspondence between them written during the war has been found), but he draws his own connection between fictional mulattas at home and abroad in his short stories.

In Frank Steward's fiction, however, that connection is implied only obliquely, as one element in a complex fictional rendering of de-raced military service. Through this oblique parallel, what was repressed in his creation of a racially unspecified American military officer returns to trouble the text's central binary between American and Filipino. While Steward's outward purpose in the "Tales of Laguna" seems to be to suppress domestic race inequalities to prioritize a linguistic, gendered, and racial divide between American and Filipino, the figure of the Filipina tragic mulatta reminds readers of the color line within the United States. The effect is to recast Steward's de-raced narrator, who has willfully forgotten race, as one who is enveloped and imbricated in a set of local racial meanings and legacies that travel with the cosmopolitan wherever he might go.

As described in chapter 1, anti-imperialists frequently characterized the Philippines as a place of danger for white American soldiers falling prey to sexual immorality, venereal disease, miscegenation, and Darwinian racial regression. Traces of this tactic appear in the black press as well: a 1903 article in the *CAM* by Army Regular Rienzi B. Lemus depicted the islands as a place where "about the only thing thoroughly accomplished . . . is miscegenation," a jibe at colonists past and present: "When the Americans arrived [the archipelago] was a handsome set of all hues and kinds, and they—soldiers and citizens, officers and men, white and colored—did not fail to leave behind them beauties who give promise to be attractive to someone. If the blood of every nation were of a different hue, a modern Filipino could well be termed a 'human leopard.'"[46] But the pessimistic, anti-imperialist elements of Steward's "Tales of Laguna" hint that the Philippines are not only a place of confused and degraded mixture to be avoided but also a later chapter of the familiar American story of sexualized racial oppression.

The parallel that "Starlik" implies between racial mixing at home and in the Philippines is similar to the one more explicitly drawn by Pauline

Hopkins in her short story "Talma Gordon," which appeared in the *CAM* in 1900, two years before Steward's "Tales of Laguna." "Talma Gordon" takes up a key question of Rudyard Kipling's "White Man's Burden": What will be the effect of imperialism on the white man? It poses this question by making it the topic officially under discussion at a meeting of the Boston Canterbury Club, an elite men's group. The subject of "vital importance to the life of the republic" they are to discuss is "Expansion; Its Effect upon the Future Development of the Anglo-Saxon throughout the World."[47] The first members to speak identify only the benefits of expansion. Because of it, the United States will win, as Kipling promised, an "exalted position . . . in the councils of the great governments of the world," and Protestantism will win more souls.

But when the most respected participant Dr. William Thornton speaks, he demands that his listeners also consider the potentially negative effects of expansion on the Anglo-Saxon race: "Did you ever think," he asks, "that in spite of our prejudices against amalgamation, some of our descendents, indeed many of them, will inevitably intermarry among those far-off tribes of dark-skinned people, if they become a part of this great Union?" ("Talma Gordon," 50). Here whiteness comes under threat from the white man's burden, but Thornton clarifies that amalgamation is only *sometimes* undesirable. Its desirability depends not only on the moral and physical development of the races in question but also on the readiness of Anglo-Saxons "to receive and assimilate the new material which will be brought to mingle with our pure Anglo-Saxon stream" (51). An expansionist policy, he argues, should only exist if such a state of readiness exists. Here Hopkins borrows the language from McKinley's declaration that the purpose of the United States in the Philippines would be "benevolent assimilation," but while McKinley's supporters in the U.S. Senate vigorously clarified that a policy of "assimilation" in the Philippines did not mean racial "amalgamation," Hopkins asserts that it will and must: there is no benevolent assimilation without the ability to accept and effectively shape amalgamation.[48]

The story concludes with the revelation that Mr. Thornton has achieved this state of readiness by himself marrying and having children with the beautiful and accomplished Talma Gordon, a woman with some small portion of African American ancestry. He relates Talma's past experiences of rejection and suffering, typical to stories of tragic mulattas, to demonstrate the evils that will follow from inevitable race mixing in situations like slavery or colonialism, but he reveals in his own marriage to Talma his own faith in race mixing's positive potential. This ending leaves the Canterbury Club's debate on expansion's effects on the Anglo-Saxon race seemingly unresolved, leaving readers perhaps to conclude on their own that only if Americans can rise to the level of the exceptional Dr. Thornton can they successfully accomplish benevolent assimilation and improve the Anglo-Saxon stock by empire's judicious intermarriages, a version of the positive eugenicism that John Nickel shows to be a theme in Hopkins's writing.[49]

Steward, as I have argued, is not so optimistic. In his pessimism, a more apt comparison to Steward's vision of mulatto empire is with Gertrude Atherton's anti-imperialist political novel *Senator North* (1900), in which two plots intersect: one about imperialism, and the other about a tragic mulatta. In the first plot, ambitious young Washington, D.C., socialite Betty Madison falls in love with middle-aged Maine Republican mugwump Senator North, a character based on real-life senator Eugene Hale. The year is 1898, and as the United States is about to plunge into the Spanish American War, Senator North convinces Betty that cooler and more aristocratic heads must prevail over the young jingoes in Congress intent on going to war. Betty unsuccessfully tries to help Senator North in this lost cause against his own party by running a salon for political discussion, and while doing so manages her secret love for the married senator by highmindedly waiting until his invalid wife dies before acting on their love. In the second plot, Betty learns that she has a half-sister, Harriet Walker, born from her dead father's twenty-year-old affair with a mixed-blood African American woman. At Senator North's prompting, Betty decides to take responsibility for past sins, both her family's and her nation's, by caring for Harriet, who looks white and whose tragic fate, the novel contends, is to belong nowhere. Betty helps Harriet to pass for white, setting her up in Washington, D.C., and in doing so introduces her to Jack Emory, one of Betty's jilted suitors. Jack and Harriet fall in love, but when Harriet tells Jack the truth about her ancestry, he kills himself, and then in guilt and grief, Harriet commits suicide as well. Betty is left to ponder the tragedy she inadvertently created and has a maturing realization that links the two plots:

> She had engaged in a conflict with the Unseen Forces of life and been conquered. She had been obliged to see these forces work their will upon a helpless being, who carried in solution the vices of civilizations and men persisting to their logical climax, almost demanding out loud the sacrifice

of the victim to death that this portion of themselves might be buried with her. Despite her intelligence, nothing else could have given her so clear a realization of the eternal persistence of all acts, of the sequential symmetrical links they forge in the great chain of Circumstance. It was this that made her hope more eager that the United States would be guided by its statesmen and not by hysteria, and it was this that made her think deeply and constantly upon her future relation with Senator North.[50]

This startling passage links three kinds of desires for the "vices of civilization": the desire of Betty's father and other white men for African American women, the "hysterical" desire of the United States to seek empire through war with Spain, and Betty's own sexual and romantic desire for a married man. Harriet was born a product of this vice, and, as such, "Unseen Forces" demanded her sacrifice, so as to destroy the liquefied vice that she carried with her still as a "solution" in her blood. What additional tragic victims would be produced as animated carriers of the two other forms of vice—empire building and adultery—are unthinkable to Betty, and she resolves more firmly to live up to her ideals of chaste political and sexual restraint. *Senator North* never dwells on the possibility that even more race mixing will result from imperial expansion but makes Harriet Wilson and the collateral damage she causes a symbol of such unintended, lingering problems. Steward's "Starlik" fills in that possibility, showing the second stage of unintended problems for a foreign tragic mulatta shamed and doomed by the vice of her fathers. In contrast, Hopkins's "Talma Gordon" admits the possibility of a continued chapter of race mixing but then defuses the risk associated with that possibility by explaining that, in fact, one can judiciously harness Atherton's Unseen Forces to fulfill the promise of racial uplift at home and abroad.

The Taint of Language

The continuity Steward draws between the effects of miscegenation at home and in the Philippines is made more explicitly in his final short story, "The Men Who Prey," which appeared in the October 1903 *CAM* , the same issue as Micaela Flores's profile.[51] This final story leaves behind the local color mode to follow more directly in the genre of turn-of-the-century U.S. Orientalist fiction such as Long's "Madame Butterfly." But in its thematic content, local domestic prejudices and regional histories are again placed in continuity with the new global project of U.S. expansion.

In "The Men Who Prey," an unidentified first-person narrator appears only in the opening framing paragraphs, as an observer introducing a story about Captain Thomas Lane. The story's protagonist, Captain Lane bears some similarities to the first-person narrator of the "Tales of Laguna": he shares the same rank, his regiment is garrisoned in a small Laguna town, he speaks Spanish, and he is romantically interested in a young Filipina. But Captain Lane is overtly raced and assigned a regional identity, in addition to his status as an American officer: he is a white Texan whose ancestors fought alongside Sam Houston in the days of Texan independence. The narrator observes, "I saw [Captain Lane] striding about the little Laguna pueblo, a veritable giant among the diminutive hombres of the bosky," a man who "sprang out the Southwest" and whose distinguished ancestors won fame not only through their frequent service as judges and congressmen but also "in ways more turbulent, and after the manner approved by the best Texas traditions."[52] Back in Texas, unofficial records of the Lane family's local fame can be gathered from "the admiring talk of local denizens, from some vague findings at coroners inquests, and the speechless testimony of a headboard here and there in local cemeteries" ("Men Who Prey," 720). How Lane will continue this local Texas legacy in the Philippines emerges in the story as we hear more "admiring talk" about him.

The first-person observer narrator quickly fades into the background, replaced with two new alternating perspectives on Lane. In one narrative point of view, the now-omniscient narrator describes Lane as he says goodbye to his pregnant wife Fanny and five-year-old daughter back in San Antonio, arrives in the Philippines, embarks on several short campaigns before being garrisoned, meets a Filipina laundress named Jacinta, initiates with her a sexual relationship (making her his "matrimoning," in the camp's pidgin terminology), and exchanges letters with his unknowing wife. This omniscient narration breaks off occasionally into segments where a chorus of Lane's comrades comment favorably on his situation, as in this unintroduced scene:

"Fellers, d'ye catch onto the K.O's matrimoning? Ain't she a beaut?" observed No. 3 of the second relief, then at the guardhouse on the long bench, waiting turn to go on post.

"Bah, she ain't in it with the top seargeant's spouse," broke in No. 2.

"I think Reddy Merrimen's senorita is a heap finer looking than either," interjected No. 1.

"Who is the commandante's matrimoning, anyway? I don't know her," asked No. 5.

"What, you don't know Huhacinta," volunteered No. 3, "the damsel who used to live in the third shack in the alley next to the corral, that the gugus call calyay saint-something-or-other? She used to live with her aunt, that damned old bugau (procuress), Maria. But she's got the swell shack now, right back of the K's quarters. She's got it rigged up in great style." (722)

Here this "admiring talk" suggests a continuation of the Lane family's un-official frontier exploits, one that will also find no official record, because "matrimoning" does not require matrimony.

By revealing continuity between the regional past to the imperial pres-ent, a continued colonial history emerges, as well as fears and doubts about the intimacies of benevolent assimilation. While the "Tales of La-guna" offer surface readers a comforting pose of linguistic superiority to Filipinas, "The Men Who Prey" makes Filipinas the route to U.S. linguis-tic and moral corruption. The invented pidgin term "matrimoning" cor-rupts both the English language and the white American bloodstream, a contamination that further links past and present, region and empire, lo-cal and global. Lane speaks Spanish more fluently than do the common soldiers who celebrate him, but he is shown using it only to assert sexual authority over Jacinta. When they first meet, Lane is impressed with Ja-cinta's rudimentary English and then "went at her in the Spanish tongue, over which his Texas birth and rearing had given him control," asking a series of questions before making her his mistress. Here one imperial ven-ture of his ancestors settling and claiming Mexican land prepares Lane linguistically for another, but Lane's linguistic ability, figured as a kind of powerful "control," only enables a duplicitous sexual affair with a power-less Filipina.

This moral and linguistic corruption finds its way back home to the United States through the name "Jacinta," clumsily pronounced "Huha-cinta" by No. 3 in the preceding quotation. Although "six generations of Southern chivalry" run in Lane's blood, he symbolically miscegenates his family by selecting that name for his legal wife's second daughter, born during his service, without telling Fanny where he got it. In a letter from home, Fanny enthuses about loving the name her husband has selected for "Baby Jacinta." Interestingly, the "foreignness" of the name's origin is disguised by the family's Texan roots—Spanish language rather than

Filipino blood is injected into the Lane family tree, but the name might not seem out of place for the daughter of a family tracing its roots back to Texan independence. In this way, the Orientalist form of Steward's tragic Amer-Asian romance reminds readers of suppressed imperial intimacies within the nation's legal borders: as in the "Tales of Laguna," American "plain citizens" are implicated in domestic racial hierarchies, and, going one step further, they are also implicated in domestic imperial histories. "Local" stories, like the history of winning Mexican land and the unrecorded exploits of Texas oral tradition, seem regionally tangential to a unified "American" perspective, but, like the story of the "tragic mulatta," they recur globally in a projection—rather than an erasure—of the U.S. color line.

As in "Starlik," "The Men Who Prey" compares the sexual exploitation of Filipinas with that of African American women indirectly, through narrative and figurative conventions that would be familiar to readers of the *CAM*. The American "men who prey" turn out to be not so different from the friars—the men who *pray*—as both are linked with U.S. histories of empire, miscegenation, and the color line. The story ends immediately after we see Fanny's letter about Baby Jacinta, with a scene where her Filipina namesake realizes that Lane has deserted her and returned to Texas. In the story's final three paragraphs, we see Jacinta's reaction through the narrator's uncomprehending gaze:

> What boots it that a Filipino leaning against a post at the Anda wharf, swoons and falls in a heap just as the launch with the officers of the — Infantry pulls off for the transport? May days are fiercely hot in the tropics; even gugus are known to succumb sometimes.
>
> Two native women standing by pick the girl up tenderly, summon a corromatta and take her to their home. . . . Pretty soon Jacinta's eyes open, and the pickaninnies standing by innocently cry out their joy, for they thought her dead.
>
> The women gaze at Jacinta stretched out upon the couch, with hair streaming, and eyes open but seeing not, and shake their heads with foreboding. The one of them goes forth in great haste and summons Isabel, the mid-wife. (722–23)

In what we can begin to recognize as Steward's penchant for dramatic, sudden conclusions, this passage castigates colonial racism, showing even the narrator's callous disregard of suffering and revealing that Jacinta's unborn child will go without a patronym even as Baby Jacinta receives her given name. While the "Tales of Laguna" indirectly criticize U.S. imperialism and only subtly cast doubt on the narrator's motives, "The Men Who Prey" overtly cues readers to reject both the narrator's and Captain Lane's callous cruelty. That Jacinta ends up pregnant is no great surprise, but disclosing this information only through the story's final word, "midwife," repeats the abrupt conclusions of the "Tales of Laguna" and leaves the reader wondering about the fate of the Filipino American child. The "foreboding" looks of the women nursing Jacinta don't augur well for either her or the baby, suggesting that another Lane family exploit will be recorded only in gossip and on tombstones. But if the child lives, he or she (probably *she,* in Steward's gendered imbalances) will only suffer the fate met by Starlik. Indeed, the phrase used in "Starlik" to describe the corruption of Spanish friars aptly describes the influence of the "Men Who Prey": "the whitened faces among the populace have revealed the trail of their lust" (390).

While all three of Steward's stories oppose U.S. Pacific expansion as a route and a return to dangerous and immoral sexual intimacies of slavery and colonialism, the most obvious iteration of this point comes with the final story—the one that races the figure of the American officer as white. But it is in the "Tales of Laguna" that Steward most ingeniously attempts to expand the terms of black Orientalism. In those stories, readers are left to decide both the narrator's race and his race's importance to understanding his perspective, making the meanings of the story contingent on the reader's basic assumptions about race and imperial authority. If the narrator is read as white, would readers of the *CAM* —or readers today— find themselves more likely to seize on opportunities to find him hypocritical or unreliable in his superior attitude toward Filipinas? And if he is read as black and "de-raced," to what degree would desire to fulfill the political fantasy of "plain citizenship" prevent such critical interrogation? Or would readers see that by being de-raced, the captain is authorized only to re-create the conditions of his own racial oppression abroad? The "Tales of Laguna" powerfully reveal the impossibility of "de-racing" U.S. citizenship when the concept itself is defined in opposition to others by race and colonial status.

Steward's use of the device of the de-raced first-person narrator is thus his most remarkable formal experiment, one that was seldom used in the era's prose writing by African Americans. Perhaps this device was used so rarely because there were few contexts in which one could indulge a political fantasy of de-raced perspectives and citizens. To the extent that the idea of a de-raced American citizen could function at all in the post-Reconstruction era, it seems most viable in stories set outside of the United States, where the binaries of American versus foreign can be marshaled to overshadow internal racial difference. Furthermore, in some foreign settings, this device is more viable than in others—for example, as I show in chapter 4, the foreign space of Africa cannot sustain the pose of the de-raced American citizen; instead, Africa was figured as the place where the United States' repressed or forgotten blackness necessarily returns. The Pacific, in contrast, offered an ideal place to negotiate de-raced American power and authority, because there African American marginalization could be concealed beneath that of the Asiatic, a figure whose constitutional right of self-determination inside and outside the United States was also in question.

Another experimental element of Steward's writing is his demonstration and possible representation of African American multilingualism, one of his key tools for breaking the supposed linkage between whiteness, authority, and civilized mission. Whether we take the narrator of "The Tales of Laguna" as a de-raced white or black officer, the stories' exhibition and thematic concern with multilingualism offer a new enactment of black linguistic proficiency that extends the African American tradition's central concern with literacy, the vernacular, and the creation of an authentic black voice. A number of late-nineteenth-century writers pointedly rejected—or like Paul Lawrence Dunbar, questioned the popularity of—representations of African American vernacular dialects, selecting instead bourgeois characters and attributing to them all the genteel linguistic ability and "plain" unmarked speech afforded to white, Northeastern, middle-class characters. Rejecting dialect in this historical context made a case for educational and social equality, as well as for the standard "Americanness" of the new African American voice, one not tied to a particular regional vernacular and not marked by the "foreign" creole languages of South Atlantic Gulluh or Louisiana creole.[53]

Steward takes such arguments for black standard American linguistic proficiency a step further, by stressing his own and possibly his de-raced black narrator's ability to encode and decode the nonstandard speech of the other, whether concealed behind accented speech or in Spanish, French, or Tagalog. While regional American dialects were treated as local details to be realistically categorized and mastered, as in Mark Twain's famous "Explanatory Note" to *The Adventures of Huckleberry Finn* about his "painstaking" accuracy in rendering the various "shadings" of local Missouri speech, Steward instead authorized himself, his readers, and possibly his de-raced black narrator to assume the position of verbal expert and analyst. Again, however, this form of linguistic empowerment functions by making object and other of the inept or imperfect foreign English speakers whose failed efforts at linguistic proficiency signal their disqualification for U.S. citizenship. If Steward constructs an "articulate" de-raced African American (to use a term that has come to invoke the dominant white expectation of African American linguistic inability), he does so at the expense of the inarticulate other.

Are all these mechanisms of African American linguistic authority undercut by ironic criticism? I suggest here that Steward's use of these devices is especially interesting for the interpretive possibility that the Filipino oppression necessary for the de-raced American's ascent to the status of verbal expert, civilized authority, and "plain" citizen echoes rather than displaces African American oppression, resulting in an ironic parody of the captain's de-raced perspective. But this, I acknowledge, is only one interpretive possibility, and what Steward's readers actually made out of his writing is unknown, especially as no reviews or commentary on these obscure stories has been found. It may be that the ambiguity and interpretive openness in Steward's writing only echoed and intensified what was, in Du Bois's words, "a time of vacillation and contradiction for the American Negro."[54] However, while reception of Steward's work is largely unknown, one of his readers was most certainly Pauline Hopkins, the literary editor of the *CAM* for some of the period in which his fiction appeared. In chapter 4, I explore how the writing of Pauline Hopkins responded to the contradictions and incoherence seen in Steward's and other contributors' representations of the figure of the black cosmopolitan. Regarding the present discussion of Steward's writing, however, it seems clear that his stories' ambiguity came from his effort to simultaneously authorize the war and criticize it, an urge that he shared with a number of African American commentators on the conflict in the Philippines.

Finally, even if it is the case that Steward's readers were skeptical about the authority offered to them vicariously through the narrator and interpreted the "Tales of Laguna" as ironic reflections on the racialized logic of global colonial hierarchies of color and purity, one troubling Orientalist element still inflects the Afro-Asian anticolonial sympathy that they provoke. That element is Steward's obsessive repetition of the figure of the sexually available young Filipina. Like Long's "Madame Butterfly,"

Steward's fiction criticizes U.S. imperialism through the figure of the care-less American military man, but, as in Long's fiction, such portrayals also draw on and reinforce sexual fantasies of Asian female passivity and pow-erlessness—a fantasy that Chata violently dispels but Starlik and Jacinta embody. Steward's young Filipinas provide flexible material for political moralizing; they can signify spoils of war, or victims of colonialism, or potentially assimilated fellow Americans, or metonyms for Filipino sover-eignty, or new incarnations of the U.S. tragic mulatta, all without a single portrayal of their thoughts and emotions from an internal perspective.

As Norma Alarcón has written about La Malinche, Hernán Cortéz's concubine and translator who in nationalist mythologies came to serve as a symbol of indigenous Mexico's conquest and victimization, the mascu-linist construction of feminine symbols for compromised national integ-rity positions female sexuality as a marker of cultural and racial purity to be policed and trivializes a specific female experience.[55] Micaela Flores's motto, "The Philippines and Filipinas for Filipinos only" resonates only ambivalently in Steward's fiction, because for Steward the Filipina's sexu-ality is endlessly available for his own writing, both about domestic preju-dices and new incarnations of the global color line.

4

Pauline Hopkins's "International Policy"

Cosmopolitan Perspective at the Colored American Magazine

When Reuel Briggs, the protagonist of Pauline Hopkins's serially published novel *Of One Blood, Or, The Hidden Self* (1902–3), catches his first glimpse of Africa, the coast of Tripoli appears as a "low lying spectral band of shore," its "nudity" covered only by the "fallow mantle of the desert." Ghostly and naked, the land evokes in Reuel a feeling of sadness and, because of the assumed "intimate relation" between a land and its people, an expectation of difference: *"Reuel realized vividly that the race who dwelt here must be different from those of the rest of the world."* As numerous critics have noted, such descriptions of Africa in *Of One Blood* follow common Africanist and Orientalist tropes; they represent its landscape as a space of otherness and imperial fantasy, just as the novel's plot adopts generic conventions of imperialist fiction made popular by writers such as H. Rider Haggard.[2] Reuel Briggs's adventure across the desert to Ethiopia, with its serpents, lions, hidden treasure, and lost civilizations, is clearly inspired and structured by such conventional writings.

Less apparent is the fact that the more-immediate origin of the language in this passage is closer to home. Hopkins drew her description of Reuel's first glimpse of Africa from another writer's essay, "Some Foreign Cities I Have Seen," which was published in same issue of *CAM* that carried the first installment of her novel *Of One Blood*. Written by an African American sailor named Nicholas H. Campbell, this article describes the author's first vision and subsequent visit to Africa while on a tour of duty in the U.S. Navy. Following this route of rhetorical borrowing—from conventional imperialist discourse, to an essay employing this discourse in *CAM,* to Reuel Brigg's tortured vision and narrative point of view in *Of One Blood*—illuminates Hopkins's embattled engagement with black cosmopolitanism as author and editor. In turn, Hopkins's apprehension of the figure of the black cosmopolite offers a striking example of the cultural problem of African American perspective in shadowing the white man's burden.

Of One Blood unquestionably echoes Campbell's essay. Immediately after the lines quoted above, Reuel's traveling companion Charlie Vance offers him a telescope, and the text (italicized here and above to stress the language taken from Campbell) describes what Reuel sees through it:

> In the distance one could indeed make out upon the deep blue of the sky the profile of Djema el Gomgi, the great mosque on the shores of the Mediterranean. At a few cable lengths away the city smiles at them with all *the fascination of a modern Cleopatra,* circled with an oasis of palms studded with hundreds of domes and minarets. Against a sky of amethyst the city stands forth with penetrating charm. It is the *eternal enchantment of the cities of the Orient seen at a distance; but alas! Set foot within them, the illusion vanishes and disgust seizes you.* Like beautiful bodies they have the appearance of life, but within the worm of decay and death eats ceaselessly. (*Of One Blood,* 509; italics mine)

Campbell uses similar phrasing and a similarly authoritative voice to describe what "the traveler" sees approaching Tunisia from the Mediterranean:

> The sea sleeps on sandy beaches, tender skies reach out boundlessly, the line of shore like a bank of mother-of-pearl. Even when a storm sweeps over her surface, the Southern sea still *fascinates like a Cleopatra,* —her frowns but rendering her more bewitching. The influence of this soft climate lulls to rest all cares, regrets, ambition, even the stern Duty call. . . . But prosperity has long turned its face from Tunisia; there is *an intimate relation between the character of the country and its people. The race who dwell here represent something very different* from the inhabitants of our hardy northern climes. The struggle against rough and adverse elements in the north, the necessity of keeping up a continual warfare in order to live, the possibility of mastering these problems of life, have developed the best faculties of our species; while the people of this soft clime lie like slaves under the too ardent kiss of an implacable sun, which has

engendered idleness and fatalism. . . . *Seen at a distance, the eternal enchantment of the cities of the Orient has a penetrating charm; but set foot within them and the illusion vanishes, although the charm of novelty still remains."*[3]

Hopkins's borrowing of key phrases, sentence structures, images, and ideas—the theory of environmental determinism, the feminization of the landscape as Cleopatra, the mood of mystical allure and enchantment belied by close contact—so nearly replicates Campbell's that her writing appears to detach itself from Reuel's viewpoint. Hopkins's verb tense switches from past to present tense as the report of Reuel's thoughts and actions merges into the narrator's surveying of the scene. Within this shift to free indirect discourse, perspective changes from the third-person report of the protagonist's thoughts ("Reuel realized vividly") to the third-person indefinite (in the first sentence, on what "one" could see through the telescope), to the second-person imperative (in the penultimate sentence, on what will be realized when "you" set foot in the enchanted cities of the Orient). One might suppose these inconsistencies to be merely the result of Hopkins's careless adaptation of Campbell's firsthand account. But inconsistency in perspective raises a more fundamental question about Hopkins's adaptation of Campbell's already generic vision of Africa, one posed more generally by *Of One Blood*'s recent readers: How do we interpret the conventional and generic depictions of Africa in Hopkins's writing?[4]

Considering Reuel's characterization, the shift in perspective in the passage quoted above may not reveal a move outside of Reuel's consciousness at all but, instead, may be the narrator's report of Reuel's own thoughts. After all, while the reader knows that the learned doctor and mystic has never traveled to the east before and cannot speak from experience about what will be seen there, Reuel may have assumed in this instance the scientific and ethnological authority to anticipate what "you" or any westerner will learn upon going ashore. The novel's irony, of course, is that if these are his expectations, Reuel learns a very different lesson in Africa. The African American scientist is passing as white to serve as the "medical man" for an expedition bound to uncover the ruins and treasure of a lost Ethiopian civilization, an adventure that he joins desperately for the money that it will earn him rather than the knowledge that will be uncovered. But what he finds is his own "hidden self," in the words of the subtitle: the lost Ethiopian civilization of Meroe claims him as Ergamenes, its long-awaited king, destined to restore Ethiopia to its former greatness. He learns that Ethiopia fell from its former glory not because of the people's "intimate relation" with their environment (either too harshly desolate or too luxuriously tropical) but because of a now-completed period of divine punishment for their worship of false idols, which led to thousands of years of retribution wherein "the white stranger was in Ethiopia but a scourge in the hands of an offended God" (*Of One Blood*, 555). Even laid low, the Ethiopian inhabitants of the city of Telassar remain the hidden custodians of their culture's riches and ancient art, science, and mystical knowledge, all kept in a state of perfect preservation. This reality contrasts with Reuel's conventional expectation that Africa is like a "beautiful body" decrepit and decayed, figured in the moment when readers learn that Meroe's arts include a process whereby flowers and "the bodies of [their] most beautiful women" are preserved from decomposition (561–62).

In this instance, then, we can interpret Reuel's conventional perceptions as a westerner, a colonialist, and a scientific authority as character flaws that are corrected when he embraces his dual hidden selves as an African American and a mystical king separated from his royal inheritance. However, the fact that Hopkins locates and parodies this colonialist point of view specifically as she found it *in African American writing* reveals that her novel is engaged more broadly with the turn-of-the-century problem of positioning African Americans within projects of U.S. and Anglo-American nationalism and imperialism. This interpretation addresses the question that a number of recent critics have asked about *Of One Blood*: "whether Hopkins manipulates the conventions of the African fantasy tale in the age of high imperialism, or these conventions manipulate her."[5]

Some readers have concluded that, despite the novel's revelation of ancient African greatness, it nevertheless succumbs to the conventions of Africanist discourse. A key piece of evidence for this argument is that the novel links Meroe to classical civilizations of Egypt, Greece, and Rome, while depicting modern Africa outside the lost city of Telassar as a mixture of ruins, "howling wildernesses" (565), and "dirty Arab town[s]" (526) offering "just enough dilapidated abandon, dirt and picturesqueness to make the delight of the artist" (512). In this way, as Kevin Gaines writes, "Hopkins's elite, Western vision of African heathenism was meant to enhance black American's race pride, but at the expense of the autonomy of African peoples, whose cultures and histories remained a blank page for imaginary conquest."[6] The role of Christianity is also a sticking point for these critics: Reuel develops his occult powers of second sight in Telassar, but by simultaneously teaching his people Christianity, he appears to these readers as a missionary figure akin to many African Americans of the day who sought to evangelize Africa as a form of racial uplift that drew on and reinforced the imperialist "civilizing mission."[7]

In this chapter, I extend this critical debate about Hopkins's contradictory relationship to imperialism by arguing that her characterization of Reuel Briggs in Africa self-consciously echoes and signifies on ambivalent constructions of black cosmopolitanism found in the *CAM*. Drawing on Hopkins's correspondence about her editorial role at the magazine and on the materials published in the magazine that she adapted for her portrayal of Reuel, I contend that Hopkins's story about a racially ambiguous figure shadowing the white man's burden both symptomizes and diagnoses the magazine's uneasy linkage between African American uplift and U.S. global power. These materials published in the *CAM* include writings by Nicholas Campbell, who provides a model for Reuel not in his profession or situation—Campbell is a sailor, while Reuel is a doctor—but in his voice and perspective, which Hopkins adapts in her formal construction of Reuel's bifurcated voice and vision. Campbell is the most explicit source for Hopkins, but I argue that Hopkins borrowed from his writing features of black cosmopolitanism that were found throughout the magazine, including the fiction by Frank R. Steward discussed in chapter 3. By placing Hopkins's novel in this textual and historical context, I propose not to resolve the question of Hopkins's conflicted relationship to imperialism but to demonstrate that she self-consciously identified this conflict when she pieced together Reuel's perspective from the textual materials at hand.

As a critical intervention, then, my argument responds less to those who wish to decide if Hopkins's novel either promotes or subverts imperialist visions and more to critics concerned with the era's theorization of black cosmopolitanism. Ross Posnock has argued that Hopkins casts Reuel Briggs as a cosmopolitan, a term that he uses to describe black intellectuals seeking to escape race and racial essentialism through a commitment to universalisms.[8] Posnock sees Briggs as modeled after W. E. B. Du Bois and William James, but by considering Nicholas Campbell and Frank Steward as alternate models, we must acknowledge that, for Hopkins, cosmopolitanism was bound up in the era's conflicted narratives of global expansion and civilization. Hopkins critiques the limitations of Campbell's and Steward's versions of the black cosmopolitan, and while she does so without transcending those limitations, she borrows from Campbell and Steward a sense of irony that challenges the idea of de-raced imperial authority. My interpretation of the novel in this context spotlights both the appeal of imagining black cosmopolitan in an era of U.S. expansion and the oppositional effects of seeking that unattainable goal. Neither Hopkins nor Steward nor Campbell creates a black cosmopolitan able to escape into raceless universalisms, but, as I argue, seeking to do so was nonetheless a profoundly troubling challenge to national narratives of a white man's burden.

From the Deck of the U.S.S. Dixie

A key source and inspiration for *Of One Blood*, Campbell's essay was one of the sailor's several contributions to *CAM*. It begins by firmly identifying the racially unmarked first-person voice as that of a civilized man. Like "many men" in the "civilized world," he writes, he harbors a "natural appetite for all that is wonderful" ("Some Foreign Cities," 3), and this curiosity is what motivates him to join the liberty party of sailors leaving the U.S.S. *Dixie* on an afternoon visit to the Tunisian city of Bizerta (Bizerte). Assuming the authoritative voice of the geographical expert, he tells us that the coastal city is destined to resume its ancient commercial importance and become once more one of the greatest ports on the Mediterranean, despite its lazy people whose crude technology and idleness make the visit seem like one back in time to "ancient days" (4–5).

In the previously quoted long passage from Campbell's article, the voice explains racial difference as a result of environment, identifying with Anglo-American racial progress: the Tunisians differ from the inhabitants of "our hardy northern climes," whose struggle against the elements and constant exercise in warfare have developed "the best faculties of our species" instead of lying idly "like slaves" in the tropical sun. Here Campbell's scientific rhetoric and loosely Darwinist ideas give what appears to be an implicit justification for slavery and empire; if environment has determined racial development, some races have been left to act like slaves while others push forward, partly through war, to improve the species. Campbell's description of his walk around Bizerte generally follows from these stated theories; he describes primitive farming and milling methods that provide "the desolate spectacle of a passing civilization" (6), "dirty, yellow streets" that are "crooked and irregular" (7), and a funeral, all seemingly symbolic of the decaying or stagnated civilization. He remarks on the racially mixed populace, containing Arabs, Negroes, Jews, and Europeans, and he notes favorably the appearance of Negro merchants and soldiers, but nowhere during the description of the visit to Bizerte does Campbell say anything that would specify his own race or suggest that his viewpoint as an African American differs from that of any "civilized" man.

This racially unmarked voice changes in Campbell's concluding paragraph, however. If Campbell's assumption of de-raced authority formed a model for Hopkins's construction of Reuel's perspective on first seeing Africa, this shift at the end may also have formed a model for Reuel's rejection of this position later in the novel. In other words, Hopkins may have taken the notion of signifying on the de-raced African American cosmopolitan from Campbell himself, who partially undermines his own de-raced imperialist viewpoint in his conclusion. Campbell's article ends with him back on board the U.S.S. *Dixie,* watching the sunset from the deck and again examining the African coastline. From this vantage point, Campbell muses that across the Sahara is "an ethnological exposition of African humanity, for from that sandy desert comes fierce types of Negro merchants and caravaneers. A colony of these fierce and untamed blacks, transplanted in the heart of American caste prejudice in 'Dixie's land,' would cause the most intrepid white Southerner of the [Senator Ben 'Pitchfork'] Tillman stripe, to quail, and to literally crawl into his boots" (11).

Here, playing on the name of his ship, Campbell's colonialist perspective gives way to a fantasy in which Africans colonize the southern United States, a space that Campbell identifies with the very ship—the U.S.S. *Dixie*—that has brought him to Africa and given him the powerful mobility and vision that he uses to mark himself as "civilized" man earlier in the article. If such a move does not undo the forms of racist authority that Campbell cited earlier in his essay, it does reveal that the white man's burden cannot be so easily de-raced because racial politics of the United States invite a re-scripting of the imperial story: its vision of civilized authority in northern Africa gives way to one of black colonizing and vengeance in the Southern United States. Echoes of Campbell's fantasy of African retribution can be seen in Hopkins's conclusion to *Of One Blood,* where Reuel brings fierce Tellasarian Africans with him back to the South, Dixie's land, to confront the novel's villain, Aubrey Livingston. In Reuel's transition from racially unidentified civilized expert to African king seeking justice in Dixie's land, Hopkins borrowed from Campbell a strategy of ironic reversal that she adapts and amplifies.

Interestingly, Campbell's final view from the deck of the U.S.S. *Dixie* creates division and contradiction within the supposedly homogeneous "civilized" entity that Campbell initially claims to represent, an ambiguous and troubling move similar to the ones that I have argued Frank Steward made in his fictions of U.S. imperial authority as well.[9] Hopkins invokes Campbell and, less directly, Steward, both writers whose work she read and edited, when she characterizes Reuel as a would-be assimilationist, seeking to submerge his race consciousness under the authoritative voices of American, doctor, and imperialist. By raising the question of what view of the world an African American from the land of Dixie should take, Hopkins amplifies Campbell's final moment of critical self-reflection and Steward's indeterminate critique of black cosmopolitanism, although none of the three writers wholly challenges the strategy of accessing discourses of colonial power. *Of One Blood* remarks on Steward and Campbell most explicitly through its formal construction of Reuel's perspective, but before I move on to to analyze that narrative device through a close reading, it is helpful to consider Hopkins's editorial role at the *CAM*. Knowing how Hopkins herself experienced a backlash against black cosmopolitanism helps to better gauge the potential implications of such unstable depictions of black global knowledge and authority.

Hopkins's "International Policy"

Of One Blood addresses a conflict about global politics and African American uplift that Hopkins experienced before and after she assumed her position as the literary editor of the *CAM* in May 1903, midway through *Of One Blood*'s serial publication in the magazine from November 1902 to November 1903, and one month after publication of Steward's "Starlik." Letters to and from the editors of the magazine during her tenure as fiction editor reveal that a major question facing the magazine was whether colored American uplift was a national or an international issue and that Hopkins's answer to this question was part of the reason that she lost her job at the *CAM*.[10]

These letters suggest that Hopkins was fired because of her political and editorial differences with the magazine's white self-appointed patron, John C. Freund. Freund, a music critic from New York who assumed a powerful influence over the editorial direction of the magazine, clashed with Hopkins over the proper place of African Americans in an expanding U.S. empire. Most Hopkins scholars examining this conflict have framed it as one between Booker T. Washington and Hopkins rather than between Freund and Hopkins, because evidence points to the fact that it was Washington's urging of a "more conciliatory" editorial policy that motivated the decision to fire Hopkins.[11] Washington was sought out by Freund and the struggling magazine's editor, Colonel William H. Dupree, in late 1903 as first a contributor and then a source of financial backing and professional support. With Freund's help, the wizard of Tuskegee apparently leveraged his influence over the magazine's content and, ultimately, a year later, its ownership. However, I focus on Freund rather than Washington in relation to Hopkins's interest in internationalism. Freund's letters to Dupree and to Hopkins cite Washington as an authority holding the same objections as Freund, but, lacking any more direct statements of Washington's position on Hopkins and *CAM*, I find in Freund's own battle with Hopkins the most direct evidence of a conflict over the magazine's relationship to a global color line.

Hopkins collected Freund's letters to prove the existence of what she thought to be an elaborate and sustained plot to control her editorial choices and ultimately silence her.[12] A few months after she was fired, she sent the letters to William Monroe Trotter, publisher of Boston's African American newspaper the *Guardian,* along with her own letter explaining her side of the story. The letters prove that Freund demanded that the magazine stop printing several types of content: criticisms of past and present racial oppression, calls for political equality, and literary material of any kind. Such content should be replaced, Fruend specified, with more optimistic reports of practical African American achievement. The letters also reveal that Freund objected to content placing the question of racial oppression on a global scale. As Hopkins tells the story in her letter to Trotter: "Little by little Freund opened his views to me and I found that he was curtailing my work from the broad field of international union and uplift for the Blacks in all quarters of the globe, to the narrow confines of the question as affecting solely the Afro-Americans."[13]

Most obviously, the work Hopkins refers to here is the partnership she had forged between *CAM* and A. Kirkland Soga, the editor of the South African publication *Izwi Labanut.* In her letter to Trotter, Hopkins calls Soga, perhaps ironically to jibe at Freund's criticisms of her, "the corner stone of my 'international policy.'"[14] Soga contributed a series of articles to *CAM* in 1903 titled "Ethiopians in the Twentieth Century" on "Questions Affecting the Natives and Colored People Resident in British South Africa," and there he specifically credits Hopkins for bringing the *CAM* to his attention.[15] Soga's pieces criticize South African legal and structural oppression, although they also make some positive statements about British control of South Africa. One is even addressed and written as a letter to British Secretary of State Joseph Chamberlain, complaining about racial discrimination.[16] Soga's motivation for criticizing British colonial practices in a U.S. magazine, as he explains it in an editorial note in *CAM,* was to direct attention of colored American readers to Africa and convince them that "we should cooperate by extending hands across the sea."[17]

But although the "corner stone" of Hopkins's international policy, her relationship with Soga was only one piece of it. This is an important point for expanding current arguments about Hopkins as an early Pan-Africanist.[18] Of particular concern to Freund was the magazine's coverage of the Filipino American conflict, as is revealed in this letter from Freund to Dupree:

> Either Miss Hopkins will follow our suggestion in this matter and put live matter into the magazine, eliminating anything which may cause offense; stop talking about wrongs and a proscribed race, or you must count me out absolutely from this day forth. I will neither personally endorse nor help a business proposition, which my common sense tells me is foredoomed to failure. Every person that I have spoken with on the subject is with me, *IT IS MR. BOOKER WASHINGTON'S IDEA.* If you people, therefore, want to get out a literary magazine, with articles on the Filipinos, I refuse to work one minute longer."[19]

The source of Freund's and "Mr. Washington's wrath" in the letter above was an April 1904 issue of *CAM* that, as Hopkins explained, contained two especially controversial pieces: an article by William Lloyd Garrison Jr. questioning Washington's program of industrial education as the solution to the Negro Problem, and another by Professor S. E. F. C. C. Hammedoe on José Rizal, the Filipino revolutionary, and, as Hopkins calls him, martyr. These articles were found objectionable, Hopkins thought, because they "not only offended the South, but, also, seemingly reflected upon President Roosevelt's Phillippine [*sic*] policy."[20] While the politics of the series on industrial education deserve more study as part of the conflict with Washington, my particular interest here is in the "articles on the Filipinos" mentioned in Freund's letter and in Hopkins's characterization of the debate.

S. E. F. C. C. Hamadoe, the author of the profile of Rizal, was an African American linguist and travel writer who contributed regular features on geography and on foreign, often colonial, cultures bearing titles such as

"Rainilaiarivany: Prime Minister of Madagascar," "The Lesser Antilles: Life and Customs of the Colored Inhabitants," "Ithamar: The Land of the Palm: Siamese History, Customs, Etc.," and "The Total World Colored Population." Hamadoe's tone in these articles, including the piece in question about Rizal, is quite neutral and objective, never taking a position on colonial politics except insofar as they give significant detail about anticolonial movements, and rarely offering the reader any other subject position from which to view these cultures and conflicts besides interested world traveler and objective geographical expert. Unlike Soga, who writes as a participant in the racial politics of colonial South Africa, Hamadoe writes as a detached, western scholar and assumes an objective, neutral tone.

Looking today at the contested article on Rizal, one wonders what was so potentially offensive to Roosevelt's policy. The article says nothing about Roosevelt's policies, instead merely describing Rizal's talent, heroism, and dedication to the cause of Philippine independence from Spain. Rizal was executed in 1896 before the United States won the Philippines, and because of this he was not an especially controversial figure in the United States; his resistance to Spain was even celebrated as more evidence against the Spanish tyranny that the United States remedied by taking possession of the islands. But perhaps more controversial than Hamadoe's text on Rizal was the choice of photographs that accompanied it. These photos depict Rizal and his generals, some of whom, such as Aguinaldo, lived long enough to fight against the United States. Significantly, one portrait of Aguinaldo bears the caption "President of the Filipino Republic," a position he was elected to under the Filipino Malolos Constitution, a document the United States rejected by forging the Treaty of Paris and taking possession of the islands. Titling the portrait in this way, a choice that was possibly made by Hopkins as editor, expresses subtle but definite respect for Filipino independence.[21]

By including such material, Hopkins was made to feel that she was defying the conservative recommendations of Freund and purportedly Washington, which demanded, in her words, "'no talk of wrongs,' or of a "proscribe[d] race,' no 'glittering generalities', no 'international aspect' of the Negro question, [and] no talk of Filipinos.'"[22] Yet, reading the magazine's issues printed between 1900 and 1904, one scarcely feels like one is reading a publication that made radical moves toward black internationalism and anticolonialism. While it includes some "talk of Filipinos," expressions of anticolonialism or direct criticisms of U.S. policy in the Philippines under the Republican Roosevelt and McKinley administrations are rare. Hopkins was apparently criticized—and silenced—for choosing to print a few pieces that only indirectly questioned U.S. policies in the Philippines. Two of the most explicit anti-imperialist pieces appear during the magazine's first year of publication in 1900.[23] Later, a few more subtle criticisms can be found, as in the November 1903 issue containing the last installment of Hopkins's *Of One Blood,* which reprints from the *Boston Transcript* an opinion piece on how the Republican administration should make use of information in the Philippine census. The editorial comment suggests that "a wise administration" will recognize the ability of Filipinos to choose voluntarily to Americanize in instances where American ideas are genuinely of greater value.[24] Perhaps even reprinting another periodical's gentle recommendation to offer Filipinos some agency in their adoption of American ways was too bold a move for Freund and Washington to countenance. Frank R. Steward's fiction might also have counted as objectionable material, for its anti-imperialist leanings, as well as its generic status as fiction—especially his 1903 "The Men Who Prey," which most explicitly directs the reader to sympathize with Filipinas against U.S. colonial power, and which was published during Hopkins's tenure as literary editor.

Outweighing such subtle criticisms, however, were a larger number of items affirming U.S. policy toward the Philippines.[25] These especially stress opportunities for African American soldiers and businessmen in developing the islands. A 1901 article titled "Manila and Its Opportunities" by Charles Steward, son of Theophilus and older brother of Frank, claims that American civilization would awaken Filipinos to "new wants and ambitions" for manufactured goods, creating potential for investments in the islands that will "ring up fortunes for some enterprising Yankees." Besides mention of the many beautiful Filipinas who have a "decided preference for colored Americans," the article draws no distinction between white and black Yankees' views of these opportunities.[26] This lack of race distinction in nationalist feeling is the topic of several other articles, including A. L. Demond's 1902 "The Negro Element in National Life," which asserts that Negroes are "pre-eminently Americans in all that we do to-day," especially in military service during the Spanish American War: "In that hour, who sprang more eagerly to the rescue, fought more bravely or died more willingly than men of our race? When Spain's army had been defeated, her navy sunk and was forced to bid farewell to possessions in the western world, the Negro played his part and played it well." With a warning against narrow clannishness or extreme race consciousness among

Negroes, Demond writes, "as the old ship of state sails out into the ocean of the 20th century, the Negro is on board, and he can say: 'Sail on, sail on, O ship of state, / Sail on, O Union, strong and great."'[27] While Campbell subtly reminds readers that the ship of state gives the African American sailor the viewpoint of Dixie's land, Demond imagines a unified ship of state with room for Negroes willing to "play their part" in future naval exploits on the world's stage.

Within this range of content, however, no clear binary between imperialist and anti-imperialist content exists. While Steward and Campbell destabilize such visions of homogeneous U.S. national identity, their writing can also be placed in a continuum with these writers' more affirmative claims to U.S. imperial power. With all of these examples, the most overt appeal is to a perspective of de-raced, civilized world power, with only more subtle moves to interrogate that viewpoint. Asking why Freund perceived such subtle criticism as dangerous and controversial reveals that it may not be anti-imperialist sympathy for Filipinos that bothered Freund but, rather, the very act of claiming the authority to speak about global politics. In other words, what if Freund was bothered not so much by the radical tenor of the *CAM*'s content on the Philippines and on other colonial sites around the globe but by the assumption of authority required to make *any* statement about world politics from the vantage point of seemingly de-raced expertise? Or, to put it differently, what if Freund's objection was to the inherent challenge of black cosmopolitanism? I want to briefly explore this point before turning to *Of One Blood*, because the threat Freund possibly perceived in black cosmopolitanism allows us to understand how Hopkins's novel, while failing to radically critique imperialism, could still offer a troubling contest to the notion of the white man's burden.

That Freund objected to any and all international content seems unlikely, especially when one notes that the first contribution made by Freund himself to the *CAM* was a series of stories about his travels to Jamaica. In fact, these articles were Freund's introduction to the *CAM*. Dupree solicited him in late 1903 to publish a condensed version of the series in the *CAM*, which Freund had previously printed in his own publication, the New York *Music Trades* newspaper. Freund agreed to have them reprinted and offered $15 toward the magazine's operations, the first of several apparently philanthropic gifts and services he donated. As Hopkins tells the story to Trotter, "we examined the articles [on Jamaica] and found them exceptionally interesting and instructive," an admiration that, combined with deference toward a generous new patron, apparently motivated Hopkins and Dupree to make Freund's articles the leading feature in most of the issues where they appeared.[28] It may be that Freund's generally favorable impressions of Jamaica seemed attractive to Hopkins because they departed from earlier antebellum tendencies to regard the island as a failed experiment in free Negro labor, one that, along with Haiti, stood as a warning to U.S. Americans of the disorder and loss of productivity that would accompany voluntary abolition of slavery.[29] But whatever motivated Hopkins to feature Freund's series, his work was not at all unusual for the magazine in its international content. Instead, the most notable difference between the voice of the civilized traveler found in Freund's piece and that seen in Hamadoe's or Campbell's writing is the racialization of its authorial voice: the voice of the cosmopolitan expert in Freund is explicitly marked as white.

I speculate that this difference may be the root of Freund's objection to the *CAM*'s other international content—its shadowing of whiteness in the never completely de-raced voice of the black cosmopolitan expert. Freund would rather have himself as the worldly patron and his "children" as more stationary, local objects of his knowledge and aid (Hopkins reports that the he was nicknamed "Papa Freund" by the workers at the *CAM*).[30] The series on Jamaica overtly identifies Freund as white ("an Englishman, though of German parentage") in an editor's note beginning his first installment in January 1904, but his race is further stressed in the content of his article, which on the first page offers the following as one of his stated reasons for traveling to Jamaica: "I am very much interested in the colored people. I like them as much as I dislike the Indians. The Negro for me as against the red man and the Malay—they are all one race—everytime!"[31] Freund's voice does not presume to be de-raced; here whiteness is not assumed but directly claimed, alerting readers that they are not encountering the voice of the black cosmopolitan.

Jamaica as Freund represents it serves as a model and source of inspiration for colored American readers, but not as a place for their future touristic adventures, ethnographic studies, or capital investment. This is not to say that trade and tourism don't matter to Freund: he lavishes great detail on subjects including U.S. commercial development of Jamaica through the United Fruit Company and the beauties of its landscape as appreciated by the sophisticated American traveler. But colored U.S. Americans are invoked primarily as those who should take heart in the high state of civilization found on the predominantly black island, and who should copy—from a distance—Jamaica's peaceful state of affairs by promoting industrial education and economic development of the U.S. South.[32] Freund is full of praise for smiling, polite, and hard-working Jamaican maids and waiters; he is impressed that Jamaican blacks serve in minor governmental positions such as customs officials, and he is gratified that racial relations between the white minority and black majority are peaceful.[33] But his references to African Americans back home tend to reinvoke homey, vernacular, literary "types" that underscore the maintenance of power relations necessary to create Jamaica's biracial paradise.

For example, in the April issue, Freund defends his idea of Jamaica as an earthly "Paradise" against a fellow traveler's objection that "nobody ever heard of there being black angels" with the following anecdote: "One day, in a cotton mill in the South, an old Negro was walking along with a little girl, much in the style of Eva and Uncle Tom, and discussing many things together." Their topic is heaven, which the girl regrets her companion cannot reach because of his race, but which the old man aspires to, based on this reasoning: "Heah am de cotton seed. Dar ain't nothing no blacker, and yet, from dis heah black cotton seed, you get de buful, buful, snow-white cotton. Now, if de Lawd kin make de white cotton come out of de black cotton seed,'pears to me he kin make a white angel out of a pore old black man."[34] The condescending invocation of Stowe's literary types works as powerfully here as does this anecdote's maintenance of a white/black color hierarchy to undermine Freund's intended criticism of racial prejudice. (Indeed, Freund's reference to literary productions of race seems to contradict his disapproval of African American literary production as a political tool in the *CAM;* for Freund, literature *does* create powerful racial images, but black writers should not attempt them.) Freund juxtaposes white geographical expertise and black local virtue, with the latter locked in the past, fixed in a regional space defined by fiction, and expressed with Christian patience, optimism, and a respectful admiration of whiteness.

Condescending as it is, Freund's series on Jamaica stands out in the magazine neither for its ethnocentrist ideas of civilization nor for its investments in trade and U.S. strategic interests. In fact, its view of Jamaica does not differ significantly from what is found in some of Hamadoe's or Campbell's representation of foreign spaces. Rather, my point is that what Freund does not do is presume the deeply destabilizing authority of the black cosmopolitan. The same controversial April 1904 issue that contained Freund's installment on Jamaica and Hamadoe's article on Jose

Rizal also contains another piece by Campbell, titled "Panama: The New Black Republic," which is politically no less replete with imperialist gestures than Freund's view of Jamaica. Campbell's ship, the U.S.S. *Dixie,* was one of the cruisers sent to monitor U.S. interests in the canal zone during the 1903 Panama revolution.[35] His article about Panama combines in three pages the geographic determinist notion that Central American political revolutions are "tropical necessities," the expansionist statement that Panama's recent revolution demonstrated its people's unanimous wish to someday "be a state in our precious union," a breezily idealized historical narrative explaining U.S. administrative control over the canal project and military intervention in the Panama revolution, and some bemused firsthand accounts of encountering colorful locals during a walk around Colón.[36] And yet, because of his de-raced voice, Campbell's presumption of authority, expertise, and global knowledge carry a complex and troubling set of meanings that are crucially different from Freund's comfortable assertions of the same.

Hopkins, who as we see here experienced a backlash when she assumed the authoritative position of the black cosmopolitan in her editorial choices, makes this issue of authority and perspective a central theme in *Of One Blood;* the novel is her meditation on black cosmopolitanism as she encountered and participated in it. While her conflict with Freund was only beginning when she assumed editorial control and as she published the African portion of *Of One Blood,* Freund's reaction to international content in the *CAM* helps highlight the subversive implications of Reuel Briggs's ambiguous relationship with narratives of white civilized imperial destiny.

Narrative Point of View and De-raced Authority in Of One Blood

These two archival findings—that the Filipino American War and the "international aspect" of racial oppression were experienced as sources of professional tension for Hopkins, and that Hopkins used part of her novel *Of One Blood* to deliberately reframe the perspective of the African American imperialist found in Nicholas Campbell's essay about Bizerte— invite us to return to her last novel with a new hypothesis. Hopkins's novel, which both echoes and signifies on the vision of worldly expertise constructed in the magazine, was where she could most fully assume and reflect on the internationalist perspective that she would be criticized for assuming in her editorial choices.

Of One Blood, while not directly challenging U.S. imperialism, raises the "international aspect" of the Negro question that Hopkins was later chastised for attempting to broach through her editorial choices. To this end, *Of One Blood* mimics—sometimes critically, sometimes not—the tendency of other contributors to view global conflict from the narrow scope of the American Negro seeking inclusion and equality on the expansionist ship of state. But even Hopkins's uncritical replication of certain imperialist ideas may have been troubling to a reader like Freund, for whom the bifurcated vision of the black cosmopolitan is itself destabilizing. I argue here that Hopkins most fully destabilizes the assumption of a white national subject representing the United States on the world stage in her representation of the country's mixed race identity, which, as in "Talma Gordon," pushes toward a new kind of cosmopolitan vision.

Because what Hopkins borrows from Campbell is perspective, I begin this section with a close reading of how the rendering of the novel's narrative point of view figures the conflict Hopkins identifies in black cosmopolitanism. Formally, through the representation of Reuel's and the narrator's perspectives, *Of One Blood* criticizes the narrow and blinkered viewpoint of the de-raced Afro-American imperialist. Reuel's vision, even more than his contested identity, is the object obscured by mystery and suspense. As a passing narrative, the novel is concerned not so much with whether Reuel is "really" black or whether the secret truth about Reuel's small portion of African ancestry will be revealed to the reader, for most readers familiar with generic treatments of mixed-race characters would have been quite confident about both of these outcomes. Rather, a more important source of narrative tension comes from the desire to find out how Reuel's perspective and the readers' access to it will expand when this truth is revealed. This tension arises because of the narrator's and readers' exclusion from a portion of Reuel's thoughts throughout most of the book.

For example, during the expedition to discover Meroe, Reuel assumes the supposedly dispassionate and objective view of the scientist, not only to his colleagues Charlie Vance and the British Professor Stone but also to the reader. While the narrator reports obvious signs that more is occurring inside Reuel's mind, the reader has no direct access to his internal thoughts, seeing only the pose that Reuel uses, in one example, to conclude an evening's conversation with his companions. During the conversation, Professor Stone expresses his radical intention to establish "the primal existence of the Negro as the most ancient source of all that you value in modern life, even antedating Egypt" (*Of One Blood*, 520), but Reuel ends the discussion abruptly, stating that "the relationship existing between the Negro and other people of world is a question of absorbing interest. For my part, I shall be glad to add to my ethnological knowledge by anything we may learn at Meroe." The narrator comments that "thus speaking, Reuel *seemed* desirous of dismissing the subject" (521; emphasis mine), a cue that his companions follow. While at other points in the novel, the limited omniscient narrator has access to Reuel's thought and emotions, here the narrator is denied internal knowledge of Reuel's motivations and can only report on how Reuel *appeared* to other characters. The effect of this suddenly externalized narrative point of view is to raise suspicion in the readers' minds, prompting them to look for disparity between what seems to motivate Reuel and what really does. Importantly, this disparity divides Reuel's "hidden self"—his motivations and identity linked to his African ancestry—from his professional self: his expressed interests as a racially unmarked but presumably white civilized expert.

Early in the novel, the reader is trained to look for and examine this veiled split in Reuel's perspective: to chart the relationship between Reuel's expressed thoughts as a dispassionate white expert and his imperfectly hidden emotions and perceptions as one whose "blood" ties him to Africa. In the first chapter, the reader almost immediately encounters information leading toward the hypothesis that Reuel has some small amount of African ancestry and is "passing" for white when the narrator speaks of Reuel's unknown origin and his friend's unconfirmed speculations that he is part Italian or perhaps Japanese, and when Reuel answers evasively a question about his position on the "Negro problem." The second chapter, in which Reuel and Aubrey Livingston accompany friends to see the Fisk Jubilee Singers perform Negro spirituals for a white audience in Boston, builds on this mystery of identity through a lesson in identifying double meanings and double consciousness. There Reuel displays the objective and neutral guise of the medical expert, one that both he and his friends mark as specifically white, while hinting at his separate perspective of a hidden self beneath the posture. One companion attempts to engage the moody Reuel in conversation by noting that the chorus of African American singers has some pretty girls in it, "one or two as white as we" (451). When Reuel gives no response, the Southerner Aubrey explains that "they range at home from alabaster to ebony. . . . The results of amalgamation are worthy of the careful attention of all medical experts" (451). Reuel responds "peevishly," telling Aubrey to not "talk shop" (451). Aubrey then scolds him for being disagreeable, encouraging him to "try to be like the other fellows," who continue the conversation about the singers' beauty until Reuel ends the discussion by "drily" declaring that "if this is to be the result of emancipation, I for one vote that we ask Congress to annul the Proclamation" (452).

The reader's unconfirmed hypothesis that Reuel is passing in this scene again produces obvious and conflicting potential meanings. While the narrator has some access to Reuel's thoughts that evening (the narrator knows, for example, that Reuel is distracted because he is thinking about his mysterious vision of a strange woman's face), the narrator doesn't look far enough into Reuel's thoughts to discover why this conversation especially annoys him. Reuel *appears* to his companions and to the narrator (who describes his tone as "peevish" and "dry") to be displeased, perhaps because of polite, if dour, gentility; he finds the loose conversation about attractive mulattas, like the tendency among "medical experts" to "talk shop" at a concert, to be ill-mannered. But if he is passing, as no doubt readers by this point suspect, his distaste for the topic comes instead from his inability "to be like the other fellows" because of concealed indignation that white men are glibly discussing sexually attractive, racially mixed women. Thus his closing comment about the results of emancipation may be more than a joke about impolite speech; it may sarcastically suggest that freedom is meaningless under the enduring conditions of white male rape and manipulation of African American women, a theme that many critics have observed in the novel's depiction of Dianthe's fate at the end of the novel.[37]

The narrator's access to Reuel's internal consciousness fluctuates, at times suggesting Reuel's hidden identity by assuming an almost Hawthornian ambiguity in reporting the character's behavior. When Professor Stone explains that the descendents of ancient Meroe will identify their long-lost king by the presence of a birthmark shaped like a lotus flower, the narrator exits Reuel's point of view entirely to remark that "it may have been the unstable shadows of the moon that threw a tremulous light upon the group, but Charlie Vance was sure that Reuel Briggs started violently at the Professor's words" (535). We later find out that Reuel has such a birthmark, which his mother had often reverently examined, but here as elsewhere the narrator preserves Reuel's secret by refusing to look beneath the veil of his white identity. This suddenly assumed narrative distance from the protagonist forces the reader to track dual interpretations of Reuel's speech and behavior as either a dispassionate, white civilized expert or an African American invested by blood and by social interest in these topics. This device works quite poorly if its purpose is to build suspense about Reuel's racial identity; it is hard to imagine that a turn-of-the-century reader of *CAM* wouldn't have quite confidently guessed that Reuel is passing in the first chapter. But the effect of the device is something other than suspense. Instead, it communicates that Reuel's racial perspective is so profoundly buried beneath his assumed identity of white expertise that the narrator, and perhaps even Reuel himself, cannot easily access the repressed secret.

Thus when Reuel catches his previously quoted first glimpse of Africa, the narrator's switch in pronouns (from reporting what "he" could see, to what "one" could see, to what "you" would see) follows the pattern throughout the first half of the novel wherein the particularity of Reuel's viewpoint is submerged beneath a pose of objective and authoritative neutrality. The narration makes a similar switch in point of view after the party uncovers evidence of the ancient civilization they sought, receding from Reuel's perspective to explain what "one" who "had visited the chief galleries of Europe" *would* experience upon making this discovery: he would be greatly surprised to realize that here was "a metropolis where science and art had its origin," created by "the people whose posterity has been denied a rank among the human race, and has been degraded into a species of talking baboon!" (538). This experienced traveler would also marvel that "where civilization and learning once reigned, ignorance and barbarism have resumed their sway" (538). But this wonder and surprise is distanced from Reuel, whose thoughts upon making the discovery, if very different from the generic civilized scholar's, are veiled from the reader. These pronoun shifts both conceal Reuel's true identity and figure the divisions that create it.

This veil is finally removed in the next chapter when Reuel wanders away from the party's ethnological excavation to stumble on the vibrantly alive lost city of Tellasar. There the problem of his viewpoint is immediately raised by Ai, the elder who greets him by asking why he wandered into the Pyramid's hidden passages: "Are you, too, one of those who seek for hidden treasure?" (546). Ai cannot be asking whether Reuel belongs to Professor Stone's expedition, because we learn that he already has comprehensive knowledge of the group through their Telassarian guide, Ababdis. Instead, he must be asking about Reuel's motives: Do they truly match those of the others in the expedition, or do they differ?

This question could also reflect on the many essays about the Philippines in *CAM* in which the economic interests of whites and blacks are aligned as "Yankees" reaping material gains of U.S. expansion. Reuel

doesn't answer Ai's question about his motives, but his subsequent enlightenment in the lost city reveals that the "undiscovered country" (448)
within him is more valuable than treasure, allowing him to more fully
distinguish himself from his companion and fellow American, Charlie
Vance, who sees the expedition as a money-making scheme. Charlie explains his own motives to Ai by saying that he comes from a "race bold
and venturesome, who know not fear if we can get a few more dollars and
fresh information" (584). Charlie's "race" may refer to whites, Americans,
or Anglo-Saxons, but in any case readers can only authoritatively distance
Reuel's motives from Charlie's *after* the text provides full access to Reuel's
consciousness and hidden self inside the city of Telassar.

Dividing Reuel's vision and subjectivity between his hidden self and
the pose of the scientifically objective yet financially self-interested white
expert pointedly recapitulates and criticizes Campbell's and Steward's assumption of the supposedly de-raced geographic authority. Campbell's
previously described environmental racism, his confident assertions about
the economic role of the port he enters, and his call for an "ethnological exposition of African humanity" all function rhetorically to authorize
him as a source of scientific knowledge in the service of civilization, despite the clear economic and nationalist interests that his writings convey.
But Campbell also reveals a different personal stake in such knowledge
by signifying on "Dixie's land," a move that Hopkins amplifies and re-
writes when her hero more dramatically distances himself from western
science in *Of One Blood*. My argument here thus inverts Posnock's claim
that Hopkins sought and failed in her novel to imagine her character's
escape from racial essentialism to universalist cosmopolitanism. Instead,
rather than lapsing back into the idea that Reuel's African blood and destiny comprise his essentialist, originary self, Hopkins shapes her novel to
dramatize a *release* from the ambivalent and complex inflections of black
cosmopolitanism that she read and participated in as editor of *CAM*. Instead of failing to remain the ideal cosmopolite, Reuel succeeds in *Of One
Blood*'s fantasy by evading that position's contradictions.

However, despite its portrayal of Reuel's release from the contradictions
of black cosmopolitanism, the novel itself does not evade those contradictions. Here I join critics such as Kevin Gaines, John Cullen Gruesser,
and Hannah Wallinger who view Hopkins as aware of Reuel's imperialist
viewpoint but not fully aware of her own. This viewpoint influences not
only the novel's Eurocentric depiction of a "civilized" lost city in otherwise
"savage" Africa but also Hopkins's sense of divine destiny guiding earthly

processes, including imperialism. *Of One Blood* lays out a theory of providential imperialism as one component of the scripturally foretold rise and fall of Ethiopia. In this account of history, the rise and fall of civilizations is a divinely willed cycle of punishment and retribution, not a factor of environmentally determined or inherited racial characteristics.[38] As Ai explains to Reuel, God "removeth kings and countries, and setteth them up again" (556). Slavery and colonization at the hands of the white race thus are not products of a pseudo-Darwinist struggle for racial superiority but a form of divine punishment for Ethiopia's ancient sin of idolatry. While undercutting expert scientific knowledge about race, geography, and evolution, Hopkins's providential view actually justifies imperial expansion for its unintended consequences.

This faith in the unfathomable divine consequences of empire is also supported by a passage at the end of the novel in which Reuel views "with serious apprehension, the advance of mighty nations penetrating the dark, mysterious forests of his native land," sadly asking, "Where will it stop? What will the end be?" While critics have read this line as a sign of Hopkins's anti-imperialist stance, they fail to consider the novel's answer to the question in the next sentence.[39] The narrator answers, "None save Omnipotence can solve this problem," for God's "handiwork" can direct caste prejudice and race pride like "puppets in his hand" (621).[40] In other words, Reuel worries about the advance of mighty nations, but we should not, if we see the divine course of all things.

For Hopkins, then, empire is a part of divinely planned white man's burden, one that will have results different from what anyone supposed. This idea is also the central premise of a series of articles that Hopkins wrote for the *Voice of the Negro* in 1905, called "The Dark Races of the Twentieth Century," after leaving *CAM*. Here, without editorial pressures from Freund, Hopkins still struggles to locate a position of cosmopolitan authority from which to enter into debates about civilization and race, and the idea of divinely determined imperial processes appears to be her solution. She begins the essays by noting the causal relationship between imperialism and the racial sciences of ethnology:

> Many causes have lately arisen to augment the desire of thinkers to know all possible about the origin and the relationship of the dark-hued races, and the time is ripe for a popular study of the science of ethnology. The rise of new power and the decline of old powers, the great expansion in the business world or the growth of commercialism, the remarkable

development of imperialistic fever among governments, has caused a searching of the obscure corners of the globe even among untutored savages for world markets and world conquests. Nor is this new knowledge and insatiable curiosity of little value. It is all in accord with the plan of salvation from the beginning. [41]

According to this "plan of salvation," imperialism and its attendant ethnological studies will bring about the "reunion" of peoples scattered after the biblical fall of the Tower of Babylon. Hopkins moves from this assertion of divine will to a supposedly systematic overview of racial groups around the world, reproducing many of the biases of civilizationist thought and racial science in the process. As Gaines observes about these essays, "despite a religious vision of human brotherhood, Hopkins's writing showed a preoccupation with constructing an authoritative bourgeois persona, a concern which seemed to preclude a more consistent critique of imperialism and its racist assumptions."[42] But to call her *Voice of the Negro* essays inconsistent in their criticism of imperialism is an understatement; rather, they overtly *justify* imperialism and the shrinking world of global commerce as human processes under a benevolent if inscrutable divine control. And yet, as I have argued, even assuming an "authoritative bourgeois persona" wielding worldwide geographical expertise was a potentially threatening move to readers like Freund. The irony that she both claims and undercuts scientific authority in assuming this authoritative voice is another example of the rhetorical move that I call shadowing the white man's burden.

For Hopkins, one of the divine outcomes of imperialism is racial mixing, which, as "Talma Gorden" anticipates, has already rendered the United States a mulatto nation, a place where people are or soon will be all of one blood. As *Of One Blood's* narrator states: "In His own mysterious way He hath united the black race and white race in this new continent," where no one is "clear enough in vision to decide who hath black blood and who hath it not" (607). Here is Hopkins's most potentially radical idea, and the one that goes the furthest in pushing toward a cosmopolitan stance freed from racialized perspective, although not from the histories of slavery that created these mixtures. A key element for communicating this future cosmopolitan possibility is Charlie Vance, who more than any other figure in the novel stands for the "typical" white American.

Charlie undergoes a dramatic character shift through his discoveries in Africa. Nicknamed "Adonis" by his friends, the handsome Northeastern medical student initially lacks all of Reuel's seriousness; he is "the spoiled darling of wealth and fashion" (581) and a model of the careless, up-to-date young American: he uses humorous slang, practices modern fads like boxing, and otherwise lives for pleasure. After Reuel's disappearance from the expedition, however, he learns "many needed lessons in the bitterness of spirit out of these African wilds" (581), benefiting from the imperial man-making that was Kipling's crucial justification for expansion. Yet Charlie's whiteness is not affirmed by this trial but, rather, is radically called into question, as a metonym for U.S. whiteness more generally. In Hopkins's earlier novel *Contending Forces,* one character asks another, "Did you never think that today the black race on this continent has developed into a race of mulattoes?"[43] What *Of One Blood* shows is that the white race has developed similarly, leaving no one, not even Charlie Vance, free to assume the false position of de-raced cosmopolitan expert and imperialist, untouched by this history of slavery and domestic racial oppression. For, as the novel makes clear, who is to say that Charlie Vance is any whiter than Reuel or Aubrey? From this implication, the novel allows *everyone* in the new mulatto nation to assume a new kind of cosmopolitan subject position by creating a new platform for global awareness in which mixed selves are not de-raced but merely impure and in which we do not assume that civilized viewpoints are American viewpoints, American perspectives are white perspectives, or raceless vision is white vision.[44]

Part of Charlie's newly gained maturity is his realizing sense of American racial intermixture and fraternal interconnection. While Reuel learns that because of racial intermixing during slavery he and his wife Dianthe Lusk and his enemy Aubrey Livingston are all in reality brother and sister—literally "of one blood"—Charlie learns to call by the name of "brother" Jim Titus, "a Negro of the old regime" who accompanies him and Reuel to Africa. When Jim and Charlie are captured by the Telassarians, Ai condemns Charlie's country's race prejudice, reminding him that "ye are all of one blood, descended from one common father" (585). Charlie at first dismisses these lessons, but as his bondage with Jim in Telassar progresses, their fellowship and shared danger changes his mind: "Ai's words were true. Where was the color line now? Jim was a brother; the nearness of their desolation in this uncanny land, left nothing but a feeling of brotherhood. He felt then the truth of the words, 'Of one blood I have made all races of men'" (590). This realization of metaphoric brotherhood underscores both Charlie's and Jim's kinship with Reuel, Dianthe, and Aubrey in an extended set of biological and legal fraternal relations that makes almost all of the novel's major characters siblings: Charlie would have been Aubrey's brother-in-law through Aubrey's anticipated marriage with Charlie's sister Molly Vance; and Jim says that he agrees to work for Aubrey because "Aubrey Livingston was my foster brother, and I could deny him nothing" (593).

In this case, then, a white nation's exploration (and intended exploitation) of Africa has the unexpectedly positive results in revealing to its characters the extensive, hidden fraternal bonds that unite and confound white and black. By going to Africa, they learn that the United States is already, in Dixon's terms, a mulatto nation. Charlie's question, "Where was the color line now?" suggests not only the color line's lack of relevance in a situation where monogenesis and miscegenation overdetermine the characters' shared blood but also the geographical disorientation that occurs when the United States cannot be defined as "white" in narratives of global civilization.

In the novel's sense of extended fraternal relations, we find the novel's strongest effort to challenge narratives of a white global mission for the United States and to rearticulate black cosmopolitanism. The figure of the United States on the world's stage is not de-raced but redefined, through an assumption of racial impurity that denies anyone the possibility of justifying or perfecting whiteness by carrying an imperial burden. Notable in these final chapters is Professor Stone's absence from the novel's conclusion and from its fraternal bonds; the British scientist's search for ethnological knowledge catalyzes both Charlie's and Reuel's transformations, but ultimately his story and his family is not theirs. History ensures that Professor Stone is not a brother except insofar as the novel insists on a common human origin for all races, so characters like Charlie and Aubrey can claim no special kinship with him, contradicting notions of a transatlantic Anglo-Saxon race mission that accompanied imperialist discourse. The United States cannot join in an Anglo-American "white man's burden," Hopkins demonstrates, because while civilizing missions may indeed be beneficial, America's mission must reflect its racially mixed fraternity and destiny, and so is united to the coming cyclical rise of Africa in a way that Britain is not. Hopkins's internationalist take on the Negro question binds the United States as a mulatto nation to a providential destiny.

What I have described here is a two-pronged strategy to deconstruct narratives of racial progress and empire. On the one hand, looking into

Reuel's bifurcated perspective trains readers in taking second looks at the utterances of black cosmopolitans assuming de-raced authority, a training that helps readers understand writers such as Steward and Campbell critically. On the other hand, the novel's challenge to civilized scientific authority and to American whiteness casts suspicion on any writers' assumption of de-raced authority. *Of One Blood* does not contend with expansion itself, which is revealed to have potentially positive effects; instead, it contends with the arrogant theories of racial mission that interpret history as a social Darwinist competition among races and civilizations and promote empire on these grounds. Yet, like Campbell's and Steward's writings, Hopkins's novel also replicates the very imperialist and racist assumptions that it criticizes, especially in its inability to fully challenge western definitions of civilization. The relationship between Hopkins and these two writers, or between Hopkins and internationalism in the *CAM* more broadly, is not one of Hopkins the radical social critic versus more conciliatory assimilationists, but one found along a spectrum of tangled, simultaneous efforts to seize the authority associated with civilized global vision and to question the nature of that authority as it is wielded by whites in power. These authors—Steward, Campbell, and Hopkins—are more or less ambivalent in how they shadow the white man's burden, but similarities in their strategies suggest a shared literary approach to the problem of their own relationships to black cosmopolitanism.

PART III

Pacific Expansion and Transnational Fictions of Race

On Friday, September 29, 1899, Admiral George Dewey's flagship the U.S.S. *Olympia* steamed into New York harbor in a grand naval procession. He and his crew were returning to the United States for the first time since they defeated the Spanish Pacific squadron a year and half earlier, a resounding victory that won the port of Manila and made Dewey a national hero. Throughout New York City, preparations were being made for the celebration's main event: a parade of more than thirty-five thousand men down Fifth Avenue to the recently constructed "Dewey Arch," a majestic wood and plaster structure for which New Yorkers were already raising money to rebuild permanently.[1]

On and off the parade route, enthusiastic New Yorkers decorated their homes, streets, and storefronts with murals, electric lights, bunting, festoons, streamers, and flags. One neighborhood's decorations particularly caught the attention of a *New York Times* reporter covering the preparations. In a segment titled "Patriotism Not All Native," the reporter interviews several residents of New York's Chinatown, asking why they decorated when Dewey had no plans to parade there. Li G. Chung, the proprietor of a store on Pell Street, answers by asserting Chinese Americans' stake in the common cause of a U.S. Pacific empire:

> We feel proud because several Chinese were on board his [Dewey's] ship when he whipped the Spaniards. They were serving there, and did not have to fight, but went up on deck and helped the sailors to handle the guns and shells, and fought just like the Americans. . . . We Chinese who are here in New York do not intend to return to China, and don't want to have anything to do with the old country. They treat us here better than the Spanish treated the Chinese in the Philippines, and we are glad they

got licked. We intend to remain in the United States and to die here, and
we want to become American citizens, and to call the Stars and Stripes
our flag too.[2]

For Li G. Chung and the other Chinatown residents interviewed, Dewey's
return was an opportunity to argue that, because of shared military sacrifice and shared national interests and feelings, the Chinese should receive
the full rights of U.S. citizenship. In a strategy resembling the patriotic accounts of African American troops that Steward and Hopkins adapted in
their writing, Li G. Chung puts Chinese Americans aboard what we saw
A. L. Demond, quoted in chapter 4, call the "ship of state."

Chung's words had another more conspicuous precedent, however.
Dewey himself had publicly made a similar argument on behalf of the
Chinese seamen aboard his Pacific squadron. Immediately after his victory in Manila, Dewey issued a request to the secretary of the Navy that
because of their valor in the Battle of Manila, the Chinese men aboard
his ship should be exempt from the Chinese Exclusion Act. "The Chinese
servants and other Chinese upon the ships of this squadron rendered
the most efficient services upon that occasion, and behaved in the most
exemplary manner," Dewey wrote: "To my mind it seems unreasonable
that men who have battled for our country should be excluded from it.
These men who have shown courage and energy in the face of an enemy
are at least worthy of the treatment accorded to any citizen of any other
country who does not come to our shores as a mendicant, or under labor
contract."[3] Dewey mentions nothing about naturalization in this initial request, only asking that his seamen be allowed to land on American soil,
but newspapers later quoted Dewey calling for their rights to naturalization as well as immigration.[4] There were about fifty such Chinese seamen
aboard the Pacific squadron, and, as Dewey notes, some of them had
served aboard these U.S. battleships for more than fifteen years—since
the early 1880s when the Chinese Exclusion Act was passed, and since
more recent efforts by the federal government to require specific forms
of written documentation for American-born Chinese. Some of Dewey's
Chinese seamen had emigrated from China before or after the Exclusion
Act, and some were born in the United States, but even the latter, if they
lacked documentation, were in effect trapped aboard the naval ships, risk-
ing deportation if they were discharged or tried to go ashore.[5]

With Dewey the hero of the hour, his request, which he submitted a second time to the State Department in December 1898, made the

national news. The *Denver Evening Post* covered the story with the head-line "Noble-Hearted Dewey: Hero of Manila Wants Chinese with His Fleet Rewarded"; the *Morning Oregonian* reported that "Chinese Behaved Well and Dewey Recommended That They Be Made American Citizens"; and the *Philadelphia North American* noted his second request with the headline "Dewey Appeals for the Chinese." When photographers came aboard the *Olympia* during the summer of 1899 to take photographs for distribution to mass-circulation magazines, Dewey had one taken of his Chinese cooks, posed not in the kitchen but on deck, a subtle statement about their position on board in light of his correspondence with the State Department. Laura Wexler has interpreted this photograph as part of Dewey and the U.S. government's "official interpretation" of interven-tion in the Philippines, noting that the Chinese cooks are not portrayed as part of the active fighting forces.[6] But Dewey's well-publicized and of-ficial comments on the service of these Chinese cooks suggest that there was no one "official version" of U.S. intervention in the Philippines and that, instead, Dewey pointed out an instance when the reality of U.S. ra-cial heterogeneity upset the era's unstable association between whiteness and imperial mission.

Whether or not the Chinese seamen had actually gone aboveboard to participate in battle or remained below in the mess became to some an important issue because it raised the question of whether these Chinese seamen were "laborers." Dewey's official requests were all refused—ul-timately by the Treasury Department, where the State Department for-warded Dewey's request—with the reasoning that only Congress could make an exception to the law that "specifically prohibits the landing in this country of Chinese laborers."[7] One editorialist, decrying this deci-sion, indignantly remarked, "Would it have been a very great stretch for the Treasury Department to have decided that sailors in the United States Navy are not 'laborers' in the sense of the law, but gallant defenders of the flag in the naval service of the country?"[8] Dewey himself clarified their role as sailors, not servants, in a letter printed in the missionary maga-zine *Woman's Work*; he explains that, although nearly all these men were employed as stewards, cooks, or messmates, "like everyone else on board they had their special stations for battle, some at the guns and others sup-plying ammunition."[9]

In these two competing views, the Chinese seamen are either foreign temporary workers whose labor was, like that of all Chinese, a competi-tive threat to whites, or they are patriotic immigrant sailors whose heroic participation in battle contributed to the American victory in Manila. A first-person account by "a sailor who served with Dewey," printed in an Oregon newspaper, veers ambivalently back and forth between these two registers of patriotic inclusion and alien exclusion, revealing an uncertain effort to manage the problem of representing Chinese American participation in the Battle of Manila. The sailor employs familiar stereotypes of Chinese Americans as workers to retain a sense of racial hierarchy despite unified efforts in battle: "These Chinese servants ordinarily used for fetching and carrying were impressed into service, and showed courage and skill. They showed as much nerve as the Americans. They aided at the whips, and in lifting and carrying the ammunition. Their faces were as impassive as when serving dinner in Hong Kong harbor." Here *servants*, not sailors, have to be pressed into service, implying an unwillingness to fight, something they then perform impassively. This is a key racial attribute in constructions of competitive Chinese labor that can underbid and outperform white workers by simply wanting and caring for less. For the Chinaman, the language suggests, he may as well be waiting tables in Hong Kong as carrying bullets for the United States, a sign of the Chinese servility and incapacity for national belonging. And yet showing "nerve," meaning showing courage, also implies a capacity for feeling that the "impassive" Chinese stereotype would deny. The Chinese seamen perform their tasks in battle, as the sailor notes, "mechanically," but still, "when some man would sing out that we had struck a Spanish ship, they were as happy as we." Here again shared *feelings* as well as effort draw the men together in national interest, complicating without dispelling the familiar domestic construct of Chinese immigrant labor's impassivity.[10]

By the time Dewey reached New York City for his homecoming celebration, both of his official requests had been denied, but the issue of the Chinese seamen still lingered in the press. An editorialist for the *New York Times* reminded readers that "Admiral Dewey is bringing back with him, on the *Olympia*, some of these Chinese servants. Under the law, unless they can prove a right to re-enter by producing certificates to show it, they cannot be permitted to parade with the other heroes of the *Olympia*'s crew, and they may not be discharged without incurring the risk of deportation." Their absence at the parade, the editorialist writes, threatened to cast a shadow on the festivities: "The people who are to crowd our streets to see Admiral Dewey and the men of the *Olympia* who helped to add to the glory of the navy, to overcome the enemy and to make Dewey an Admiral, will know, if this little handful of Chinese are not seen, that his enjoyment and theirs are impaired by what will seem to be an unjust and cruel exclusion."[11] A few days earlier, the *New York Times* reprinted another paper's suggestion that local customs officials find a "loophole" to allow the Chinese to land, thereby saving the country "from the ungracious role of refusing to accord due honor to every man who served with credit under Dewey."[12] Thus when Chung and other residents of New York's Chinatown decorated their homes and businesses for the parade and spoke to the press about their reasons for doing so, they visually and orally participated in a continuing public debate, spurred by Dewey's return and the new era of U.S. overseas colonial expansion, about the possibility and terms of national belonging for the Chinese in America.

The preceding discussion demonstrates some major points of this book as a whole and of my final two chapters in part III in particular. First, as with the accounts of African American soldiers and sailors in part II, we see here another example of individuals considered to be nonwhite claiming access to U.S. citizenship and equality through narratives of participation in the project of U.S. empire. As I contend throughout this book, visions of this kind of imperial contribution were powerful tools for exploiting the popular but logically unstable linkage between whiteness and America's role as a world power or empire. This exploitation is the tactic that I call "shadowing the white man's burden" in this book, and we see it functioning here in multiple ways: the *New York Times* claims that a pall would be cast over New Yorkers' enjoyment if these Chinese sailors are *not* seen in the parade, but, had they been included, another set of anxieties stemming from the troubled linkage between whiteness and Dewey's imperial conquest might have soured the party as well.[13] Left aboard Dewey's ship indefinitely, the Chinese seamen remain a kind of haunting supplement to the United States, always just outside of its borders and yet inhabiting the very ships that symbolized the newly emerging U.S. world power. In chapters 5 and 6, I extend my analysis of texts that shadow visions of white empire by examining the writings of Winnifred Eaton and Ranald MacDonald, mixed-blood Asian American and Native American writers who find in narratives of U.S. Pacific expansion and transnational racial affinity the opportunity to redraw their own racial definitions and terms of national belonging.

Like Steward and Hopkins, Eaton and MacDonald create their redefinitions by entering into a rhetorical and narrative contest over how to account for U.S. racial heterogeneity in a racially conceived imperial mission. As we saw Steward and Hopkins contend with white writers who placed blacks "at home" in rural, premodern, local-color scenarios or represented them fighting for empire in stereotypical terms culled from these domestic settings, the writers I discuss in part III contend with forms of racialization that would deny the participation of Asian and Native Americans in promoting U.S. cultural, economic, or military influence abroad. Eaton's and MacDonald's countertexts do so in terms that differ depending on the repertoires of racialization available for and made applicable to Asian and Native Americans. In the case of the Chinese seamen, we see their military service compared with the work of waiting tables, an appeal to a stereotype generated in the domestic context of U.S. immigration but that would simultaneously place the Chinese abroad—in Hong King harbor, not in New York's or San Francisco's Chinatown. While whites sought to position blacks at home, contained in the rural past, the terms for containing Chinese participation derives from domestic conflicts over immigration by projecting the Chinaman abroad, in foreign lands. My examination of Eaton and MacDonald extends this discussion of alternate terms of racialization to each of their cultural contexts.

Second, my discussion of responses to Chinese American naval service offers another example of the ways in which U.S. empire and domestic racism did not always neatly overlap and echo one another but, rather, were variably interrelated in representations of a new U.S. world power. While we saw Dixon striving to unite these stories in *The Leopard's Spots,* representations of empire and domestic racial segregation or exclusion were not always coterminous and mutually reinforcing. Thus, in chapter 5, I focus on strands of discourse and storytelling that trouble the supposed alliance of U.S. immigration policies and empire, revealing the two to be more variable and opposed than some scholars have noticed. For example, in *At America's Gates: Chinese Immigration during the Exclusion Era, 1882–1943,* historian Erika Lee claims that immigration laws were "central aspects" of U.S. imperialism during this period, suggesting that the former were essential supplements to the latter, with both composing and reflecting a powerful sense of white U.S. national identity. Noting the extension of the Chinese Exclusion Act to Hawaii in 1898 and to the Philippines in 1902, she writes, "The 'white man's burden,' the term used by American imperialists to describe the United States' responsibility to uplift and civilize savage peoples abroad, also involved the protection of Americans from the foreign menaces plaguing the mainland United States."[14] In Eaton's and MacDonald's writing, I focus on visions of empire that instead exploited confusion over the meaning of the "white man's burden" to offer alternative racial constructions of U.S. empire and U.S. citizenship. Like Dewey's and Chung's arguments on behalf of the Chinese seamen, Eaton's and MacDonald's textual arguments could be seen as historical losers in that they were unable to overcome the powerful force of law and custom behind formations such as the Chinese Exclusion Act. But neither were they isolated, radical visions that lost to a hegemonic, unassailable conception of the white man's burden. Instead, their textual arguments reveal a set of tensions between race and empire that could overshadow even the most affirmative celebration of U.S. Pacific expansion.

In part III, I closely examine some alternative views of white, Asiatic, and Native American racialization, conjured up in the new conceptual spaces created by U.S. expansion in the Pacific, in order to better understand the contested fields from which our modern-day terms of racialization emerged. Thus even when examining a text that exemplifies Erika Lee's understanding of complementary U.S. empire and Chinese exclusion, one can recognize it as responding to an active debate rather than reifying a foregone conclusion. A text that seems to neatly weave together U.S. Pacific expansion and Chinese exclusion into a coterminous white man's burden at home and abroad is Joseph Jarrow's melodramatic play *The Queen of Chinatown*, which opened at the Star Theater on Broadway in August 1899, just a few weeks before Dewey's much-anticipated homecoming.[15] A brief discussion of Jarrow's play can demonstrate how its terms of racialization are better understood in the context of the shadow that Dewey's missing Chinamen threatened to cast over the upcoming party.

Jarrow partly based his play on a sensational murder that had topped the headlines in New York City fifteen years earlier: the murder of the prostitute Elizabeth "Beezie" Garrity by her lover, the notorious gang leader Dan Driscoll.[16] But Jarrow updates the story by setting it in the present, when sailors are returning home from the Spanish American War, and by adding a sordid story about a white slavery ring in New York's Chinatown. The play's hero and his sidekick are a lieutenant and a sailor who served on the U.S.S. *Oregon* in the battle of Santiago, Cuba, and both are in search of the lieutenant's kidnapped sister, who has been abducted by Hop Sing, a Chinese gambling den proprietor. Aiding in the kidnapping are the dastardly Dan Driscoll and the tragic fallen woman Beezie Garrity, the so-called Queen of Chinatown, although she is quickly won over to the lieutenant's cause to save his sister. One advantage of setting the play in Jarrow's present moment was that, by filling it with topical references, Jarrow could easily harness the audience's boundless enthusiasm for America's recent victory and the upcoming celebration for returning sailors. In the first scene, characters give three cheers to Admiral Dewey, and his victory is gratuitously mentioned several times throughout the play. But ideologically, the play's references to current events further imply that after defeating the Spanish abroad, the next step is to defeat a foreign menace at home in Chinatown.[17]

The play draws this connection by linking the defense of white womanhood in the "foreign" territory of Chinatown to the current U.S. hostilities with Filipino insurgents. Early in the play, a newspaper seller shouts headlines stressing this simultaneity of national interest: "Extra—extra, sir. All 'bout the abduction of a beautiful young girl—great battle in the Philippines—de land forces wid the half of Dewey's marines knocked de niggers to smithereens—casualties—Aguinaldo captured—His losses, one thousand killed, wounded and captured. Our army, three wounded, our navy, nary a man."[18] This complete victory predicts the melodramatic play's resolution, where good of course prevails over evil, and the lieutenant succeeds at his task of foiling Hop Sing with the same resounding success as the headline announces for U.S. military forces. Paralleling Chinese at home and Filipinos abroad, this line racializes both as "niggers," a move that pointedly alters the terms of Dewey's and Chung's arguments for naturalizing the Chinese. While Chung makes the Spaniards the enemy against whom the Chinese can be incorporated into American national interests, and while Dewey likens the Chinese to "citizen[s] of any other country who [do] not come to our shores as a mendicant, or under labor contract," Jarrow draws his color line to clearly divide European Americans from Asiatics, reinforcing the notion of a "white man's burden" that binds together overseas expansion and immigration policy.

Furthermore, the play solidifies its category of whiteness by recruiting characters of various European ethnicities and social classes to the side of the U.S. Navy. Two comic immigrant characters, Mr. and Mrs. Huffnagle, a German American man and his Irish American wife, live in the neighborhood and come to assist the lieutenant, suggesting an example of homogeneous European American whiteness uniting through the symbolic situation of empire. As Matthew Frye Jacobson has noted, "questionably white" European immigrants such as Irish and Germans seemed whiter when they fought on the side of the United States against imperial others such as the Filipinos. Here the lieutenant's apparent extension of that overseas fight to a New York ethnic enclave makes Chinatown a space demanding U.S. military control by a newly unified, homogeneously white populace. Also aiding in this project are Freckles and Columbia, a young couple working the streets as a bootblack and a newspaper girl; they initially help Hop Sing by luring drunken sailors into his gambling house as easy marks, but upon first sight of the lieutenant, even before they hear about his abducted sister, they are won over to his cause and turn against Hop Sing. "Say Lieutenant, I like your face. I want to sail in your ship," Columbia says, using one of the play's many nautical metaphors to express instant unity binding the white working class to the more genteel officer in the face of Chinese difference. Columbia herself, as a metonym for the United States, climbs aboard a ship that sails against Chinese cultural invasion, with no place for Chinese seamen above deck or below.

Jarrow's melodrama might seem to merely deepen the grooves of an accepted white man's burden wrapping back around into Chinatown from abroad, but reading the work in the context in which New Yorkers viewed it—in light of Dewey's return and under the shadow of his missing Chinese seamen—we recognize that it opposed competing notions of Chinese American racialization that were also generated through the signifying opportunities of Pacific expansion. Jarrow's likening of Chinese to Filipinos notably absents the Spaniards as enemies, locating U.S. empire as a conflict between white and Asiatic, not Anglo-Saxon and Spaniard. His characters triumphantly recall victories at Manila and Santiago, but without mentioning the Spanish, disallowing Chung's comparison in which the U.S.'s difference from Spain hinges on its "better treatment" for Chinese at home than Spain's for the Chinese in the Philippines. While Jarrow simplifies a binary between homogeneous European whiteness and homogenous Asiatic otherness, Chung complicates that binary by including Spain as a triangulated term.

To best understand how a text like Jarrow's *Queen of Chinatown* reasserts the contested linkage between whiteness and empire, we must see how it tried to dispel alternate racial formations that were also pieced together from the signifying opportunities of Pacific expansion. In this final section, I examine such contests over U.S. racialization for their insight into the flexibility and instability of race as a tool in narrating international relations and, conversely, of narratives of international relations as tools in constructing race as a national or a transnational category. The point is not to idealize or recommend Dewey's and Chung's arguments for national inclusion. Resting on the idea of military inclusion for the Chinese at the very moment that the United States was violently opposing Filipino independence and contemplating Chinese exclusion from the Philippines, the limits of their appeals (whether to only fifty Chinese seamen or even to every Chinese American immigrant) are still drawn through the exclusion of the non-American imperial object undeserving of democratic self-determination. Instead, these arguments and the arguments of Eaton and MacDonald demand our attention because they suggest both the possibilities of transnational racial identifications during this era and their necessary limitations, insofar as stories about crossing national borders during this era inevitably navigated and negotiated the discourse of U.S. expansion and global power on the world's stage.

This brings me to a final central argument featured in this last pair of chapters. In the example of Jarrow's play and Chung's argument, we see a circular pattern in which racializations of Chinese Americans are refigured through imperial comparisons either with the Filipinos or with the colonized Chinese in the Philippines. Both examples cannot be fully accounted for by a projection model of U.S. racialization, which describes racial definitions and policies as developing domestically before being projected outward onto the field of Pacific empire. While scholars of U.S. empire have pointed out instances where "a reserve of racial understanding inherited from American slavery and Indian wars" inform and predict U.S. Americans' perceptions of Filipinos,[19] these arguments on behalf of Dewey's Chinese seamen are an example of a way that U.S. domestic racial perceptions, such as stereotypes of Chinese laborers, could instead be revised or adapted through shifting visions of U.S. overseas empire. In other words, domestic racial hierarchies and definitions of nonwhite and questionably white residents were negotiated through the shifting lens of U.S. interests abroad.

In chapter 5, I examine Winnifred Eaton's attempts to recalibrate U.S. domestic racial categories of "white" and "Asiatic" by viewing them through the shifting lens of international relations in the Pacific. In her fictions of Japanese American romance, Eaton borrows from the set of racial meanings categorizing the Japanese as white that were being used to narrate commercial and geopolitical contests over Asia. In Eaton's fiction, this sense of Japanese whiteness becomes a tool to pry apart and fracture the juridically and culturally ascendant conception of homogeneous Asiatic otherness in the United States. In this chapter, my understanding of the field of U.S. Pacific empire is not restricted to the Philippines and other territorial possessions but includes the various nations and imperial powers that were seen as actors on a world's stage vying for Pacific geopolitical power. I broaden this focus in order to challenge what I call the "frontier model" of Pacific expansion, a model that isolates Pacific expansion from multipolar European-centered contests for geopolitical power and in doing so misses an important symbolic register through which U.S. Americans interpreted their nation's new Pacific empire. The Philippines and Hawaii were widely understood as weigh stations for commercial influence in China, and defeating Spain meant not only winning the rights to certain territories but also being recognized as a new world power with global rights and responsibilities. Thus, rather than seeing "empire" as symbolically located only in relations with the new Pacific possessions, I am interested in various narratives of imperial and international competition that were sparked by Pacific expansion and the shifting racial narratives that accompanied them. As I demonstrate in chapter 5, these were part of the repertoire that Eaton used to make her bid for reordering U.S. racial categories and hierarchies. By accessing international narratives about Slavs, Anglo-Saxons, and Japanese, Eaton sought to alter the terms that writers like Jarrow used to sharpen a white/Asiatic binary at home.

In chapter 6, I continue to focus on competing empires in the Pacific by examining the way that Ranald MacDonald alternately framed his autobiographical narrative about visiting Japan in either U.S. or British Canadian narratives of Pacific expansion, fitting himself ambivalently in each because of his mixed-race Chinook heritage. What it meant to be a "half-breed" and a proponent of British Columbian or U.S. American Pacific progress was the problem that MacDonald faced in trying to tell his story. In this chapter, I compare his approach to the problem with alternate versions of his story written by other U.S. American writers, who characterized MacDonald as an object and artifact, not an agent of Pacific commercial expansion. This discursive contest over MacDonald's story provides several examples of racialization that do not project domestic conceptions of "the Indian" outward onto Asiatic others in an isolated Pacific frontier but, instead, access the international landscape of Pacific expansion in narrative attempts to redefine domestic categories and definitions of Indian and half-breed at home, within and across national borders.

5

How the Irish Became Japanese

Winnifred Eaton's Transnational
Racial Reconstructions

In Winnifred Eaton's 1906 novel *A Japanese Blossom*, war becomes a crucial testing ground for racial differences and similarities. The novel tells the story of Kiyo Kurakawa, a Japanese widower who returns to Japan from the United States with his new wife, Mrs. Ellen Kurakawa, an Anglo-American widow. Together with her two children, she experiences the challenges and novelties of moving to Japan and gaining a new family, for the widower already has children of his own. The dramatic conflict that finally unites the Japanese and American sides of the family results from the outbreak of the Russo-Japanese War (1904–5), which raises mild tension between the two parents because of their initially differing ideas about war and sacrifice. While Mrs. Kurakawa thinks that her husband should put his duty to his family first, Mr. Kurakawa feels compelled to risk his life fighting for his country. As he explains his patriotic obligation to his wife, "I seemed to be a living example of the evolution of an Oriental mind long swayed by Occidental environment. . . . Now I know that I can never be other than what I am by every inherent instinct: a true Japanese."[1] This revelation might seem to confirm the opinion of Lafcadio Hearn and other early-twentieth-century "experts" on Japanese culture that Japanese assimilation to western civilization was merely a mask behind which remained an irredeemably Oriental mind.[2] But in *A Japanese Blossom*, this unmasking provides, instead, a proving ground for the Kurakawas' mutual affection and for American respect for Japanese militarism. Mrs. Kurakawa reacts to her new husband's revelation not with dismay but with pride. She tells him she had not expected him to change, but that "*I*, as your wife, was willing to become one of you, if you would let me"

(113), and the entire family, American and Japanese, rallies together to join in the Japanese spirit of patriotic self-sacrifice.

That is, all of the family members except one: the Irish nursemaid Norah. In the novel's ensemble cast, Norah provides the comic relief that audiences would expect from an Irish maid. She alone approaches Japan with the assumption that it is a "haythen land of savages" (68), and when homesick she wanders the streets in search of "the soight of the face of a foine cop" (63), humorously assuming that policemen in Japan will be Irish, like those she has seen in the United States. Like Mrs. Kurakawa's American children, Billy and Marion, Norah gets into comic mishaps because of her cultural ignorance of Japan (for example, her fear of foreigners causes her to temporarily lose the Kurakawas' infant). But unlike the American children's problems, the maid's cannot be solved by herself and require the help of Mrs. Kurakawa. Significantly, Norah's difficulty assimilating to Japan extends to her failure to join in the spirit of Japanese patriotism and self-sacrifice during the war. While the rest of the family eagerly arise on the morning that Mr. Kurakawa leaves for the front, Norah lies in bed grumbling and later threatens to leave the family in their greatest time of need. The Irishwoman's difference from her Anglo-American employers is even marked on her body; when the Japanese Kurakawa children greet their new family, the foreign face that "frightened them most" was Norah's (30).

Eaton's depiction of Norah as physically different and inferior to the English-descended members of the Kurakawa family is unsurprising: the Irish, like several other European ethnic groups during this period, were still undergoing the discursive and political process that would render them white in the public mind.[3] But what role does the third term of Japan play in this contrast? In this racial triangulation, we see another example of the phenomena that this book examines: a writer using narratives of empire and international relations to modify domestic U.S. racial groupings and comparisons. In this instance, however, the dynamic is different from what we might suppose based on current scholarship on racialization and empire during this period. Matthew Frye Jacobson's explanation of the "racial alchemy" that formed our twentieth-century U.S. conception of homogenous European whiteness, when contrasted with Eaton's triangulation of Irish, Japanese, and Anglo-American characters, opens a new window onto the reconstruction of racial identity in the era of U.S. overseas empire.

Jacobson argues that visions of empire were a significant arena in which the modern-day conception of "Caucasian" whiteness cohered, taking the place of earlier nineteenth-century U.S. conceptions of fractured and hierarchical European races. According to Jacobson, an important "throughline" in American history was that "some questionable peoples would win inclusion based upon an alchemic reaction attending Euro-American contact with peoples of color." In other words, Irish "Celts" (such as Mrs. Huffnagle in Jarrow's *Queen of Chinatown*) seemed whiter when fighting alongside Anglo-Saxons and for the cause of Anglo-Saxon civilization. Jacobson suggests that this "homogenizing magic" operated at the turn of the century because of the era's heightened attention to issues of extracontinental empire: "The manufacture and maintenance of Caucasian whiteness depended . . . upon national encounters with 'barbarian dominions' even more problematic than the immigrants themselves— from constant (and constantly narrated) contact with 'black morsels' like the nations of the plains, Mexico, Hawaii, Samoa, Cuba, Puerto Rico and the Philippines."[4]

Jacobson's model might lead us to anticipate that Norah would appear whiter in contrast to the nonwhite "morsel" of Japan. Instead, we see that Winnifred Eaton attempts this alchemy in her novel by using a less-successful formula for whiteness than the one that Jacobson says triumphed in this era. It is her Japanese characters who seem whiter as they fight alongside Americans against another questionable ethnicity, the "Slavic" Russians. In *A Japanese Blossom*, Norah's presence (and that of other minor characters of non-Anglo-European ethnicity) serves to further highlight this qualification of the Japanese to stand—and fight—alongside Anglo-Saxons as equals. Eaton's Celts, Slavs, and Gauls are the questionably white (and questionably civilized) foreign barbarians whom the reader is encouraged to exclude from the shifting boundaries of whiteness.

A Japanese Blossom was not the only work of Eaton's to attempt this losing bid in the discursive battle for whiteness, nor was Eaton the only author to devise such a formula for whitening the Japanese. Rather, this formula was developed and contested in a number of fictional and nonfictional writings around the Russo-Japanese War. Examining this unsuccessful formula provides a greater understanding of the alchemy of whiteness by suggesting that American racial reconstruction took place in a more complicated international milieu than whiteness studies have recognized. Unlike other more domestically focused accounts of U.S. racial formation, Jacobson's looks across national borders to ask how U.S. racial categories were rearranged through perceived contact with the foreign realm of empire.[5] But despite this wider lens, his account is limited in its conceptualization of Pacific imperialism through the model of an expanding frontier. My argument here is thus not primarily with Jacobson or with whiteness studies more generally, which have often worked within a dominant paradigm in American studies that defines an object of study that is inwardly absorbed and isolated from European-centered contests for global power. Rather, my argument is with the frontier model itself as a powerful but limiting frame for understanding Pacific expansion at the turn of the twentieth century.[6] This is not to wholly deny that U.S. military and economic contact with Native America, Hawaii, the Philippines, Samoa, China, or Japan can be usefully interpreted as a series of chapters in a continuing mythic American encounter with "the West" or that a pattern of racialization organized and linked together, in Richard Drinnon's account, a "metaphysics" of Indian hating extending from North American Indians and Mexicans to Chinese and Japanese immigrants in the United States to Filipinos and Vietnamese in the twentieth century.[7] Rather, my analyses here and in the next chapter demonstrate that these continuities depend on a vision of American expansion into a frontier isolated from the shifting racial and cultural meanings of multipolar global contests for power. This conceptual isolation from contested global color lines is part of the fantasy that must be identified and undone.

Expansion in the Pacific was not only perceived as an extension of the boundless American frontier outside of which stood the unquestionably nonwhite other. Expansion also meant joining the European-centered contest for geopolitical control over Asia, and this required re-imagining the United States as a one of several "world powers" with a complicated set of global alliances and responsibilities that were envisioned and represented through the shifting lens of race. Two of these powers were Japan and Russia, whose conflict in the Russo-Japanese War (1904–5) provided a narrative opportunity for locating the United States diplomatically and racially in the world. Thus the domestic drama in which vying immigrant groups claimed and secured "whiteness" was played not just on the stage of empire understood as the extension of a frontier between white and nonwhite, civilized, and savage. It was also played out on the stage of global diplomacy, where race was used as a flexible tool for locating the United States in contests for geopolitical power. Most importantly, then, study of the discursive skirmish over whiteness that surrounded the Russo-Japanese War—a foreign war in which the United States was not a combatant—globally integrates the frontier model of U.S. empire. It deepens our understandings of both early-twentieth-century racial formation and the cultures of U.S. imperialism by practicing what Paul Giles has called "critical transnationalism," the assumption that U.S. literature and culture reflected and negotiated questions of global power.[8]

Placing Eaton's popular romances at the center of this analysis helps to foreground the construction of Asian American identity as a corollary to this reconstruction of whiteness. Recent scholarship on Eaton tends to represent the author as a trickster figure who adeptly hid subversive messages about race and gender equality in conventional packages.[9] The fact that this half-Chinese, half–British Canadian, New York transplant pretended for most of her early career to be the half-Japanese Onoto Watanna—and in one instance wrote an entire novel under the Japanese pseudonym using the first-person voice of an Irish American servant—are for these critics instances of her performative de-essentialization of race. But such interpretations fall into the trap of what David Palumbo-Liu calls the "uncritical postmodernization of Asian-American identity." This inadequate critical strategy rushes to endow ethnic American literature with the oppositional force of postmodern elements like indeterminacy and mimicry, and in doing so "elides the constituent historical and conceptual elements of ethnicity" that should be central to such criticism.[10]

Eaton's works do highlight the plasticity of race, but to see how, we must understand their participation in her era's labored decision that the Japanese are not white. That Eaton manipulated the foreign and domestic interests engaged in this decision makes her work a case study in understanding the transnational processes of racialization. Recognizing her particular role in this process furthers the recent project to "denationalize" Asian American literature, which, in part, seeks to think through the influence that global historical specificities, including U.S. imperialism, have on local Asian American sites of intervention.[11] Eaton provides an example of an early Asian American novelist who resisted the emerging notion of an Asian American ethnic identity at home by participating in an effort to characterize Japan through its diplomatic standing abroad. Her efforts to harness the discourses of international relations and cosmopolitanism in order to contest ascendant ideas about race reveal an important and underexamined tension in the evolution of an Asian American ethnic identity.

Saxon versus Slav versus Asiatic

After the Meiji Restoration in 1868, Japan launched an aggressive campaign to achieve power and equality among western nations by adapting and successfully implementing western political, industrial, military, and cultural practices.[12] With Japan's victory over China in the Sino-Japanese War in 1895, its participation with western powers in the military campaign against the Chinese Boxers in 1899, and its winning of the diplomatic status of extraterritoriality from Great Britain and the United States in 1899, Japan had seemed to reach this goal. As an American consul to Japan told readers of an 1899 *North American Review,* "when an Empire has, within a quarter of a century, turned its back upon Oriental customs and superstitions and written its name so brightly in modern history, it may justly claim the applause and respect of the world when it is about to take its place in the ranks of civilized nations."[13] Yet the metaphor used in the title of this article—"Japan's Entry into the Family of Nations"—suggests the racial problem of consanguinity that arose from this transformation. If equal diplomatic status makes Japan "family," what does this imply about Japan's racial status or the racial status of the family itself?

As Joseph H. Henning has shown, numerous ethnologists and political commentators of the day met this problem by asserting that no miscegenation of the "family" had occurred at all, because the Japanese were in fact also white.[14] Writers like William Elliot Griffis and George Kennan strained ethnological evidence to argue that the Japanese actually descended from white and Malay (not, like the Chinese, Mongolian) ancestors, a lineage that explained their capacity for progress. Ethnologist Arthur May Knapp went so far as to argue that Japanese progress resulted from their descent from the Aryans, a pedigree adulterated by only small amounts of "alien" influence.[15] In Henning's analysis, such racial reorganizations did not trouble assumptions of white superiority; rather, they were "a new and effective means of preserving the accepted hierarchy of races."[16] Coming to terms with a nonwhite nation as an equal was easier if one simply decided that the nation was in fact white. A writer in the *Nation* satirically identified this tendency in 1904 when he suggested that Secretary of State John Hay arrange a ceremony of "blood adoption, by which the subjects of the Mikado may acquire the standing of a white race, and become entitled to share what we cannot prevent them from possessing themselves." Such a ceremony would lessen the contradiction of a Japan that participated and won in "a game which only white nations could play," thus breaking the "fixed law of 'sociology'" outlining the "cosmic process of wiping inferior races off the map."[17]

But Henning's analysis misses the fact that the categories of white and nonwhite were so unstable at this time that asserting Japanese "whiteness" does not have to signify denial and self-delusion merely because it flies in the face of our contemporary racial classificatory systems.[18] When whiteness itself is accepted as a rhetorical construct, these arguments can be understood not only as an effort to reconcile an ideology of white superiority with Japan's unprecedented rise to power. They can also be examined for their productive power, both in shaping the racial categories that triumphed in these battles for whiteness and in revising popular conceptions of the place of the United States in the world. In so doing, they spotlight the competing domestic and international agendas that formed the crucible in which our modern ideas of whiteness coalesced.

The Japanese may have briefly appeared to win the status of whiteness on the international stage, but such arguments had little influence in the legal battle over Japanese racial identity occurring within the United States. Because U.S. naturalization laws extended citizenship only to immigrants who were "white" or "of African nativity or descent," deciding whether or not the Japanese were white became an important juridical problem. In several U.S. naturalization cases between 1894 and 1922, courts decided that the Japanese applicants were not white but "Mongolian," part of the "yellow" race, and therefore like the Chinese ineligible for citizenship. Through such decisions, the courts hardened the line that would include "questionable" European immigrant groups, like Celts or Slavs, in the monolithic category of whiteness while homogenizing and excluding the Asian "race" from citizenship.[19]

But however ineffective legally, the losing arguments in these cases are clearly efforts to revise domestic racial categories in light of diplomatic events. In an 1894 law review article, legal scholar John Wigmore answers the domestic question about the status of Japanese immigrants by appealing to international relations, as well as ethnography: "Having as good a claim to the color 'white' as the southern European and the Semitic peoples, having to-day greater affinities with us in culture and progress than they have with any Asiatic people, isolated as they are to-day from Asia in tendencies and sympathies," the Japanese should be allowed citizenship, and the courts should interpret the statute "in the direction indicated by American honor and sympathy."[20] In 1902, Takuji Yamashita developed this idea that international "affinity" granted the Japanese special status in his prerequisite case for U.S. citizenship before the Washington State Supreme Court. Yamashita argued that the 1899 U.S. treaty that granted Japan extraterritoriality demonstrated the distinction between China and Japan in the minds of legislators. While U.S. laws specifically restricted Chinese immigration, U.S treaties granted only Japan of all Asian nations this status of international equality. Like Wigmore, Yamashita finds it relevant to his case that his race is one "which has shown itself in a brief period of years capable of taking its place in the front rank among the most highly civilized and enlightened nations in the world."[21]

The idea of Japan's special "affinity" with the United States to which both Wigmore's and Yamashita's legal arguments appeal was widely held in the 1890s and early 1900s. At the turn of the twentieth century, both Americans and Japanese represented Japan to U.S. audiences as particularly allied with the U.S.'s new overseas mission to spread commerce, freedom, and enlightenment in Asia. Japan would not only aid in maintaining the Open Door to free markets in China but was especially qualified to assist the United States in "modernizing" China by instilling in the Chinese a desire for U.S. commodities and culture. The strength of this bond became a widespread topic of discussion during the Russo-Japanese War, where, as one magazine columnist noted, "One of the most interesting and extraordinary of modern international phenomena is the spontaneous and general sympathy of the American people with the Japanese in their terrific struggle with Russia."[22] Another claimed that he had never known a conflict in which the United States was not an active participant where there was anything like "the unanimity of opinion or intenseness of sympathy which is felt in the republic for Japan."[23] The practical reason for this preference was clear to these commentators: Russia sought imperial expansion and opposed free markets, while Japan was committed both to protecting U.S. access to Chinese markets and facilitating Chinese westernization. As another writer explained, "In this war, Russia stands for reaction and Japan for progress."[24]

These commentators vary in their treatment of Japanese racial identity (one writer marvels that these genuine sympathies can exist when Japan is of an "utterly alien" race),[25] but they commonly stress the racial difference marking Russia as a force for barbarism. In 1900, expansionist Josiah Strong wrote that "whether the Anglo-Saxon or the Slav is to dominate is the spinal column of world politics, of which all other questions are only the ribs."[26] For political scientist Wolf von Schierbrand, this was the racial feeling that most guided U.S. sentiment in the Russo-Japanese War; influencing the United States was "the deep racial antipathy between the Slav and the Anglo-Saxon, the irreconcilable differences in the conception of life and its ideals, of government and policy." In contrast, he writes, "the 'Jap,' our pupil, in this war stands for most of the things this nation is striving for."[27] Another commentator on the war wrote that "Russia is in race, customs, art, thought and general culture more yellow than white, more Asiatic than European," and in fact had far more in common with China that did Japan.[28] Readers of the *North American Review* who might be inclined to side with Russia were told that of the two combatants, Russia has "the least claim to the part of defender of the Aryan Race and of European culture."[29] Meanwhile, wrote another commentator, "Japan stands for the essentials of Anglo-Saxon civilization."[30] Japanese propagandists strongly encouraged such formulations by placing in American periodicals articles that described the war as a struggle not between Japanese and Russian national interests but between "Saxon" and "Slav," with Japan taking the side of the Anglo-Saxon.[31]

The notion that this coming racial conflict would determine the future global politics seems to have originated in the United States with William Dudley Foulke's *Saxon or Slav: A Study of the Growth and Tendencies of Russian Civilization* (1887, reprinted 1898), and was largely influenced by British political thought. However, one reason this notion appealed so strongly derived from domestic racial tensions in the United States; the Saxon versus Slav showdown clearly meshed with U.S. nativism and rising concerns about increased immigration from eastern Europe. Prescott Hall's influential 1906 study of immigration warns against assimilating the racial element of the Slav, a category that includes Russians, as well as Poles, Slovaks, Bohemians, Lithuanians, Croatians, and Bosnians. Hall locates in domestic labor conflicts that same elemental racial divide, regretting "the displacement of the 'English' by the 'Slav' in the Pennsylvania mining fields."[32] Yet while the term "Slav" and the theory of Slavic inferiority were in common circulation in domestic discourses of immigration and labor dispute, the standing right of Russian or Polish or other Slavic immigrants to become naturalized citizens was never legally challenged. Anglo-Saxonists like Hall wanted to set legal limits for Slavic immigration, but they never questioned the immigrants' qualifications for citizenship as "white" persons under existing naturalization law, as they did with Chinese and Japanese immigrants. In light of this cohering juridical assumption of Slavic whiteness at home, then, it is all the more surprising that on the international field of the Russo-Japanese War, it was the Japanese who were more frequently and enthusiastically represented as compatible with the progressive Anglo-Saxon in general and U.S. interests in particular.

American enthusiasm for the Japanese cause was so intense that Eaton's fanciful novels about Japan were read and promoted as insights into the conflict. Virtually all of the reviews of her *Daughters of Nijo*, released at the height of the conflict in spring 1904, make mention of the war, despite the fact that the historical novel was set in Japan of the 1870s and contained no Russian characters. As one reviewer explained, "coming at a time when the war in the east is a topic absorbing public interest, this new romance of Japanese life seems to acquire a decided importance in the list of newly published novels."[33] Some booksellers listed *Daughters of Nijo* as their top seller for May 1904, and that year, Eaton—in the guise of her Japanese persona, Onoto Watanna—was sought after for interviews on the topic of the war, which she happily gave. In one she gushed, "Isn't it splendid the way my people have been giving it to the Russians? I guess people here will not have so much to say about Asiatics being an inferior people now." Later she says of the Japanese: "Talk about their being Asiatics! I guess you will find that most of the people in Asiatic Russia are Asiatics, and a much poorer kind that the Japanese." In contrast to Russia, "Japan's greatest hope is to become the 'Light of Asia,' and her leaven is bound to have good results in China."[34] Here Eaton contests the contemptuous dismissal of the Japanese as Asiatics by pointing out that they are racially superior (because militarily more skilled) to their fellow Asiatics, the Russians. Her strategy fractures the ascending notion of European "Caucasian" whiteness by casting Russians as "mostly" Asiatic, a move that counters the coalescing juridical and domestic acceptance of the Russians as a white race. It uses the new signifying spaces opened up by U.S. Pacific expansion to fracture homogenous whiteness, a signifying move that Eaton would develop further in her fiction.

Japanese War Games

Enthusiasm for the war clearly influenced Eaton to write two subsequent works that deal explicitly with the conflict: *A Japanese Blossom* and "The Wrench of Chance," a short story that appeared in *Harper's Weekly* in 1906. Both works explore Japanese racial identity in comparison to Slavs, Celts, and other competitors in the discursive battle for whiteness, and both promote American identification with Japan on the international stage. In *A Japanese Blossom,* Eaton most fully explores the racial implications of an American-Japanese alliance through the boyish military enthusiasm of Ellen's twelve-year-old son Billy. Before his stepfather leaves for the front in Manchuria, Billy tells him that when he grows up, he wants to be a Japanese soldier and a Japanese citizen (124). But does racial difference prevent Billy from filling these roles? This question is addressed in scenes where Billy plays war with his younger Japanese stepbrother Taro while their father is away. When Taro suggests that Billy pretend to be a Russian admiral to fight against Taro as the Japanese naval hero Admiral Togo, Billy reacts with anger: "*Me* a Russian?" (137). Taro answers, "Yaes, Because you loog jes' same." This "insult" turns Billy purple: "I don't. Father says when I wear your old kimono I look Japanese. I'll be Togo. I'm the oldest" (137). They finally resolve the fight by forcing their baby brother Juji to play the Russian, because Russians "all cry and pray and make a big noise" (138). Billy's outrage at the suggestion that he looks just like a Russian questions the assumption of visual similarity between Russians and Anglo-Americans, replacing it with the possibility of a more fundamental martial likeness between Anglo-Americans and Japanese.

Eaton further undermines the assumption of shared whiteness among Europeans with the introduction of another character into the boys' war games: a French boy who lives down the street. Alphonse, the French boy, is marked as visually different and physically less powerful than both Taro and Billy. Although at age fourteen the eldest of the three boys, Alphonse is "a little fellow," with "very black and furtive" eyes and "a tiny little mouth that he would not keep closed" (197). When Alphonse insults Japan by saying that the Russians will win the war, Taro responds by, in Billy's words, "lick[ing] the Frenchy till he squeaked for mercy" (154). According to domestic U.S. politics, Alphonse's status as a member of an equal white race would be unquestioned; although French Gauls were one of the European racial groups that ethnologists ranked below the Anglo-Saxon, French whiteness and fitness for citizenship in the United States was practically unquestioned at the beginning of the twentieth century. (Prescott Hall praises French immigrants as in "every way desirable to the [U.S.] population."[35]) But in this scene of international conflict, Alphonse's racial difference is heightened by his connection with the Russians, emphasized vocally: the Russians cry and the French squeak. Indeed, according to Billy, it is the weak but blustering French boy who is most "like [Russian Admiral Petrovich] Rojestvensky—he bluffs" (154). This low ranking of the French draws not from domestic prejudice but from U.S. perceptions of European rivals for world power, who, as diplomatic historian Michael H. Hunt explains, were arranged in "a clear and fixed pecking order even for whites." Beneath the Anglo-Saxons and the Germans were the Slavs, and beneath them were the French and other Latin peoples. Purportedly held back by effeminate sentiment and a lack of discipline and vigor, the French were regarded as being "of small account in international affairs."[36]

The force of international politics in ranking and linking the boys' racial characters becomes clearer when the three boys fight again after the Kahmrahn (Kam Rahn) Bay incident (1904), in which the supposedly neutral France appeared to break international law by allowing Russian warships to receive supplies in a French-controlled port. The news outrages Billy and Taro, as it does the rest of the town, and the boys decide to seek vengeance on their French neighbor. After easily capturing the boy, Taro observes that both of the boys cannot unfairly team up on Alphonse, and Billy offers a solution: "Japan doesn't want to fight France *yet*. You leave him to *me*. [France] interfered in what wasn't their affair, and now America's going to do the same" (196). But Taro sees a solution that doesn't violate American neutrality: "You be England . . . she our honorable ally," and Billy eagerly accepts: "'I am English, then,' shrieked Billy; 'all our people come from England originally. Mamma said so'" (196–97). Here Billy's pure Anglo-Saxon lineage further qualifies him to champion Japan and distances him—both racially and politically—from the continental powers of France and Russia.

This movement seems patterned after the influential military theorist Alfred Thayer Mahan's characterization of early-twentieth-century world politics as a coming struggle pitting older "land" powers like France and Russia against more modern "sea" powers like the United States, Great Britain, and Japan, which shared interests in open markets. Mahan believed that racial characteristics contributed to this major geographical division, making the struggle for power in Asia also a showdown between the Asiatic, the Teutonic, and the Slavic, with the insular Japan more drawn to the side of the Teutons to aid in "rejuvenating" the Asiatic with free trade. Despite an elemental racial difference, Mahan writes, "in the kind and methods of their power, the Teutonic group and Japan are one," just as France was drawn toward the side of the Slavs by strategic rather than racial interests.[37] Eaton's *A Japanese Blossom* builds on this discourse of international politics, using its new alliances and oppositions to fracture the notion of homogeneous European whiteness and to make compelling the emerging idea of Japan as a racially compatible member of the family. Billy might look like a Russian soldier, but racial mission beings him closer to his little Japanese brother.

While the Japanese and American Kurakawas unite against the clearly inferior Russians and French, the family's internal power relations are more complicated. How do Japan and the United States relate to one another within the family? Billy is older than Taro, and although he is impressed with his little brother's courage and fighting ability, the American boy is the victor when the two square off early in the novel. His superiority in age and strength might metonymically suggest Anglo-American racial superiority, but what do we make of the gendered relation between Kiyo and Ellen, which casts Ellen as the inferior in the relationship, striving to adapt to her husband's world? Perhaps it was popular enthusiasm for militant Japan that authorized Eaton for the first time in her writing to fully invert the popular *Madame Butterfly* convention of an adoring Japanese woman enraptured by an American man. Nonetheless, the potentially troubling implication—that Americans might emulate Japanese ways rather than vice versa—is forestalled by characterization of their marriage as extraordinarily equal and Kiyo's fatherhood as most gentle, good-humored, and wise. Kiyo seeks Ellen's approval before joining the Japanese army, and she tells him that she had "always felt like a mother" to her husband (234). Indeed, her domestic authority might be understood as the real power in the household.[38] (Ellen's daughter Marion carries on this motherly role to her stepfather by providing him with a Bible at the front.) In turn, Mr. Kurakawa provides a wise, gentle influence for the occasionally bloodthirsty and jingoistic Billy; when Billy asks his stepfather to bring him back buttons from dead Russians' uniforms, Kiyo respectfully reminds his stepson of the dishonor associated with scavenging trifling souvenirs (191).

In creating this balanced relationship between an American woman and a Japanese soldier, Eaton followed—and attempted to extend—a rhetorical bid for Japanese racial kinship that seemed compelling during the Russo-Japanese War. Other texts of the era similarly used the backdrop of the war to promote the idea of Japan as a potentially equal member of the family. Two years earlier, Archibald Clavering Gunter's 1904 novel *My Japanese Prince* presented a similar vision of an alliance between the United States and Japan that distances both from "Slavic" Russians. Its heroine Hilda Armstrong, an American businessman's daughter, chooses to marry the dashing Japanese Prince Okashi Sendai over the blustering Russian Baron Serge Schevitch as the two men fight for both her heart and their countries in the Russo-Japanese War. While Schevitch insists Russian "six foot men can whip [Japanese] five foot monkeys," his faith in Russian racial superiority is belied by the novel's depiction of Prince Sendai as both eminently modern and augustly aristocratic.[39] One character describes Sendai as "the expert engineer, the great bridge-builder, the profound mathematician, he who is even in modern democracy the

most aristocratic representative of one of the great houses in Japan" (37).
While the novel's French characters side with Russia, its British show "the
usual Anglo-Saxon admiration" for Japanese heroism and scientific progress (76, 236), and its Americans seem content to ally with whichever side,
Russian or Japanese, will be most profitable. Racial difference is hardly an
issue in Hilda's marriage to Sendai. At first, Hilda's father tells his daughter that "American women had better marry their own countrymen" (99),
a statement that uses the political trope of "nation" rather than race to
describe Sendai's difference. Such national difference is suggested as much
by Schevitch's "soft Slavic tones" (15) as by Sendai's ardent "Oriental passion" (250). Yet some characters—like the Armstrong's Chinese servants
and the cunning Chinese official they meet in Manchuria—are clearly
outside of the wider racial line drawn around the various "civilized" nations in Armstrong's social set.

Mingling with these "civilized" nations of Europe and Asia causes both
Mr. Armstrong and his daughter to recognize the social and economic
benefits of Hilda's marriage to Sendai. At the novel's end, Mr. Armstrong
encourages his new Japanese son-in-law to visit New York to help out
with plans for bridges over the East River: "With your engineering ability I think we can get the contracts and make a raft of money" (244). The
comically modern and high-spirited American girl Hilda is less interested
in money than social standing, which Sendai, who is appointed military
attaché of the Japanese embassy to the British Court of St. James, can also
provide. As she triumphantly writes in her journal: "The English Court!
Look out for your prestige, Mesdames Marlborough and Roxburghe.
What are your puny titles, scarce two hundred years old, to that of a *dai-
mio* prince, whose house for two thousand years has record in the history
of Japan?" (255). Marriage to Sendai gives the Armstrongs the benefit of
Japanese scientific modernity and aristocratic respectability, empowering
Hilda to compete for prestige on a global stage. Their match is a modern
one, suggesting the rapprochement of two new Pacific powers poised to
join—and rejuvenate—the system of European diplomacy. Gunter's vision
of strategic Japanese American kinship thus echoes political commentator
Frederick Wells Williams's 1904 diplomatic prediction that, as a result of
the growing alliance between these two "newly arrived" and "first class"
Pacific powers, "the bottom drops out of that system whereon was based
the diplomacy of nineteenth-century Europe."[40]

In *My Japanese Prince*, U.S. relations with Japan are imagined not as a
campaign against a racial other on an extended Asian "frontier" isolated

from world politics but, rather, as a novel and potentially disruptive entry into the European-dominated balance of power in Asia. As in Eaton's *A Japanese Blossom*, the complex web of international relations creates a romantic landscape that challenges the concept of a shared European racial identity positioned in opposition to a homogeneous conception of "the Asiatic." But if Eaton maps racial affiliations according to international diplomacy rather than domestic prejudice, where does she place the Irish maid Norah? It may be that, as a colonized people, the Irish fall even further below the Slavs and the French and make an even sharper contrast with the ambitiously colonizing Japan. In the text's particular construction of Norah, however, global politics is a less-significant factor than domestic U.S. racial constructions in triangulating her with Japanese and Anglo-American civilization.

Eaton casts the Russians and the French as racial others through the dynamics of global alliances and strategic interests, but she renders Irish inferiority by invoking a more familiar prejudice against immigrants at home. This domestic definition of the Irish abroad as "bad immigrants," echoing familiar ethnic stereotypes about Irish- Americans, in some ways resembles the hegemonic efforts described in chapter 2 to affix African American soldiers to familiar domestic racial hierarchies by firmly locating them in local domestic settings and denying them symbolic access to the position of the civilized global cosmopolitan or imperialist. In other words, Eaton, like Steward and Hopkins, is fighting a discursive battle over who, on the one hand, can claim access to the dynamic transnational and international racial signifying systems invented to make sense of a rapidly changing global landscape of power relations and who, on the other hand, is cordoned off from that unstable terrain in the supposedly fixed and familiar racial roles of the domestic United States. Eaton implicitly claims this privilege and power for the Japanese but insists that racial meanings of Irish Americans be defined domestically.

An Irishman Abroad

In *A Japanese Blossom* as in Eaton's other writings, the Irish are inherently less adaptable to civilized conditions than the Japanese, less capable of class mobility, and less willing to fulfill the duties of patriotic citizenship. This familiar, domestically sedimented characterization of the Irish is particularly evident in "The Wrench of Chance," Eaton's short story published a few months after the release of *A Japanese Blossom*. In the short story, Michael Lenahan, an Irish sailor and fugitive from English justice, seeks anonymity and protection from the law in a small Japanese hamlet. Finding himself "alone with a race of people he calls 'oogly haythens'" (78), Lenahan makes the best of his situation by taking advantage of the small town's ambition to adopt western learning.[41] Here Eaton emphasizes the comedy of the delicate and polite Japanese attempting to learn western civilization from the boorish and crude Lenahan, a man of "the lowest type" (79). Engaged to teach at the university as a "Professor of English," Lenahan changes his title to "Professor of Irish," an act of "characteristic effrontery" that inadvertently suggests the inferiority of his teaching (79). Years go by, and Lenahan, while still despising the Japanese, decides to make himself more comfortable in his adopted home by requesting from the town's governor two things: Japanese citizenship and a Japanese wife. Both of these requests are granted, giving Lenahan two responsibilities that he cannot fulfill. His chosen wife, a seventeen-year-old student of Lenahan's named Yiguri, is forced to be a "victim to the house of the Irishman" (80), submissively but unhappily suffering his "savage" manners: he drinks, he smells, he orders her around like a slave. The beautiful Yiguri clearly outclasses Lenahan: her "exquisite" features show her "patrician blood," heightening the text's indignation that she serves "the beast of the town" merely because of his status as a western man (82, 80).

If Lenahan abuses the power that Japanese law gives him over his young wife, he also fails the responsibilities of citizenship. Five years after becoming a citizen and marring Yiguri, Lenahan by chance learns the man he thought he had murdered still lives, and thus he fled the law for nothing. He immediately decides to return to Ireland, but because he is too cowardly to tell Yiguri that he is deserting her, he invents a convenient lie: that he leaves to fight for his adopted country in the Russo-Japanese War. This news elates the patriotic Yiguri, who thinks herself the wife of a soldier: "I am the wife of one both brave and noble, who will give his life for honorable Dai Nippon! . . . I had misjudged my husband. The gods made him a hero—not a beast!" (85). Lenahan's lie ensures that his wife remains his devoted servant even in his absence.

Had Eaton made Lenahan an Anglo-American or a British soldier, the story would seem to be another of Eaton's clever variations on the popular *Madame Butterfly* formula that she adapted and sometimes satirized in her writings. Instead of tragically loving her western husband and his foreign ways, this Japanese maiden despises them, and he only tricks her into devotion by assuming the pose of a "real" Japanese man. By making Lenahan Irish, however, his flaws register not as those of a westerner but as more specifically those of an Irish immigrant. Lenahan is not merely crude, dirty, and savage; more importantly, he is incapable of assimilating to the superior culture around him. He takes the privileges of citizenship without the sacrifices of military service; his thin allegiance to this adopted country dissipates as soon as exigencies change. Like *A Japanese Blossom*'s Norah—and unlike the readily adaptable Anglo-American Kurakawas, Lenahan is an undesirable immigrant.

However, Eaton partially redeems Lenahan at the story's end. After some Japanese patriots in a teahouse overhear the drunken Lenahan's true story, they indignantly press him into actual military service for Japan. Lenahan unwillingly goes to the front, where he fights alongside the Japanese and dies in service, finally earning part of the reader's respect and all of Yugiri's, who had lost faith in her husband after having been informed of his plan to desert her by a suitor aware of the Irishman's original intention. But Eaton is careful to point out that fighting alongside the Japanese does not mean he has assimilated to their ways. Lenahan's physical difference marks him even in uniform: he snores, while the Japanese soldiers sleep quietly; he sleeps heavily, while the Japanese soldiers sleep lightly; he fights the Russians with a wailing banshee cry and Irish song, while the Japanese soldiers fight silently. Indeed, Lenahan's similarity to the Russians and the Chinese—and his inferiority to the Japanese—is implicitly communicated through the sounds these characters make in battle, as was the case in Billy and Taro Kurakawa's war games. The wounded Japanese are "as silent as the dead" (94); in contrast, a Chinese peasant emits a "loud squeal of terror," Russians fight "with grunts and mutterings," and Lenahan's singing is "a strange and almost eerie sound" (93). The novel's conclusion is decidedly ambiguous, for the sight of Lenahan's corpse once again fills Yugiri with respect for her dead husband and anger for the suitor who told her that Lenahan deserted her, but with dramatic irony the reader knows that she is wrong in assuming that her husband told the truth and her suitor didn't.

Eaton lets both the Anglo-American Billy Kurakawa and the Irish Michael Lenahan play the parts of Japanese soldiers, but only Billy has the class status, patriotism, and racial stock to truly become a member of the family. The explicit fictive question in these works is whether Irish or Anglo-Americans can better assimilate to Japan, but in answering that question, Eaton makes the implicit argument that the Japanese are more qualified than the Irish for responsibilities of U.S. citizenship and equal social status at home.

Significantly, Eaton's next novel, the *Diary of Delia* (1907), departs from her usual subject matter of Japan but continues her exploration of the limitations of Irish assimilation. Her title character Delia is another Irish maid; Delia proves her value and loyalty to the Wolleys, the New York family who employ her, but the upstairs-downstairs relation between master and servant remains securely intact. The class difference that initially prevents the marriage of one of the fashionably socialist, middle-class Wolleys to their highbrow capitalist neighbor dissipates by the novel's end, but Delia's class difference remains unquestioned, no matter how much money she saves, because it is bound up with the idea of her racial difference. Both class and race prevent the narrative possibility of Delia's romantic involvement with an Anglo-American character, a limit that is never marked for Eaton's Japanese female characters in her other works. Delia's suitors are Irish and French immigrants, but had Eaton made Delia a Japanese maid, the character's chance of entering the Anglo-American social set through romantic attraction would have risen considerably. In a trope commonly associated with Asiatic racialization, Eaton's Irish remain foreign and unassimilable.

Turning Asiatic

Eaton's narrative strategy to rank the Irish—like the Chinese—ethnically below the Japanese was ultimately a losing one. It lost in the courts where Japanese naturalization and whiteness were on trial, and it lost in the obvious sense that few U.S. Americans ask anymore whether the Japanese (or the Irish or the Russians) are "white." But this discursive gambit exemplified in Eaton's writing is more than just a historical footnote to the seemingly inevitable triumph of modern-day racial categories. Rather, it invites us to understand the numerous appeals this vision offered as an alternative ordering of racial and cultural alliance through the realm of international relations.

First, the idea of a modern, empowered Japan symbolically eased the uncomfortable transition from hemispheric to Pacific empire insofar as Japan appeared—unlike China or the Philippines—to actively and successfully embrace the benefits of western influence and American commerce. Partnership with a happily Americanized Japan thus reinforced the notion of an empire for liberty at a moment when it was particularly strained by resistance to U.S. expansion. Second, this fantasy of partnership allowed Pacific expansion to be figured as joining with another, modern power in a new transpacific bond that would displace older, European conceptions of diplomacy and eastern empire, evading the fear that the United States was simply joining what Mark Twain had called "the European game" of colonialism.[42] And finally, the notion of Russian racial difference provided a convenient ideology for positioning the United States as a progressive force in future conflicts over Asian land and markets, as well as in narrating the *rapprochement* between the United States and Great Britain at the turn of the twentieth century.[43] While Caucasian whiteness could be reaffirmed, as Jacobson writes, in the face of the more obviously savage and nonwhite Filipinos, it had to simultaneously overcome the strategically effective characterization of Russians as Slavs opposing globally shared Anglo-Saxon interests.

Just as important as understanding these appeals is recognizing the domestic forces that specifically contested this popular vision of Pacific power. How was the idea of Japanese whiteness criticized or revised by writers seeking to mark a definitive line between the Caucasian and the Asiatic? Through what rhetorical moves did ascendant notions of homogeneous white and Asiatic racial identities defeat Eaton's alternative vision? Examining both sides of this discursive skirmish as it played out during and after the Russo-Japanese War reveals the ways that the idea of Japanese-American alliance shaped the terms of American racialization.

Eaton scholars have speculated that changing, post-1905 perceptions of Japan accounted for *A Japanese Blossom*'s sales being lower than those of previous Onoto Watanna novels.[44] As Dominika Ferens points out, when Eaton began writing *A Japanese Blossom,* "Japan's popularity had reached a high point on the East Coast, but by the time the book came out voices alarmed at Japan's expansionism had begun to dominate."[45] Instead of a helpful younger sibling who could aid in the mission of Americanizing the Pacific, the militant expansionist Japan began to appear as a potential rival for Pacific empire.[46] The military devotion to country that Eaton depicted as so similar to patriotic America's began to be perceived as a key aspect of Japanese difference. For example, in 1906, Thomas F. Millard warned about Japan as a competitor and potential military threat. Due to the "hypnotic effects" of Japanese propaganda, "the average person in America and England now finds himself imbued with the impression that Japan is a miracle among modern nations, . . . [and] that the Japanese people are the most patriotic, most agreeable, and the 'cutest' even known," but, in fact, Japan seeks to extend its power eastward, "to some, perhaps all of the territories to which she sends emigrants."[47]

In addition, after 1905, opponents of Japanese immigration on the West Coast became more vocal as the working-class, labor-dominated Asian Exclusion Leagues and mainstream middle-class newspapers like the *San Francisco Chronicle* joined forces in warning against the "yellow peril" at home. Japanese immigration was at its height during these years, and West Coast anti-Japanese activists responded by lobbying for laws banning marriage between whites and Japanese and restricting Japanese immigration.[48] While Millard uses fear of a yellow peril threatening military invasion, another method for contesting the notion of transpacific kinship was satire of the Japanese immigrant as a presumptuous intruder at home, as Wallace Irwin's *Letters of a Japanese Schoolboy* demonstrates. In one of these comic pieces originally published in magazines in 1907–8, the fictitious Japanese immigrant Hashimura Togo writes a letter from his new home in California to a New York newspaper, saying that although Chinese, Koreans, Negroes, and Poles are members of the Yellow Peril, "the Japanese gentleman must not be written down on this list":

> Derby hat, American pant, Tuxedo overcoat, have rendered him completely white of complexion and able to vote for President when asked to know how. Please do not include him in Yellow Peril, because he will not be there. Let Japanese help to do by pushing out all-coloured Yellow Perils coming to this country together with all patriots of star-stripe banner Yankee-doodle dandy, banzai!

After negatively describing the Korean immigrant Mr. Whee and the Polish immigrant Mr. Gumowsky, Togo asks, "Which is more better citizen, thank you—Mr. Whee of opium smoking and Gumowsky of whiskey-drunking or Japanese Boy of derby hat, frockaway coat and all other white manners of civilizedation?"[49] Here Irwin has Togo reiterate the essence of Eaton's argument, but while Eaton is serious, Irwin is joking; Togo misses at civilization the same way he misses at correct spelling.

A major battleground for the possibility of transpacific alliance and Japanese American racial kinship was the contest over Japanese admission to San Francisco public schools. The incident drew national attention for the way it pitted federal against local authority and set the notion of Japan as a civilized peer among "world powers" against the notion of Japanese immigrants as inferior, nonwhite aliens. In his December 1906 State of the Union Address, President Theodore Roosevelt reprimanded the San Francisco school board and other anti-Japanese agitators who had offended

Japan with the prejudicial treatment against its citizens. Roosevelt, attempting to mend relations with the Pacific ally, came to the defense of Japanese immigrants, calling the school segregation a "wicked absurdity" and asking for the Japanese the same "fair treatment"—including the right of naturalization—that he would expect for "Germans or Englishmen, Frenchmen, Russians, or Italians" or for any stranger "from any part of civilized Europe."[50] For Roosevelt and others attentive to the potential for U.S. capital investment in Asia, offending Japan was a diplomatic mistake. David Starr Jordan, president of Stanford University, also chided his fellow Californians in the *Independent*, saying that "Japan is a nation of the first class, and we can no more turn the Chinese exclusion act against her than we could against France or Germany."[51]

In both Roosevelt's and Jordan's comments we see hints of Eaton's losing strategy—to place Japan on the same diplomatic level as civilized European world powers and thus place its citizens on the same level as immigrants from these countries. Californians reacted indignantly to the president's message, claiming that he was intruding on a state matter that he failed to fully understand. One Irish American editorialist in the *New York Times* outlined the many reasons why Japanese immigrants could never be likened to European ones; another *New York Times* article reported that California's secretary of state categorized the Japanese with a different list of "strangers" than did Roosevelt: unlike Europeans, "Japanese, Chinese, Korean, or any other Mongolian" immigrants were all unfit for naturalization.[52] Here again an ascending notion of homogenized Asiatic otherness clashes with the strategically powerful conception of Japan as a member of the civilized diplomatic family.

Winnifred Eaton's response to the San Francisco public schools debate reveals a confused and divided effort simultaneously to defend the notion of Japanese military kinship with the United States and to develop a new, more cosmopolitan alternative to the white/Asiatic binary. Eaton read at least one of these pieces by indignant Californians in the *New York Times* and published a rebuttal in the *Eclectic*. She might have selected to criticize this article among the many others that appeared because it was written by a woman, a special correspondent to the *Times* identified only as M. E. C., who comments that the problem with the Japanese is not that they are like the Chinese but that they are not enough like them; the humble Chinese know their place as servants in California. She describes a conversation among strangers in a San Francisco train car who bemoan Roosevelt's misguided words and the problem of the haughty Japanese. "Japan's got the big head," one complains. M. E. C. explains that Japan's victory in the Russo-Japanese War and its treaty with Great Britain are to blame. Before the war, races knew their stations: "We were the dominant Caucasian race, he was the inferior Asiatic race—the race from which came our servants." After the war, "gone was the old deference of the Japanese" as the immigrant's "intense egotism" grew and he tried to "arrogate to himself the same privileges we would give to the European immigrants of the better class." Among the characters on her train car is an "irrepressible American boy" who in his brash enthusiasm seems to be a character type similar to Eaton's young jingo, Billy. The American boy shouts, "Oh, those Japs think they can lick all creation, since they licked Russia, but they can't lick Uncle Sam!"[53] While Eaton allies her personification of vocal young American jingoism with martial Japan, M. E. C. opposes the two.

Eaton counters M. E. C.'s complaints in her article "The Japanese in America," partly by encouraging readers to identify with Japan's pride rather than criticizing it: "Of course, crowned with her new war laurels, Japan's vanity is more apparent at the present time. How was America after the war with Spain? At such a time would it have been well for another nation to speak sneeringly of it as an 'inferior nation'"?[54] Here Eaton sticks with her strategy of comparing Japan and the United States as military powers with parallel successes in Pacific empire building. American readers should understand the Japanese because of their common experience of victory and shared attitude of jingoistic bravado. Eaton also takes issue with M. E. C.'s claims that American war correspondents for the Russo-Japanese War returned from the war with deep mistrust of Japan. According to M. E. C., war correspondents from all over the United States traveled to Japan with complete enthusiasm for the Mikado but upon their return "voiced eternal condemnation for everything Japanese." What changed their mind was learning about Japanese national traits of dishonesty, conceit, and, above all, "the hatred which these Orientals have for the white race."[55] Eaton dismisses this evidence as "audaciously false," asserting that she had read "omnivorously" all available books by these same correspondents, and "with one or two exceptions, they almost all over-praised Japan."[56]

One of these exceptions Eaton read might have been Jack London, who in his reports on the war for William Hearst developed another important attack on the notion of Japanese whiteness. Undoubtedly, M. E. C. had London, a fellow Californian, in mind as evidence for her claim; London's war correspondence in the *San Francisco Examiner* and *Collier's* magazine detailed his solidifying understanding of Japan's immutable difference. While in early reports London praises Japanese discipline and martial ability and differentiates the Japanese from more timid Koreans, he makes it clear that both nations are racially "Asiatics." For London, the Japanese patriotism that Eaton found so admirable—and so similar to American behavior—marks their otherness. To explain the military maneuver that lost the lives of many Japanese soldiers but won Japan's first major land victory over the Russians, London proffers that "the Japanese are Asiatics, and the Asiatic does not value life as we do."[57] Here on the field of battle London identifies the same racial threat that white workers were decrying back in San Francisco: how can whites compete with Asiatic workers—or soldiers—when they value their lives less than the white man does, when they will accept losses that the white man would not accept? Furthermore, he explains, the Japanese view the war in racial terms: not as a contest between Saxon and Slav but between Asiatic and white. London reports being disturbed when a Japanese civilian said to him after the battle, "Your people did not think we could beat the white. We have now beaten the white" (107).

London identifies the Japanese as "Asiatics" through a domestic, local, and class-based perception of dangerous competition for imperiled whites. His strategy is another one that, like Eaton's treatment of the Irish, would define a U.S. racial grouping according to domestic, not international, meanings, thus shutting down the possibility of inscribing a new global color line around the Japanese as civilized family members. While Gunter, the New Yorker and ex–Wall Street stockbroker who wrote *My Japanese Prince,* could more easily imagine his Japanese characters as civilized, almost-white catalysts in a fantasy of mobile American capital and diplomatic power, London viewed the Japanese primarily through his Spencerian notions of racial competition in wage-earning as well as war. As Colleen Lye argues, London portrays the Japanese in his war correspondence as a potential military threat that mirrors the perceived economic "yellow peril" of Chinese immigrants in California, an influential racial formation that links "the Asiatic" with the forces of modern capitalism driving U.S. Pacific expansion.[58]

Like the other American and British war correspondents, London witnessed the war from the side of Japan and under the supervision of the Japanese government. But viewing the conflict sparked London's uncanny realization that, as a white man, he should be racially aligned with the Russians. This realization comes to him like "a blow in the face" (106)

· one day, as he witnesses the aftermath of a Japanese victory. To provide
the reader with the proper background, he explains that he had been
traveling with "Asiatic soldiers" for months and his "mind had settled
down to accepting without question that the men who fought had eyes
and cheek bones and skins different from the eyes and cheekbones and
skins of my kind" (106). This accepted idea is shaken when London peers
into a guarded house and views his first blue-eyed Russian prisoners of
war: "I caught myself gasping. A choking sensation was in my throat.
These men were my kind. I found myself suddenly and sharply aware
that I was an alien amongst these brown men who peered through the
window with me. And I felt myself strangely at one with those other
men behind the window—felt that my place was there inside with them
in their captivity, rather than outside in freedom amongst aliens" (106).
More disturbing is the sight of a dead Russian's body piled in a cart filled
with Russian uniforms and rifles: "From the rear projected a naked foot
and leg. It was the leg of a man who must have stood over six feet tall,
and it was white. It moved up and down with the joggling two-wheeled
cart, beating ceaseless and monotonous time as it drew away in the distance" (107). London cannot explain the significance of this image as
it haunts him throughout the day; for example, he writes that when he
later saw a Japanese soldier astride a Russian horse and wearing Russian
boots, "somehow my mind reverted to the white foot beating time on the
joggling Pekin cart" (107).

Here we see London shift from a detached spectator to one whose racial
identity is dangerously at stake. The global diplomatic forces that placed
the American war correspondents on the side of the Japanese, and that
placed London outside the window sharing the gaze of the Japanese soldiers, disturbingly contradict what London represents as the undeniable
visual reality of European whiteness possessed by London and the Russian
soldiers. The Russian soldier's leg, an uncanny and unexplained image that
recurs to him involuntarily throughout the day, begs a psychoanalytic explanation. Like Freud's fetish, the foot rematerializes a binaristic division
by providing an insistent reminder of irreducible difference between Asiatic and white. Eaton and Gunter celebrated potent Japanese masculinity,
but London finds it a horrifying appropriation of the white male power
signified by the giant Russian soldier's leg. Whether or not Eaton actually
read London's account, clearly his was the kind of report she countered in
her fiction.[59] While Billy Kurakawa seamlessly identifies with the idealized
Japanese soldier, London sees only immutable Asiatic difference. While

Billy must be reminded by his wise Japanese father to chivalrously eschew souvenirs scavenged from the bodies of dead Russians, London's Japanese soldiers cravenly steal Russian boots that they can never fill. Faced with the notion that he "looks just like" a Russian soldier, Billy angrily rejects mere visual likeness in favor of vocal and martial similarity. Such visual evidence stuns London with its unquestionable force.

By reminding readers of Japanese and American martial similarity, Eaton's rebuttal of M. E. C. also responds to London's war correspondence. But Eaton's article in the *Eclectic* also makes another, contradictory counterargument when it suggests a more cosmopolitan alternative to London and M. E. C.'s manifest division between Asiatic and white races. At a time when representing the Japanese as military peers had inadvertently raised the undesirable specter of a Japanese military threat at home and abroad, Eaton partially revised the strategy she had developed in her fiction to make a new appeal to a denationalized and deracialized world. In the final lines of "The Japanese in America," she describes her own perspective on the conflict being waged in San Francisco:

> I am not Oriental or Occidental either, but Eurasian. I must bleed for both my nations. I am Irish more than English—Chinese as well as Japanese. Both my fatherland and my motherland have been the victims of injustice and oppression. Sometimes I dream of the day when all of us will be world citizens—not citizens merely of petty portions of the earth, showing our teeth at each other, snarling, sneering, biting, and with the ambition of murder at our heart's core—every man with the savage instinct of the wild beast to get the better of his brother—to prove his greater strength—his mightier mind—the superiority of his color.[60]

In one of the only published writings where Eaton ever admits her Chinese heritage, she also claims her Irish descent, identifying herself with the colonized nations that she ranked below the Japanese in her fiction. She manages this move by representing herself as a racially mixed "world citizen," a cosmopolitan who longs for the day when race, nation, and military power will be irrelevant. In this world, perhaps, the Irish can finally be Japanese.

These references to "snarling wolves" clearly counter London's "Call of the Wild" social Darwinism and M. E. C.'s claim that violence and race war will result from any effort to "assimilate to one another the Caucasian and Asiatic races." Eaton's cosmopolitan vision comes as a surprise after examining the degree to which patriotism, strategic global alliances, and racial and national chauvinisms structured her Russo-Japanese War fiction. But her seemingly contradictory tactics have one thing in common: both reject an unproblematic divide between white and Asian. In her fiction and the above-quoted passage, there is neither a meaningful, discrete category of Asian or Asian American identity encompassing the ethnically Japanese, Chinese, and Korean, nor is there an opposing notion of Caucasian whiteness. Eaton's identity as a Eurasian, which she embraces in this passage, symbolizes the futility of the supposed racial divide bridged in her ancestry—others will someday learn to accept the unity that she embodies. While this cosmopolitan vision is more attractive for its pacifism and rejection of parochial racial prejudices, no less than her fiction does it dispute the racial formation necessary for "Asian American" oppression and resistance in the United States. Apparently, being ethnically Irish and Chinese as well as English and Japanese is rhetorically acceptable only when a high ground of postracial and postnational cosmopolitanism places Eaton above the meanings she helped assign to these groups in her fiction. As in the cases of Pauline Hopkins's black cosmopolitan and Steward's de-raced imperialist narrator, Eaton looks outside the borders of the United States for a position from which to evade local U.S. racial hierarchies. In her fiction, she found the position of Japanese military prowess; in this essay, she switches to the position of the de-raced, hybrid cosmopolitan.

In her evasion of a binary opposition between "white" and "Asian" racial identity, Eaton reveals a foundational tension in early formulations of Asian American cultural identity. Such a category of identity could only become meaningful in a dialectical exchange between domestic and international struggles for power, making the perceived meaning of U.S. Pacific expansion a central problem in efforts to imagine the Asian American cultural experience in the early twentieth century. Thus Eaton's writing both complicates and enriches our understandings of the long-standing portrayal of "Asia" as immutably threatening and foreign. By furthering the popular notion of Japanese and Anglo-American kinship, Eaton contested this process and yet also shaped and perhaps ultimately reinforced it by likening Japanese military prowess with the accomplishments of U.S. empire, contributing to what Gary Okihiro calls the "closed loop" wherein model minority becomes yellow peril.[61] Of course, this is not to say that Eaton herself could be called a representative author of a denationalized Asian American literature. While she invoked transnational and cosmopolitan interests to evade prejudice against an emerging Asiatic ethnic identity at home, her Russo-Japanese War fiction nonetheless reinforced and drew from racisms underwritten by nationalist agendas for global power. Rather, as the first Asian American novelist, Eaton offers striking insight into the way that the category of "Asian American" accrued meaning by contesting alternate racial formulations structured by U.S. global ambitions and alliances. As Colleen Lye notes, "the making of Asiatic racial form . . . is necessarily a story about the international context in which American race relations take place."[62]

In this chapter, I have not explored reception and influence, as I did in my discussion of Kipling's "The White Man's Burden," but examined the narrative strategy of a writer who used literary form to redraw racial boundaries and affinities in the midst of a larger cultural conversations about whiteness and empire. However, using Kipling's poem as a window onto those cultural conversations prepares us to understand why Eaton would look to Pacific empire as a discursive terrain from which to storm the U.S. definition of whiteness. Already the source of various kinds of anxiety about the definition and stability of whiteness, the story of Pacific empire and its perceived route to "world power" status among European nations was material that Eaton could adapt, joining and harnessing various legal, diplomatic, and ethnological discourses of Japanese whiteness to contest racial formations of the Caucasian and the Asiatic at home. And paralleling Eaton's writing with Steward and Hopkins, we see that all three writers strained against counternarratives that sought to affix U.S. ethnic hierarchies and identities by representing them in local, domestic contexts, untroubled by the conflicting and shifting color lines of war, world politics, international capitalism, or imperial expansion. Each of these writers used vexed narratives of U.S. empire and the active sense of confusion about the racial meaning of the white man's burden as vehicles to redraw color lines globally.

In addition, Eaton's writing provides vivid evidence for another of this book's central arguments, one that comes to the foreground in this last section. As an example of the transnational terrain of U.S. racialization, the conversation about Japanese whiteness that Eaton joined complicates historical narratives of U.S. expansion that excessively isolate a Pacific "frontier" from multipolar processes of European empire-building, global economic relations, and transatlantic anxieties of influence. Rather than a story of westward expansion projecting "America" onto the peoples and territories of a sequestered global frontier, Eaton adapted a strand of discourse that represented Pacific expansion as an opportunity to review parochial-seeming U.S. racial hierarchies, sedimenting some domestic prejudices and dispelling others. In doing so, she claimed the discursive power to access the codes of modernity, mobility, civilization, and power associated with the narratives of international relations.

6

American Indians, Asiatics, and Anglo-Saxons

Ranald MacDonald's Japan Story of Adventure

In 1847, a twenty-four-year-old half-Chinook Indian, half-Scot named Ranald MacDonald signed onto the crew of the *Plymouth,* a whaling ship out of New York. He was about to act on a plan that had been forming in his mind since he left his apprenticeship at a bank in Ontario three years earlier. His plan was this: when the ship was full and ready to return home, the captain would give MacDonald a small boat and strand him off the coast of Japan, a land that was then strictly closed to most of the outside world. The captain reluctantly agreed to this strange scheme, and the plan was carried out. Alone in his boat, MacDonald landed on an island off Japan, where he was immediately turned over to the Japanese government. The Japanese finally imprisoned MacDonald in Nagasaki, but, despite his confinement, he was treated well; his captors set him to what he found to be the enjoyable work of teaching English to several Japanese interpreters. Some of these pupils would go on in a few years to interpret the negotiations between Commodore Matthew C. Perry and the Japanese emperor for the "opening" of Japan, a fact that has today resulted in a few historians and some local historical societies crediting MacDonald for playing a role in diplomatic history.[1] After nine months in Japan, MacDonald was rescued when a U.S. naval ship came to retrieve another stranded group of American shipwrecked sailors. But instead of returning to America onboard, he set out on his own from China to Australia, India, and then Europe, before finally returning in 1853 to live out the rest of his years in British Columbia and Washington State.[2]

This chapter is about a number of subsequent attempts to tell—and publish—this story of transpacific contact, along with the racial, national, and colonial frameworks used to shape the story's meaning. Years later,

MacDonald collaborated with Malcolm McLeod, another son of a Hudson's Bay Company officer, to write his story. The two men saw the work through several significant revisions between the 1850s and the early 1890s as they attempted to explain the significance of MacDonald's strange adventure in terms that would be recognized and valued by readers and publishers in the United States and Canada. Yet, despite their efforts, only a few chapters of their account appeared in print during their lifetimes, in a local newspaper in Kettle Falls, Washington, in 1893. In 1923, almost thirty years after his death, MacDonald's narrative was finally published in its entirety by the Eastern Washington State Historical Society in a limited edition of one thousand copies; it quickly went out of print until its reissue by the Oregon Historical Society in 1990.[3]

But while the authorized version of his story awaited publication, two other accounts of MacDonald's life and accomplishments appeared in print: Elizabeth Bacon Custer published a local color travel sketch featuring Ranald MacDonald in *Harper's Weekly* in 1891, and Eva Emery Dye made MacDonald's story of travel to Japan the focus of her historical romance *McDonald of Oregon: A Tale of Two Shores,* published by the Chicago-based McClurg and Company in 1906. In different ways, these two successful efforts to publish McDonald's story contested the terms within which a racially mixed and regionally marginal figure like MacDonald could be written into narratives of U.S. world power. In this chapter, I interpret MacDonald as a figure who shadows the white man's burden by casting himself as a racially indeterminate participant in imperial projects—a figure similar to Frank R. Steward's narrator, Pauline Hopkins's mixed-blood protagonist Reuel Briggs, and Winnifred Eaton's Japanese soldiers. MacDonald's struggle to fit into dominant narratives and conventions of national and racial progress stretches and deforms them, revealing their suppressed contradictions and permeable borders. In contrast, Custer and Dye attempt to locate MacDonald as an object, not an agent, of imperial expansion and international politics.

For all three versions, a key factor in interpreting MacDonald's adventure was figuring out how to identify him racially. In different ways, each writer counted MacDonald's Chinook-Scotch ancestry as important to his supposed contribution to international diplomacy. In doing so, they drew on various contested ethnological theories and racialized categories that were prompted by alternate visions of North American and overseas expansion. Custer's and Dye's writings each take issue with different aspects of MacDonald's racial identity. Custer's concern is the racial identity of the Scotch-Indian half-breed, whose role in national narratives of expansion was caught between the passing cultures of the British and French fur trade companies and the coming of U.S. settlement of the northwest. And for Dye, her issue is the origin of the northwest American Indian tribes, whose ancient ancestral ties to Asia were at the turn of the century being constructed in the emergence of modern anthropology. Dye affiliates MacDonald both with the global category of the Asiatic and with a U.S. pioneering spirit, making him a usefully flexible symbol for American global mission. For his part, MacDonald treats with ambivalence both of these issues—the racial identity of the half-breed and the ethnological ties of American Indians to Asia—as he seeks to position himself as an agent, not an object or artifact, of imperial narratives.

My comparison of these versions of MacDonald's story supports several main arguments of this book. First, it attends to a rhetorical and narrative contestation over who could represent an imperial project on the world's stage. MacDonald, like Steward and Hopkins and Eaton, claims the authority to look globally for alternatives to the terms of U.S. racialization. He does so both by actively assuming the position of an agent of civilized Pacific expansion and by countering more influential or more widely read countertexts that would place him locally as a nonwhite domestic figure contained within national definitions and narratives. Second, MacDonald's story complicates colonial binaries not only by casting an American Indian in the role of diplomat to the Japanese but also by linking his accomplishments to the colonial competition for Pacific influence by the United States and Great Britain, a linkage that prevents us from isolating MacDonald on a conceptual Pacific frontier, removed from geopolitical conflict among multiple empires. And third, these writers' different versions of MacDonald's story demonstrate that U.S. expansion was not wholly conceptualized by projecting preexisting racial constructs of "the American Indian" out onto new frontiers in the American west, the South Pacific, or East Asia. Rather, the various visions and understandings of transpacific power that I study here conjure up new ways to imagine the identity and role of northwest American Indian tribes and their mixed-blood descendents at home and as part of a new world power.

As in the case of Winnifred Eaton, MacDonald tells a story about his own connection with the Japanese, a people who were ethnologically and culturally a fascination for U.S. Americans during this era, and in doing so he textually reshapes narratives of U.S. expansion. While Eaton tries to revise U.S. ethnic definitions and hierarchies by recalibrating them against the Japanese as a civilized world power, MacDonald renders his interaction with the Japanese as a diplomatic contribution to Anglo-Saxon progress in the Pacific, disrupting the association of whiteness with imperial authority and international status. In this way, both Eaton and MacDonald find in Japan a rhetorical and narrative reference point from which to locate and relate categories of U.S. ethnicity and narratives of international relations.

Placing Eaton's and MacDonald's writing side by side also reveals the permeability and the power of the U.S.-Canadian border for both of these racially mixed writers. Both writers have complex histories that situate them at different times during their lives as either British Canadian or U.S. nationals. MacDonald never sought to be a professional writer like Eaton, but, like Eaton, he realized that the United States offered a larger market for sales, and, like Eaton, he adapted a story of his own identity to that market. But in writing their U.S. American identities, both writers sought further to influence the competing racial categories and meanings employed by national narratives of U.S. expansion and global power. Thus, while we could consider MacDonald to be a Native border theorist representing the kinds of transnational or hemispheric identities that have attracted recent scholarly attention, to do so might ignore the powerful and determining role that competing national and imperial narratives played in his self-representation.[4] Examining MacDonald's relationship to narratives of state power and identity, I do not appropriate him as a U.S. American rather than a Canadian writer but identify the U.S. Canadian border as an important force in shaping the alternate racializations that MacDonald, Custer, and Dye negotiated when telling his story.

Writing from the U.S.-Canadian Borderlands

MacDonald begins the 1893 version of his story, titled *Japan Story of Adventure,* with a statement that would seem to clear up any confusion about his citizenship: "Native and denizen almost throughout all my life, of the Columbia Valley of the Pacific Slope of America, I claim to be, in the broadest sense, a true American. True it was the British Flag that covered my cradle, but that makes no difference. The Oregon treaty of 1845 [sic] made me a citizen of the United States of America."[5] The movement of the border to the 49th parallel in 1846 when he was a young man seems to have clearly reassigned MacDonald's national identification from British Canadian to true American. Yet in 1888, an earlier, unpublished version of his narrative was titled *A Canadian in Japan,* and an 1891 draft opens by merely stating, "the British Flag covered my cradle."[6] A number of early and partial drafts and letters demonstrate that MacDonald's national identity was revised in an effort to find a meaningful context and a publisher for his story. Various versions were titled "The Dawn of the Pacific," "English in Japan," "'Japan' by a Canadian," "A Columbian in Japan 40 Years Ago," as well as several versions titled "Japan Story of Adventure."[7] These alternate drafts represent a series of efforts to assign his adventure national and imperial significance. For his strange journey to Japan to seem both legible and consequential, it needed to be rendered as the story of a particular national subject contributing to a grand sweep of history by taking a role on the world's stage.

MacDonald's partner in creating these versions of his story was his editor and coauthor, Malcolm McLeod.[8] An Ottawa lawyer and politician, McLeod was, like MacDonald, a mixed-blood son of a Hudson's Bay Company (HBC) employee born in the northwest, but McLeod, who was less than one-half Indian, studied law in Edinburgh, Scotland, and as a young man subsequently moved east to Ontario. His law career was somewhat unsuccessful (by the 1890s he was plagued with financial problems), but his most significant contribution to Canadian history was as a promoter of the Canadian Pacific Railroad (CPR). Indeed, he originally saw MacDonald's story as important because he related it to the railway project.

Even before the pair had begun collaborating on MacDonald's autobiography in the 1880s, McLeod had told his friend's story in a series of letters written under the pen name "Britannicus" to promote the CPR in major Canadian newspapers like the *Montreal Gazette, Ottawa Times,* and *Ottawa Citizen.* In one January 1874 letter published in the *Montreal Gazette,* MacLeod/"Britannicus" presented MacDonald's unusual transpacific adventure as a precedent that justified the destiny of Canadians in furthering British influence over Asia, especially over the rapidly industrializing Japan. MacDonald's experience as the first "teacher of English in Japan" was evidence, he wrote, that as early as the 1840s Canadians had "contributed to . . . the communication of British thought and sentiment to a people, who, of all others I know of, have the closest affinity of spirit to the British race. They, in fact, in heart and mind are the British of the East. They require but the *iron link* to bind them in cognate bonds."[9] Building this "iron link," the CPR, was largely a tactic to unify Canada and, in the 1850s, to protect its western coastal territory from further U.S. expansion north of the 49th parallel. McLeod also saw it as an important opportunity to forestall a U.S. empire in the Pacific. "Give to the United States . . . the transit trade between the two oceans, and they, in a trice, will cover the seas," McLeod warned in another "Britannicus" letter to the *Montreal Gazette* dated December 1873: "On the other hand, let Britain, still 'Mistress of the Seas,' but hold and use as her own the ocean-link which her Canadian sons propose to forge her, and her flag may [fly] for another thousand years. . . . In this sense, the work is of highest Imperial necessity—as an iron bulwark of British empire."[10] This rhetorical strategy was to write British Columbia (not even part of the Confederation of Canada until 1871) into a mythic history of Canadian progress and to allow mixed-blood writers from the hinterlands (like MacDonald and McLeod) to legitimately occupy the subject position of "Britannicus."

In late 1880s and early 1890s, as McLeod and MacDonald renewed their energy in revising the latter's autobiography, adding many pages that extended this thematic connection between MacDonald's travels, the CPR, and the British empire. Still these efforts to make MacDonald speak as a crucial agent of the British empire failed to attract New York and Montreal publishers, who asked for advance subscriptions to guarantee profit. MacDonald began to seek subscriptions from his friends and neighbors, but his neighbors in eastern Washington were particularly unconvinced by his story's imperial framing. During these decades, MacDonald resided not in Canada but in a small town in eastern Washington called Fort Colville. The fort had been the site of an important Hudson's Bay Company trading post under his father's command during Ranald's boyhood, but the town's present inhabitants—who had only recently become U.S. citizens in 1889 when the territory entered the union as the forty-second state—resisted MacDonald's efforts to insert himself through the land's colonial past into Canadian history. In one 1891 letter to McLeod, MacDonald describes trying to secure subscriptions for "A Canadian in Japan" from his friends and neighbors. "Many took exception to the [title]," he writes: "I believe that A Columbian is more preferable to Canadian on this side of the line. . . . I observed when I told them "A Canadian in Japan" &c. there appeared to be some dissatisfaction, in fact some told me that I was no Canadian and ought to have another name." MacDonald urged McLeod, "by all means call it A Columbian, not that I object to A Canadian as Canadian but for the success of the work."[11] MacDonald's identity and the meaning of his travels, themselves irreducible to a single national context, were thus caught between two competing empires, each with their own claims on the history of the northwest and the future of Pacific empire.

Finally faced with failure in Canada, McLeod relented and revised his friend's story to be that not of a "Columbian" but of a "true American," written to a U.S. audience and to be published in the United States. (It was at this time that MacDonald, confident the work would finally be published, hired a photographer to take his picture for inclusion in the printed book; Figure 5).

McLeod admitted the necessity of this revision in a letter to MacDonald about American presses in San Francisco and New York: "British *stuff,* cock crow, and particularly Canadian, is more obnoxious in the Golden Gate than in cosmopolitan New York, where I may yet have to try the thing in its new and more acceptable shape."[12] The more acceptable "true American" revision makes MacDonald speak as an American and omits previous claims that MacDonald was "the first instructor—apostle in a sense—of English thought, influence, and power for the good of that people, then in darkness in such matters," and that Japan "promises to become, ere long, the New Britain of that further Ind."[13] Instead, it declares MacDonald's travels more generally as a "pioneering development" (72) in opening Japan to western trade and influence: "In receiving my teaching and its incidental advocacy of international relations in the general principles of comity of nations, they followed their own spontaneous desire for that" (252). But McLeod, an ardent British imperialist, had difficulty fully revising to foreground MacDonald's participation in a specifically U.S. American narrative of progress. His revision omitted MacDonald's stronger (and slightly ironic) statement of his contribution to U.S. American history, made in one of his letters: "In all this I flatter myself that I have broken the seal that made Japan a Sealed Empire to the West—at all events cracked it so bad that it made it easy for Commodore Perry to do the rest of the business and secure a commercial treaty. . . . I in the meantime to wait for my reward from the Gov't."[14]

For MacDonald, neither a reward from the U.S. government nor his less facetious hope of acceptance by U.S. publishers arrived. When MacDonald died in 1894, McLeod gave up his effort to publish *Japan Story of Adventure,* leaving behind in that final revision an unusual and stylistically rather awkward text. The culmination of McLeod's and MacDonald's efforts, the version of *Japan Story* that began to be published serially in 1893 and that was finally printed in its entirety in 1923, remains a palimpsest of previous drafts and intentions. It retains long passages about Canadian history, describing accomplishments of "old Nor'Westers" of the fur trade days and suggesting that MacDonald helped solve the British

Figure 5. Photograph of Ranald MacDonald. William Compton Brown Papers (CG 196, 15-150), Manuscripts, Archives, and Special Collections, Washington State University Libraries, Pullman, Washington.

empire's historical quest to find a Northwest Passage (112, 102). In the new national context, such passages seem like digressions, but their implicit effect is to render the Oregon territory not an empty frontier for U.S. expansion but a site of international and multipolar imperial competition. And compounding this problem of internationalizing the U.S. frontier is a different kind of problem for readers: the final version of *Japan Story of Adventure,* like the previous drafts, is flawed by a particularly turgid and clogged prose style that occasionally verges on incoherence in its embedded constructions and formal diction.

MacDonald's biographer, Frederic L. Schodt, attributes this awkwardness to McLeod's shortcomings as a stylist and storyteller, but, as I argue below, the narrative's stylistic features are inextricable from the writers' goal to speak within conventional imperial conventions.[15] *Japan Story* is the culmination of a frustrated effort "to be read, and to be *readable,*" as Mary Louise Pratt puts it, a challenge faced by writers who engage in "the dynamics of self-representation in the context of colonial subordination." For Pratt, specific kinds of readerly attention are necessary for understanding these texts in which "colonized subjects represent themselves in ways that engage with the colonizers's own terms," through partial collaboration and appropriation of the idioms of the conqueror.[16] In this rhetorical struggle, we can see *Japan Story* as, in the word of composition theorist Donald Bartholomae, "the record of a writer who has lost himself in the discourse of his readers," and the text's incoherence as the part of strained effort to locate MacDonald in "a context that is finally beyond him."[17]

This context remains *beyond* MacDonald in part because of the complexity introduced when the grandson of a Chinook chief assumes the role of pioneer, explorer, and Anglo-American diplomat. But this context also remains beyond MacDonald because it continually shifted along with geographical borders and the different constructions of racial identity that accompanied U.S. and British empire. When the border between the United States and British Columbia was settled in 1846, Ranald MacDonald was one of approximately three thousand British subjects, mostly retired HBC employees and their racially mixed families, living south of the 49th parallel.[18] Left unsettled by this movement, MacDonald found himself not entirely at home on either side, residing in the "vague and undetermined place created by the emotional residue of an unnatural boundary," to adapt Gloria Anzaldúa's description of the geographical and psychological borderlands that were created two years later with movement of the Mexican border.[19] As MacDonald states in the 1893 *Japan Story of Adventure*, "In truth I am and have ever felt myself to be a man of two flags; proper, in a way to both. Yet let me say, scarcely quite content with either" (92). Despite efforts to insert his adventures into competing imperial histories on either side of the border, *Japan Story of Adventure* and its textual history communicate a sense of dislocation that neither national narrative could encompass. In doing so, it renders the Pacific northwest not as an isolated frontier but the site of crucial international trade and diplomacy that MacDonald extends through his work in Japan. As with many nineteenth-century Native American autobiographers, MacDonald's apparent adoption and exhibition of the terms of assimilation belie a complex negotiation of national and imperial narratives.[20]

To give an example of both the text's awkward style and MacDonald's sense of national and racial dislocation, consider this passage, which was added in the 1893 "true American" revision, explaining this claim to Americanness:

> But further: on this point I may state that on my mother's side, I am by direct legal succession, of the blood of the sole King (known to history as such) of the Columbia, and of the Pacific Slope in those latitudes, *viz:* King Com-Comly of Washington Irving's *Astoria,* the truly royal host of the Astor expedition there in 1811–1813 and of all other whites since, in his realm. (74–75)

The sentence is packed with context in an effort to contain the contradiction of claiming American Indian national belonging. Its endeavor to marshal authority by stringing qualifications and details together with colons, parentheses, and Latin terms is characteristic of the narrative voice throughout: a voice that strives for learned authority and strings together modifiers and embedded phrases to forestall the readers' judgment upon completing the sentence.

MacDonald's mother was Koale'xoa, one of Comcomly's daughters, known to the English as Princess Raven and later as Princess Sunday. Here, identifying his maternal grandfather through Washington Irving, a writer renowned as the father of American literature, offers readers in the United States a way to detach MacDonald from his father's affiliation with the British empire. Irving's *Astoria* (1836) was a popular account of John Jacob Astor's failed attempt to break into the British-dominated fur trade. Astor's men lost hold of their settlement at Fort Astoria during the War of 1812, when it was captured by the British and renamed Fort George, the place where MacDonald would be born and where his father was stationed before being promoted to the position of HBC chief factor at Fort Colville. Reprinted in 1846, Irving's narrative clearly demonstrated to American readers the importance of winning the Oregon territory to redeem this early U.S. claim. King Comcomly, MacDonald's grandfather, plays a major role in Irving's text; the chief generously welcomes the American traders and urges them to continue their fight to hold the fort against the attacking British, a conventional imperial trope wherein the colonized recognizes the superiority of the colonizer—and, in this case, picks what is represented as the superior of two colonizing forces. And yet MacDonald's words insist on a lasting sovereignty for Comcomly, who is a "king" and not a "chief," and who remains the host "of all other whites since" even after his death.

Here we see a vexed effort to make MacDonald speak proudly as an American and an Indian, but some other passages added to Americanize *Japan Story of Adventure* openly criticize the United States for its racial prejudice. An earlier typescript, speaking of British colonial destiny, declares, "Britain still lives!" as the "Mother of Nations,"[21] but the 1893 "true American" revision adds quickly that Britain is "Mother of these United States of America; the grandest political brotherhood on earth!" (84). If this addition was meant to appease MacDonald's patriotic neighbors in Washington State, its complimentary nature is compromised with this next qualifying statement:

> I say brotherhood, yet must confess, that it, sadly lacks that, in its inherent hate of race; its castes; its doom of black and Red, and Yellow, and Brown, and all other shades of Heaven-painted humanity within its borders. How, or why it is so, I leave to the framers, rather, to the successors of the framers of the original Declaration of the United States of America—the first New England of America—to state. *Are* "all men equal"?

In pointing out that its symbolic brotherhood fails to extend beyond the perceived barriers of race, MacDonald seems to be describing his own exclusion from the national family Despite his stated U.S. citizenship and residence within U.S. borders, here the reader is left with the implication that MacDonald himself is not a successor to the framers of the Declaration. Rather than attempting to seamlessly suit himself as an agent of homogeneous national expansion, MacDonald calls attention to racial difference and inequality within the nation, placing himself ambivalently inside and outside its populace.

In such passages, MacDonald's writing effects the alienation of the colonial mimic, who, in Homi Bhabha's formulation, reveals "nations split within themselves, liminal signifying spaces internally marked by the discourses of minorities [and] the heterogeneous histories of contending peoples."[22] One aspect of this heterogeneous history is the conflict between whites and Indians that would be fought out in the northwest; another is the conflict between contending empires of Britain and the United States, an imperial competition that U.S. Americans tended to overwrite with myths of an empty or a wild frontier. The imperial contest between Great Britain and the United States mattered for MacDonald's story, not only because of unfixed national citizenship and his text's publication history but also because of the alternate forms of racialization that shifted with the movement of the U.S.-Canadian border.

For MacDonald, as for the other sons of HBC traders living in the Columbia River Valley, to be a mixed-blood Indian in the United States meant something different than it did during his childhood under the HBC. Fur trade historians note that a number of factors—including geographical isolation from British settlements, the institutional promotion of intermarriage with Indian women, and the frequent transfer of employees and their families from one part of fur country to another—created among British fur trade families a particularly distinct and cohesive culture, one whose greater acceptance of race mixture was troubling to the American settlers who began arriving in the 1840s.[23]

Reverend Cushing Eells, one of the first U.S. missionaries in the Pacific Northwest, recalled a conversation that can serve as an example of these different attitudes. Eells writes about once speaking with MacDonald's Scotch father, Archibald McDonald (Ranald preferred the spelling "MacDonald"),[24] while staying with Ranald's family at Fort Colville in 1842. According to Eells, "Chief Factor A. McDonald asked me who fifty years hence, would probably compose the inhabitants of this country. He answered the question himself by saying substantially, 'The descendents of the Hudson's Bay Company.'" Then Eells reports the answer given to the same question by Dr. Marcus Whitman, an early U.S. missionary to the region and a strong promoter of U.S. territorial claims: "Dr. Whitman said, with reference to the same class of persons (of mixed blood): 'Fifty years hence they will not be found.'"[25] In the mind of Dr. Whitman, who one year later led the first wagon train of one thousand U.S. emigrants over the Oregon Trail, the mixed-blood descendents of the Hudson Bay Company would disappear once coming U.S. settlers occupied the land.

The fur traders' descendents in this territory did not disappear, but by the century's end, many were either classified as white or residing on reservations.[26] Their fate was shaped by the influence of these new U.S. settlers and by the 1846 treaty. The new U.S. territory's Provisional Government, which granted voting rights to "every free male descendent of a white man of the age of twenty-one years and upward" who inhabited of the Oregon territory at the time of its organization, protected these mixed-race individuals from the colonial subjugation that threatened the northwest tribes. But over the next three decades, the rights of the mixed-blood sons of fur traders were legally and politically contested as new territories and states were carved out of this country and new laws for distributing and guaranteeing land rights were passed.[27] By the end of the century, what it meant to be "half-breed" in the Columbia River Valley had changed drastically, not only because Indian hating was more virulent and explicit in U.S. settler culture than it was under the particular cultural and economic conditions of the fur trade but also because of a historical shift: by the 1890s, the Enlightenment idea that Indians could be assimilated had given way to later notions of scientific racism. Even in British North America, the fur trade ways had begun to fade into the more marked racial hierarchies of the metropole, leaving MacDonald with no place to return home.

Left in this ambiguous position, MacDonald sought to write himself into public narratives of national progress, but to do so he had to account for a number of private family issues that influenced his own construction of a public identity. MacDonald claims in *Japan Story of Adventure* that he grew up knowing nothing about his Chinook heritage. His mother died a few days after his birth in 1824, and his father Archibald remarried a year later, to a woman Ranald describes as "a Swiss (German Swiss) young woman, or girl of 16 or 17—Jane, daughter (born in Switzerland) of one of Michael Klyne, 'Postmaster' (as the office was then called) of Jasper House, a trade outpost of the Hudson's Bay Company" (94–95). Although his earliest years were spent among the Chinooks, MacDonald claims that it was not until later in life that he learned Jane Klyne McDonald was his stepmother and that he was half-Chinook. MacDonald writes that this revelation partly explains his subsequent lack of worldly success: "In effect, the discovery made me, at this time, withdraw within myself, abandoning, at once, pursuits, in high honorable enterprise in British Columbia, which in course might, I flattered myself, have placed me in a better—i.e., conventionally higher, and more comfortable position, as to worldly means, than is mine now to command" (98).

However, there are several problems with this story as it conflicts with the historical record. The lives of the HBC's highest officers are remarkably well documented in letters, records, and histories, and these sources agree that Jane Klyne was born not in Switzerland but in British America and that she was *métis*.[28] Before her marriage to Archibald, Jane was rumored to have been one of the HBC territorial Governor George Simpson's "bits of brown," a term he gave to the young Indian and mixed-blood women who accompanied him on his cross-country trips. As one chatty historian (herself a relative of the McDonalds) puts it, the truth of such rumors were of no matter, because "[Jane] made Archie McDonald a splendid wife whom he rewarded by teaching to read and write and to make a Yorkshire pudding as good as any British housewife's."[29] Jane's ancestry was no secret to visitors. On his first visit to Fort Colville the late 1830s, Cushing Eells wrote of Mrs. McDonald that although "a native of the country, she possessed rare excellence;" and another missionary called her "a pleasant wife who is nearly white & speaks good English."[30]

Keeping Jane's mixed ancestry a secret at this time would have been impossible, as virtually all fur traders' marriages in the British northwest colonies of Rupert's Land and British Columbia were made "in the custom of the country," as they termed it, with Indian or mixed-blood women. (Indeed, Oregon histories frequently identify Narcissa Whitman, Dr. Whitman's wife, and another female missionary as the "first white women" to cross the Continental Divide in 1836, although a few known exceptions belie the claim). Until 1821, the HBC officially prohibited employees from marrying British or Canadian women and bringing them along to the northwest. Trade, not settlement, was the company's aim.[31] The result was, as historian Sylvia Van Kirk argues in her history of fur trade women, a distinct culture in which sexual relations with native women were not illicit or peripheral but, rather, an open, accepted, and essential part of the economic and strategic concerns of empire.[32]

As MacDonald's narrative explains it, the HBC made it "a matter of public policy, therefore—apart from private consideration, in such remote isolation from other female help—to allow, and even encourage, the blood-bond of marriage by white with the native women" (82). Many of these marriages, including Archibald and Jane McDonald's, were later legalized in Protestant churches, and it was ordinary practice for fur trade fathers to claim and give English educations to their mixed-blood children, as McDonald did for Ranald and his thirteen half–brothers and sisters. But as MacDonald stresses in his narrative, his parents' original wedding ceremony was itself legal under Chinook sovereignty: "In Chinook realm, Chinook law (custom sanctified) governed—the world over—as to any marriage, or any matter of personal contract, as marriage is. At the time in question, there was no law of any foreign country, not even of Britain, or England, or the United States, or of any such, of any force at the Gate of King Com-Comly, where in fact his word was law" (87). In MacDonald's explanation of this "public policy," he authorizes himself as an agent of empire both by linking his parentage to the diplomatic and commercial strategies of the HBC and by rendering the Chinooks a sovereign nation with legal powers equal to those of western nations. Both inherited associations effectively qualify him as a proponent of commerce and international relations in Asia.

But if some elements of MacDonald's narrative appear to embrace Chinook authority and resignify it to be legible in terms of international relations and sovereign power, why does MacDonald not accurately represent about Jane Klyne's ancestry and, instead, so insistently repeat—three times in the passage quoted above—her Swiss European birth? Given the cultural context in which Ranald grew up, it seems unlikely that he would not have known his stepmother's métis origins. MacDonald's biographer Frederic L. Schodt theorizes that possibly he and McLeod were trying to shield the reputations of Jane and her children, most of whom had moved to eastern Canada in the 1890s.[33] Van Kirk and Pollard note similar examples of "erasing" maternal native ancestry in several Canadian and U.S. fur trade family histories and memoirs.[34] Further evidence of this motivation is seen when McLeod and MacDonald appear to be protecting the identity of another woman in the 1893 *Japan Story of Adventure:* MacDonald refers to a relative of Princess Raven who married an HBC chief factor and who later in life told MacDonald about his biological mother's marriage; he attributes to her "the refinement and intelligence, with sincere piety, of the best of the purely white race—a lady in every respect. I have not permission to give, thus publicly, her name" (92). In a footnote, however, MacDonald states that he has "no objection to do so privately, on proper inquiry." That name, Mrs. George Barnston, was penciled in the margin next to this passage in the handwritten manuscript of the 1893 "true American" published version, held in the Northwest Museum of Arts and Culture archives.[35] This evidence suggests that by the time MacDonald attempted to tell his story to broad national audiences in Canada and the United States, Indian descent had become a matter for discrete private, not public, communications. This understanding likely influenced MacDonald's and McLeod's own choices about how to represent MacDonald's native ancestry as a factor in his public accomplishment of international diplomacy.

Japan Story of Adventure is quite circumspect about the associations it implies between MacDonald's parentage and his unusual travels and accomplishments. It overtly represents his journey as motivated by an innate personal desire for adventure, as the title implies, and by a distaste for the dreary concerns of banking. But stray passages and earlier drafts suggest a more complex set of racialized motivations and explanations of his adventure. In one passage from an earlier draft, MacDonald speculates that his treatment by the Japanese, which compared favorably with that of other shipwrecked U.S. sailors held in captivity, was influenced by a shared racial bond: "(Bronzed somewhat by sea life), I was not unlike them. Apart from that, there seemed to be some subtle undefinable sort of racial sympathy between us."[36] In the 1893 edition, this passage was revised to eliminate the notion of racial sympathy: "In look, facial features, etc., I was not unlike them; my sea life and rather dark complexion, moreover, giving me their general color—a healthy bronze. I never had a cross word with any of them; and I think I passed rather as a favorite amongst them" (241). Whatever MacDonald thought about racial kinship between Japanese and American Indians before his visit to Japan or later in life, he and McLeod changed their minds about how and whether to communicate this idea in their story. Perhaps to stress these elements would detract from their effort to position MacDonald as an agent of British or American imperial progress. In other words, such statements of racial affinity between MacDonald and the Japanese would render him as shadowing rather than affirmatively carrying the white man's burden.

In a passage that explains his decision to leave the bank as not a decision to leave "home," MacDonald's narrative also hints at a motivating sense of alienation: "Home, in the strict and ordinary sense, I had not. To my mind's eye, and to that of the heart, there was no resting place, yet, in my moving world of waters; no olive branch yet, to the winged search" (118). He explains that this was because his father could be called to move anywhere in the far-reaching HBC territories from Alaska to Labrador, but perhaps this sense of homelessness seemed more pressing when he signed onto the *Plymouth* in 1847, at the same time that his father's Fort

Colville was being claimed by the United States. MacDonald follows this sentence about homelessness with more explicit discussion of the role of his race in his motivations:

> Further than that: In spite of all my training for civilized life—so called: in spite of all my magnetism of comfortable and endearing hospitality— sweets of a home, but which, still, is not a home; and in spite of all possible influences and suggestions to win such "higher life", I felt, ever, and uncontrollably in my blood, the wild strain for wondering freedom *im primis* of my Highland father of Glencoe, secondly, and possibly more so (though unconsciously) of my Indian mother, of the Pacific Shore, Pacific Seas, in boundless Dominion. (118)

Here as elsewhere in MacDonald's text, the heterogeneous histories that displace him from any single, legible national context end up having the effect of dislocating national territories and destabilizing imperial narratives. In this passage's single convoluted sentence, MacDonald attributes his desire to roam to racial impulses coming from both his father and his mother, although his mother's influence is at once prioritized and suppressed as the more "unconscious" in parentheses. This maternal influence seems to be what draws him *toward* Japan: the chain of MacDonald's appositive phrases identify his mother with the Pacific Shore *and* the Pacific Seas, suggesting obliquely that her Indian blood ties her to the Pacific island of Japan. The combination makes MacDonald's maternal influence an important factor in his contribution to Pacific trade and diplomacy; rather than being solely motivated by an ever-westward-moving germ of Anglo-Saxon progress, it is his Chinook blood that orients him toward Pacific adventure, and both lineages contribute to his intended narrative of imperial accomplishment, a move that starkly shadows the white man's burden by disassociating whiteness and Pacific progress. In this passage, MacDonald's accomplishment is still defined in national terms, but it is Canadian rather than U.S. nationalism: the final phrase in MacDonald's list of appositives is "boundless Dominion" (as in the Dominion of Canada, the name given the North American British territories when consolidated as a constitutional monarchy in 1867). The phrase "boundless dominion" suggestively maps British Canada's boundless expansion into the Pacific.

MacDonald's narrative is cautious about outlining any racial meaning for this journey, but his friends and relatives did not hesitate to interpret

his voyages as racially motivated. Archibald McDonald saw his son's unexpected running off to sea as a result of racial inheritance. Writing to the
former HBC trader who had tried to set up Ranald as an apprentice bank
clerk, McDonald expressed his "keen disappointment": "Much better to
dream of less for them . . . and to endeavor to bring them up in habits of
industry, economy, and morality, than to aspire to all this visionary greatness for them. All the wealth of Rupert's Land will not make a half-breed
either a good person, a shining lawyer, or an able physician, if left to his
own direction while young."[37] Eleanor Haskins Holly, a friend of Mac-
Donald in his last years living in Fort Colville, told the story years after
his death that Ranald decided to go to Japan after a love affair in Ontario
was doomed by racial prejudice. When MacDonald "found that the strain
of Indian blood in his veins was considered a bar to his marrying a young
girl who had won his heart," he realized "that some social prejudice existed toward him on account of his Indian blood." As Holly tells the story,
"he stated that it was then that he decided to go to Japan, of which he had
heard and read, and from which he was convinced that the North American Indians originally came—'The land of his ancestors,' as he termed
it."[38] And years later in 1916, a younger cousin adhered to a racial theory
in explaining MacDonald's relatively kind treatment in Japan: "Ranald's
mother was the daughter of an Indian chief on the Pacific Coast, hence
his complexion was that of the Japanese only unusually larger, which I
think [was] the true salvation of all the prisoners. No doubt the Japanese
Governor, who employed Ranald, possibly thought Ranald was one of his
tribe, etc."[39]

Recent scholars and writers have continued this association between
MacDonald's adventure and his race in less-essentialized terms. Postmodern novelist Gerald Vizenor's *Hiroshima Bugi: Atomu 57* expands on Mac-
Donald's supposed belief in a racial bond among Indians and Japanese in
pastiche form. And historian Jennifer S. H. Brown represents MacDonald
as an example of the "lone independent figure," a type among the mixed-
race children of the fur trade who "found individual ways to express a
continuing consciousness of their part-Indian identity and their affiliation to the Northwest without becoming assimilated to or classed with
'halfbreeds' or métis as a social and political group."[40] In other words, for
Brown, journeying to Japan *was* MacDonald's unique statement of his
own racial identity.

But I would warn against simplistically confirming the existence of
these racial motivations. For my argument, MacDonald's journey to Japan

was overdetermined by the imperial context of competition for Pacific empire. While his "real" motivations are irrecoverable and perhaps, as with all human motivations, unknown even to the subject they motivate, this process of drafting and revising racial identity and expressed racial motivations in MacDonald's narrative reveals the complexity of telling any story that both engages and complicates imperial binaries by shadowing the white man's burden. If we view the figure of "the Indian" as the paradigmatic object of U.S. continental expansion, MacDonald disrupts that binary of white American versus Indian, especially as it would be projected outward in stories that made Asia seem a new western frontier for American expansion. Thus the Japanese cannot be viewed as "more Indians" when MacDonald alters what being an Indian means, both by his claim to civilized, modern mobility and by his explanation of his ancestors' participation in the history of diplomatic alliances in the northwest.

For MacDonald, the Chinooks of his childhood were a sovereign nation engaged in legitimate diplomatic arts with the HBC, and as the product of those unions he inherits a legacy that particularly qualifies him for extending civilized diplomacy to Japan. In other words, making his Chinook lineage a key element of his ability to participate and guide Pacific expansion and to claim U.S. belonging complicates any notion of the United States as a white imperial power in isolated conflict with the Indian on a global frontier, and thus its treatment in MacDonald's story had to be carefully managed, sometimes with awkward results. It was this complication that struck both Eva Emery Dye and Elizabeth Bacon Custer, both of whom recast the racial meaning of his story in versions that sought to stabilize the linkage between whiteness and U.S. national expansion.

Elizabeth Bacon Custer: Taking MacDonald Home

The wife of the famous deceased general met MacDonald briefly in 1890 and described the meeting in an 1891 travel sketch she wrote for *Harper's Weekly* titled "An Out of the Way 'Outing.'" Custer's article details her travel on a new railroad line built between Spokane, Washington, on the Northern Pacific Railroad, and Revelstoke, British Columbia, on the CPR. The new line passed nearby Fort Colville, where she met MacDonald and heard his story. About one-half of her article is devoted to describing their meeting; the other to encouraging tourism with praise of the surrounding landscape. The railroad line was being built to open up mines, she explained, but her interest in the west was not commercial: "If I had had the building of this road," she writes, "it would have been wholly on account of the superb scenery."[41] She praises all that is unspoiled and criticizes the process of modernization of which her tourism and the railroad she rides on are a part. Troubled by encroaching signs of modernization such as an advertisement posted in front of a quaint old mission, Custer writes, "I felt I should like to go . . . through our Eastern States, and beg people to hurry out here before all this interesting country is leveled off, smoothed down, and made tame and commonplace" (534). The story of national progress she tells is not one that champions industry and settlement but one that regretfully accepts those movements while representing the west as a romantic and ineluctably disappearing landscape for the consumption of herself and her eastern audience. Her portrayal of Mac-Donald fits seamlessly into this romantic construction of the west.

During her visit to Fort Colville, MacDonald shows her around, paying "reverence to her husband's name" and apparently greatly enjoying her company. He tells her of the HBC days and of his world travels, informing her that, as she quotes him, "I flatter myself that I was the instigator of Commodore Perry's expedition to Japan." But Custer gets the details wrong, stating that MacDonald first was greeted warmly in Japan and then imprisoned cruelly in China, a mistake perhaps made because Mac-Donald's accomplishments scarcely mattered to her. As she explains to her readers, "I found that it made little difference what he said, his manner of telling what he had to say was something I was not likely to encounter everyday" (535). As she notes, MacDonald's extreme formality—"the grandiose style of an old-school gentleman"—made him seem a novelty in her travels that would amuse her readers:

> I can scarcely think of anything more incongruous than this aristocratic old man, with his high flown expressions . . . and the tumbled down, dilapidated and untidy old buildings around him. And yet the two clothes he wore, and the straggling gray hair and beard, looked to me far more interesting than the dressed up and commonplace-looking man who occupied a panel on the family album, and represented Ronold [sic] when he was in the outside world. Then another incongruity was the slip he sometimes made into every-day talk, and the introduction, in the very midst of his most lofty flights of rhetoric, of slang phrases, which seemed all the more absurd associated as they were with the stately language of by-gone days. (534)

To illustrate this effect, Custer carefully reports much of MacDonald's story by putting it in MacDonald's words, and then describing her own amusement at what she perceives as "slips" in his performance of polished manners. When MacDonald says, "in pathetic tones," that he has traveled the world but "no matter how far I roamed, my mind always reverted to this little amphitheater," she undercuts any seriousness in his sentiment by describing her own reaction: "It was difficult after this really eloquent flight of oratory to keep the corners of my rebellious mouth from quivering with laughter when he added, with his hands waving about him, 'It is my home, it is not for me to sneeze at'" (535). Being familiar with the sense of homelessness MacDonald creates in his autobiography and its revisions, this statement seems striking for its suggestion that MacDonald was working through this question of his proper location even in his conversations with strangers, but from Custer's perspective, the real point of interest is MacDonald's "incongruity" of speech.

In other words, Custer recognizes MacDonald as a mimic, as one who strives but just perceptibly fails to speak in the tones of civilization, and it is this colorful failure that she appreciates, for like the coarse dress that she prefers to gentlemanly clothes, it marks MacDonald's novelty as part of the old western world of Scotch and French traders and Indians that she relishes as a tourist. Writing in the mode of the local color sketch, Custer assumes the role of the metropolitan visitor, the same role that Steward assigns his narrator in the "Tales of Laguna," but without Steward's challenge to the genre's power relations. Like the wilderness that she wants her eastern readers to witness, MacDonald is part of a romantic landscape for the consumption of her *Harper's* readership. While listening to MacDonald, it strikes her that "some people I know at the East would enjoy this witty, dramatic and versatile man, and how I should like to . . . set him in the midst of people who get so tired of each other and long for novelty." As she tells him, "Oh, Mr. McDonald, how I should like to take you home with me!" To which MacDonald responds with a deep bow, saying "Oh Madam, take possession of me. I am yours" (535).

Custer takes possession of MacDonald and the borderlands that she visits not by erasing the heterogeneous histories of the fur trade but by resignifying their racial and economic histories as quaint artifacts of the past. She takes possession of these artifacts as souvenirs, objects for display that simultaneously objectify and erase European colonial history prior to U.S. settlement. For example, although she reports MacDonald's reminiscences of the fort's HBC days and describes remnants of its built environment in the form of old cabins and walls, she simultaneously erases the history of the fur trade (as well as the native trade routes that crossed the land before there was European contact) in her repeated regret that the future will bring "traffic and bustle" to the "isolated and wild" country (534). In the new U.S. national narrative of expansion, the HBC days become quaint, static, and precommercial: something to reflect on only in the leisure of tourism.

Similarly, Custer erases MacDonald's claims to international diplomacy by affixing him in the local tourist landscape. His claim to preparing Japan for Commodore Perry's treaty appears as only the amusing, linguistically inferior speech of the local. No matter what stories he told her about world travel, Custer writes, "it was hard for me to connect that distant world with this peaceful old man, who seemed never to have left the green basin shut in by the mountains about us" (534). Like the land itself, MacDonald only makes sense as something static, isolated, and ahistorical about to be transformed by inevitable U.S. progress. He *seems* to have never left home because she scripts this region in the racial terms of U.S. national expansion, and within those hegemonic terms MacDonald as an Indian can never be anything but local and colored. As discussed with Steward and Hopkins, where the emphatic placement of African Americans in local, domestic, and vernacular spaces rather than on "foreign terrain" was a rhetorical strategy for maintaining a linkage between whiteness and U.S. imperial identity, Custer's placement of MacDonald in a firmly "shut in" terrain guards against the potentially destabilizing notion that he is at once a half-breed, an HBC descendent, and an agent of U.S. empire and commerce in the Pacific.

When MacDonald read Custer's essay in *Harper's* a year after their meeting, he was outraged, writing in a letter to McLeod that apparently "she had come to the wooly west to pull wool over me and exhibit me as a show, as Barnum would his Wooly Horse."[42] What particularly angered MacDonald was Custer's racialized descriptions of the MacDonald household. Custer wrote that upon being introduced to MacDonald, she mistook him for the head of the household of "half-breeds," although in fact he was unmarried and living with his cousin's family. She then pokes fun at her own mistake; when MacDonald treats her so chivalrously and begs her to "take possession of me," she writes that she was afraid of jealous anger on the part of the woman she took to be MacDonald's wife: "I glanced at the squaw, wondering if any of the savage instinct remained in her, and how she would look upon this open trespassing upon her preserves. . . .

I afterward found out that she was Mrs. MacDonald, but the wife of the older man's nephew; so the tomahawks ceased to float in the air before my imaginative eyes" (535).

MacDonald complained about Custer's word choices of "squaw" and "savage instinct" in his letter to McLeod and submitted a rebuttal to the *Kettle Falls Pioneer* defending himself and his cousin's wife: "The application of the word squaw to the lady of the house was utterly inappropriate. Mrs. MacDonald, the wife of my cousin Donald, was well born[,] as well educated and with as fine a literary taste . . . and with as fine an appreciation of habit of the proprieties and duties of civilized life as any of the circle to which Mrs. Custer belongs." As he tried to explain, her parents' marriage was legitimate, customary, and a function of the diplomacy of the British empire with the powerful kingdoms of the Pacific slope: "There were no white women in the country at that time, so she was of semi-Indian blood—but then, if not still, the red blood was the true blue sovereign lordship of the country."[43] But MacDonald was insisting on a category of racial identity that was being overwritten by U.S. frontier politics and culture. In Ranald's mind, he and Mrs. MacDonald are half-breeds, and as such they assume a respectable position inheriting the legacy of the British fur trade with its royal alliances to sovereign Indian nations. In Custer's mind, Ranald and Mrs. MacDonald are half-breeds, and as such they are Indians marked by all the signifiers of savagery: "squaws" as servile wives, tomahawks, jealous violence, and an antithetical relationship to an inevitable and mobile modernity. This is why Custer finds MacDonald's elaborate manners so amusing: in an era when Native American speech was often rendered in inarticulate grunts and stoic silences, MacDonald assumes the speech of the civilized white man. Of course Custer's personal experience with the U.S. Indian Wars might have influenced her stark perspective on Indian identity: as an editorial in the local newspaper hypothesized, "Why this lady should have so turned against and so sneeringly commented on the dress, and even doubting the veracity of MacDonald, is a mystery, unless, since her brave and fearless husband was so foully butchered by the Indians, she has an abhorrence for anyone with Indian blood."[44]

This encounter between Custer and MacDonald presents an imbalanced rhetorical contest over the question of who could be imagined as representing the expanding United States as a force of modernity. The question mattered because the wrong answer complicated a powerful component of U.S. national identity: the story of a homogenous people righteously moving westward, with Indians positioned as largely as uncivilized antagonists and always doomed to disappear. Custer's strategy for maintaining this story in the pages of *Harper's* removes MacDonald temporally and spatially from its narrative of U.S. westward expansion and modern progress. She accepts MacDonald as neither a geographically mobile "true American" participating in the story of American futurity nor an agent of British empire extending the historical quest for the Northwest Passage, because in her terms of racialization, these parts cannot be played by Indians. And what fails to fit that category of "Indian," Custer can take possession of as souvenirs of the fur trade's mixing of French, Scottish, and Native cultures: a quaint static difference that, like the landscape with which it is identified, will no doubt soon disappear.

Eva Emery Dye and the Anglo-Saxon Asiatic

A year after Custer's essay appeared in *Harper's*, MacDonald received a letter from Eva Emery Dye, another U.S. American writer who would tell his story in print. A first-time author, Dye sought information for a book she was writing on Oregon history, and she had been directed to the sixty-eight-year-old Ranald MacDonald as one of the few remaining HBC descendents who remembered the fur trade days. She was considering titling her book "The King of Columbia" after HBC chief factor Dr. John McLoughlin, but MacDonald told her in his reply that he already laid claim to the title "as the only living descendent of the once powerful King Kum Kumly." He filled his letter with her requested reminiscences of the fur trade days, but he also made a request in return: in his postscript he asks, "Don't be so hard on me as Mrs. General Custer."[45] Dye did "take possession" of MacDonald's story, eventually writing an entire book about it in 1906 titled *McDonald of Oregon*. (Dye restored Ranald's father's spelling of the patronym; to avoid confusion, I call her "Ranald McDonald" character "Ranald" rather than changing the spelling back to MacDonald.) Dye claims in the conclusion to her book that Ranald himself asked her to write his story, but as Frederik Schodt points out, there is no evidence in their existing correspondence of such a request—MacDonald's letters, instead, ask her for assistance with his ongoing efforts to publish his own version.[46] In taking possession of MacDonald's identity and story, however, Dye did not follow Custer in denying his claim to mobility; rather, she turns his Pacific adventures into a tool for narrating her story of Anglo-Saxon progress.

Earlier I referred to *McDonald of Oregon: A Tale of Two Shores* as a historical romance, but the genre in which Dye wrote could as accurately be called romantic history. Dye's aim was not to write fiction; she drew extensively on primary documents and personal interviews so that she could better imagine her subjects, and while she invented dramatic situations and dialogue, she mostly used actual historical figures as characters. To write MacDonald's story, she tracked down a draft of *Japan Story of Adventure*, remembering MacDonald's mention of it in his correspondence. The manuscript she found was an earlier version (without the "true American" revisions of the 1893 manuscript); it was being held with McLeod's papers at the Parliament Library in Ottawa. At Dye's request, McLeod's papers were moved to the British Columbia Provincial archives, where she traveled to view them and hired a group of stenographers to copy the manuscript.[47] The book she wrote drew on these materials, combined with her own correspondence with MacDonald and her years of research on the fur trade and Oregon history, all framed and interpreted through her lens of heroic westward expansion into the Pacific.

Dye is best known to literary critics and historians today as the writer who promoted Sacagawea from the background of Lewis and Clark's famous expedition to her mythic position in its foreground as guide, interpreter, and symbol of Native American acquiescence. Dye's account of the Lewis and Clark expedition in her book *The Conquest* (1902) is widely credited as the first of many fictional and historical accounts to represent Sacagewea as an important figure in the mission.[48] *The Conquest* was Dye's most popular work; frequently reprinted, it was also, like one of Winnifred Eaton's novels, adapted as a stage play by the Broadway impresario David Belasco. Of course, while Dye's treatment of Sacagewea was new, the role that she invented for her was far from original. Dye's Sacagawea was clearly patterned after a preexisting literary history of "good Indian" figures who recognize the superiority of the American settlers and their conquest of North America, including Catherine Maria Sedgewick's Magawisca, Washington Irving's Comcomly, and especially the Pocahontas of early American theater[49] (Dye explicitly compares her Sacagwea to Pocahontas, even making the former a princess to better fit the mold).

Considering this U.S. literary tradition helps us anticipate the role that Dye would give MacDonald. In *The Conquest*, Dye sums up Sacagawea's contribution in these terms: "Madonna of her race, she had led the way to a new time. To the hands of this girl, not yet eighteen, had been intrusted the key that unlocked the road to Asia."[50] In *McDonald of Oregon,* Dye's Ranald plays a similar role in opening the road to Asia. Consistent with conventions, his function as "good Indian" is contrasted to that of his foil, the Yakima chief Kamaikan, another real historical figure whom Dye casts as the "bad Indian" for his role in organizing an alliance of tribes against the United States in the Yakima Indian War of 1855. This opposition is made overtly in a passage describing an imagined meeting between the two when Ranald was a boy in Fort Vancouver: "As Ranald, with irradiating eyes, talked with the old chief, little each guessed their different destinies,—one to battle against the westward march of nations, the other to light a torch to lead them on" (59).

But while we can align Dye's Ranald with Sacagawea and her literary predecessors, Dye also suggests another lineage when she declares Ranald's contribution in her introduction: "As a hero of the vanguard [of American westward expansion] Ranald McDonald ranks along with Sir Alexander Mackenzie, Lewis and Clark, and Commodore Perry. Beyond, and more so than any of these, he belonged to that Asiatic America so swiftly succumbing to the Anglo-Saxon" (vi). Not a sidekick or a feminized helpmeet, Ranald "ranks" with these masculine figures of Anglo-Saxon American exploration and progress, and yet "beyond" and "more so" he is an Indian. Or rather, he is an "Asiatic American," a key dislocation of American Indians in Dye's version of MacDonald's story. Dye's casting of Ranald as both Asian and Indian folds on top of the merging of British and U.S. American interests that are joined in this passage, making Ranald's body a tool for composing the global relations among these forces. Here, as in the other texts I examine in the preceding chapters, novel forms of racialization render newly imagined confrontations on the world's stage.

In one early scene, a group of Dye's Scotch HBC tradesmen discuss the supposed racial ties between Indians and Asians after some shipwrecked Japanese sailors wash up on the shore of Oregon in the 1830s:

> "We doubt not that this whole continent has been peopled in that way," agreed the traders at Fort Vancouver. "Have we not noticed the similarity of complexion and customs? . . . The conical grass huts of all these coast tribes are woven exactly like those of the Chinese," said one, "and our Indian mats are Oriental in pattern. In his patriarchal government, his nomadic home, his Shamanistic religion, the American Indian is an undoubted Mongolian." (73)

That origin might not specifically be Japanese, for "some argued for the Japanese, others for the Chinese, and others for the Malays," but its influence potentially extends across the hemisphere: "'Who knows but the word Mexico itself may be from Macao, and why may not the name of our Killamooks be traced to Kilmuck Tartars?" (75). Here a theory of racial origins works to render Asia, the Pacific islands, and the Western Hemisphere as territory related by its Asiatic inhabitants, suggesting a continuity between expansion on the North American continent and to the south and east. Settling Oregon was building a "road to the Orient" (332), a sequence indicated by Dye's original choice for a title, which instead of *McDonald of Oregon: A Tale of Two Shores* was *Ranald McDonald: A Chronicle of Oregon and Japan*. In this transpacific vision, Asia and the Americas appear as new frontiers filled with the same kind of Indians the United States had been contending with for a century.[51]

Dye appears to be projecting frontier racial definitions and narratives outward onto the Pacific, but her categorical statement "Asians are Indians" arises out of its reverse, "Indians are Asians," which reenvisions expansion at home according to her ideas of the United States as a new Anglo-Saxon world power. The connection explains some content in *McDonald of Oregon* that otherwise seems to be unrelated to MacDonald's travels. The 1855 Yakima Indian wars, to which Dye devotes about one-fifth of the book, are rendered not as one among many U.S. Indian wars but as an ultimate showdown between east and west, centuries in the making. Describing the failed council meeting between Washington Territorial Governor Isaac Stevens and representatives of the Yakima, Nez Perce, Walla Walla, Umtilla, and Cayuse tribes that started the war, Dye writes, "On the site of a future city not alone met these specific tribes and whites, but all ages, all time, since the ruling races bent westward and all the nomads east, fleeing from each other until the globe was circled. Today, in Walla Walla, the circuit ended, Asia faced America. Would there be a truce?" (346). Stevens sought to trade the tribes' titles to land for money and reservations; Dye represents his doing so as standing "ready to clasp commercial hands with that Asia toward which the white man had so long traveled" (362). By making her Indians read as Asians, she borrows from the perceived significance of Asian overseas expansion, turning the Oregon settlement into a crucial climax of global and millennial proportions—more than just another chapter of expansion occurring in the new world frontier. The American frontier, instead of providing an isolated, exceptionalist national identity for the United States, appears as the culmination of a global process of Anglo-Saxon and Asian racial interaction that accounts for past, present, and future world history.

Dye's racialized historical narratives are sweeping and epic, making it all the more strange that she centers them around MacDonald's idiosyncratic story. But rather than being confused or troubled by Ranald's mixedness and his national dislocation, Dye seizes upon them to make him a bridge in her story in three ways. First, Ranald's journey to Japan substantiates Dye's racial theories about Japan and Native America; second, his lack of conscious understanding of that racial linkage reinforces the status of North American Indians as colonial objects; and, third, the trajectory of his life under the British and American flags both binds together and narrates the succession of British and U.S. American colonial power in the Pacific Northwest.

Ranald's desire to visit Japan stems from a kind of unconscious racial memory that guides him even in childhood: "If ever a baby loved water it was Ranald, down there by the sea looking over toward Asia" (22). This notion of Dye's clearly departs from Custer's local cloistering of Indians in North American landscapes. When Ranald's father is surprised to find that he has run away from his position as an apprentice bank clerk ("Gone to sea? Who ever heard of an Indian going to sea? What could have induced the lad born to the land and the fur trade to turn himself into a sailor?"), the narrator chides him and all readers who would be surprised by this news: "Had Archibald McDonald forgotten that birthplace beside the Pacific? Had he forgotten that Cumcumly was literally of the sea, born of long ancestry that had ridden the billows unhampered and unterrified?" (199). In Dye's version, it makes perfect sense that Ranald would head west, because his racial origins lie across the Pacific, just as it would make sense for U.S. Americans accustomed to displacing Indians to follow him.

In making sense of MacDonald's trip to Japan, Dye drew on emerging anthropological theories that attempted to link Native Americans culturally, linguistically, and morphologically to Asia. In Dye's historical moment, the notion that Indians migrated to the Americas from elsewhere was not a new concept, but what was new was the scientific (rather than scriptural) methods being used by anthropologists to theorize the route of migration. Because of a biblical view of monogenesis, migration had since the sixteenth century almost always been assumed, with a number of groups assigned responsibility for peopling the Americas. These included, as one scholar wrote in 1841, "the Atlantides, Phenicians, and the Carthaginians, the Hebrews, Egyptians, Hindoos, Chinese, Tartars, Malays, Polynesians, the Northmen and the Welsh."[52] But in the late nineteenth and early twentieth centuries, newly professionalized scholars drawing on methods of forensic, linguistic, and cultural anthropology attempted to distinguish their new scientific approaches. For example, John T. Short, in an 1880 study titled "The North American of Antiquity," used chapter divisions to clearly differentiate "The Origin of the Americans as Viewed from the Standpoint of Science" from previous theories.[53]

Yet, as Vine Deloria Jr. has argued, such ethnological theories distinguished themselves from religious doctrine without departing from fundamental colonial assumptions that attempted to undermine Native perspective and sovereignty.[54] Deloria's critique gains particular force in our current moment, as contemporary archaeologists increasingly challenge the Bering Strait theory, which essentially states that North Asian peoples following herds of prey walked over the Bering Strait when it was dry land during the last ice age 11,000 years ago, and then moved south to disperse rapidly over North and South America. This theory, which was articulated in the 1930s and became orthodoxy by the 1960s, is currently in question because of a lack of corroborating evidence in the face of new archeological finds suggesting drastically longer timelines and different possible routes of migration or multiple migrations, including maritime routes.[55] As these new theories emerge, critics such as Deloria raise the question of what colonial work was performed for white scholars by Bering Strait theory, with its relatively recent date of entry, assumption of low technological capacity, and authoritative disregard for Native migration traditions. Despite scientific objectives, layers of distorting racialist meaning confound efforts to make sense of human migration.

Coincident with the rise of scientific theories of Asian migration, Dye's construction of Ranald's voyage reveals a particular ideological corollary wherein early versions of this scientific racial theory were adapted and promoted as part of a vision of transpacific empire. But more than this, *McDonald of Oregon* also reinforces certain fundamental assumptions of colonial knowledge in its representation of anthropological power relations. By presenting Ranald's story as a kind of anthropological artifact, Dye makes establishing who has the authority to produce knowledge about North American Indian origins a central part of her book's colonial agenda. *McDonald of Oregon* never attributes the theory of Asian-Indian racial kinship to any of its indigenous characters; instead, their animate and inanimate bodies communicate the evidence for them. Describing

Ranald's grandfather, the narrator writes: "Now Cumcumly had not the least idea in the world where he came from. If his ancestors had drifted overseas in past ages he knew it not. But his Mongolian face, with eyes turned obliquely upward at the outer corners, told of an Asiatic past" (17). Speaking for him, his physical features provide a kind of craniometric evidence of a history to be interpreted by some other civilized agent, and his understanding of the past is represented as an absence. In fact, Dye casts Native American traditions as obstacles to ethnological study: as one Hudson's Bay Company man says, "if only the Indians had not that foolish superstition that the names of the dead must never be mentioned, we might have more to guide us. . . . As it is, their history is lost in a single generation" (74).

Here, finding indigenous history will require losing indigenous beliefs. In other places in the text, however, Native legends do provide data for someone else to reinterpret: "All those Indians [living around the Mackenzie River] have a clear tradition that their ancestors migrated from the westward, and crossed an arm of the seas" (74). And when Cumcumly wants Ranald's mother's body buried at sea, the narrator asks, "Was it an inherited tradition that every Indian should go back to the Celestials in the west? The bayous beyond Astoria were filled with the dead, each in that almost priceless carved coffin, the cedar canoe, and every head was turned toward Asia" (19). Whatever these burial traditions mean to Cumcumly or to the other tribes, Dye's reader is authorized and invited to interpret them according to her given theory, a move that renders Indian human remains as forensic specimens for racial science.

Dye continues these conventions of imperial knowledge by representing Ranald as sharing this unselfconsciousness; he is entirely unaware of the supposed racial reasons for his interest in Japan. Embellishing his manuscript, Dye invents several moments when Ranald observes the familiarity of the Japanese and their language and customs, but he can only wonder "at their resemblance to the tribes of Northwest America" (218). When one of the Japanese praises his courage by saying that he has a great heart, "Ranald smiled, for was that not his grandfather's words, 'shookum tum tum,' a great heart, when he rode the Oregon sea looking toward Japan? And somehow these Japanese looked like his grandfather" (228). (Compare this to MacDonald's account: "Again they observed, 'You must have a great heart to leave in a little boat etc.' I could only smile at the compliment, given, I believe, in all the sincerity of their good nature.")[56] In Dye's version of this scene, Ranald's smile is another form of physical, bodily evidence that someone else—here the reader—must interpret, because Ranald himself develops no theory to explain the resemblance that makes him smile, only noticing that similarity "somehow" exists. In this way, his adventure appears as another version of the Chinooks setting funeral boats out to sea: an unselfconscious but racially readable body moving seaward with its head facing Asia.

For Dye, Ranald's travels are evidence of not generally Asian but specifically Japanese origins, a notion that surged in popularity at the turn of the century along with cultural interest in Japan. Writing in 1880, one researcher declares as "plausible" a scientific theory resembling Dye's: "If the original people of this continent were not Japanese, at least a considerable infusion of Japanese blood into the original blood has taken place from time to time, either by intentional colonization or by the accidents incident to navigation," citing as possible evidence the same phenomenon noted in *McDonald of Oregon:* "the great number of shipwrecks which are continually being cast upon our Pacific coast by the Japanese current."[57] The political mood of transpacific alliance with Japan clearly influenced such speculations: a *Popular Science Monthly* essay by Edward Sylvester Morse elaborates on the "tangible evidences" of Japanese and American Indian similarity in crafts, customs, and physical appearance with an anecdote about a visiting Japanese commissioner at a state reception in Philadelphia, who, upon being introduced to a "full blooded Omaha Indian" also in attendance, began trying to converse with the Omaha man in Japanese.[58] Here the scene of a mobile, civilized Japanese official participating in international diplomacy suggests part of the attraction of the Japanese as American "relatives," even while it renders the commissioner as comic for mistaking an Omaha man for a countryman. As in Dye's formulations, only Morse, the white speaker, appears able to correctly identify the two racialized guests and make scientific sense of their mistake.

With some writers like Winnifred Eaton "whitening" Japan, Dye's association of American Indians with Japanese could make the former seem more assimilable and likely to embrace European influences, as Japan was seen as doing. But Dye makes it clear that the American Indian branch of the family has declined. In this, Dye's theory of Japanese migration and subsequent degeneration resembles one being argued in her day by the French naturalist Jean Louis Armand de Quatrefages de Bréau.[59] Cumcumly's lodge is described as "suggestive of deteriorated Japan" (17), and when the Japanese remind Ranald of his boyhood among the Chinooks, he thinks, "How far away those days seemed now, and yet all about were reminders, as if those beloved Indian companions had suddenly become refined and civilized" (218). If part of the appeal of Japanese kinship draws from enthusiasm about Japan as a transpacific partner in trade and diplomacy, Dye's formulation carefully distinguishes between "civilized" nations deserving of international diplomacy and the supposedly savage tribes denied that status.

Here Dye again departs significantly from MacDonald's version, which contains its own attempt to bring racial science to bear on the origin of the Japanese. In a passage describing a Japanese man's face as "scarcely Monghol," MacDonald explains: "Aryan, or not, I regard the Japanese intellect the most subtle—finest and keenest in the world. My friend says he considers it *pre* and *supra* Aryan, with a literature pre- or *ante* Aryan, and has a theory of their genesis which—he contends with much learning and force—naturally and logically explains it. On that question I cannot enter here" (259). The "friend" propounding this theory was McLeod, MacDonald's coauthor and editor, speaking obviously through this passage: earlier drafts of Ranald's story contained long chapters elaborating McLeod's hazy theory of the Aryan origins of the Japanese.[60] By switching the ethnological theory supported by Ranald's story from one of Japanese Aryan civilization to one of Native American degeneration, Dye's version refuses Ranald the position that McLeod tried to claim for both coauthors: that of a civilized racial expert who draws—rather than is defined by—the flexible color lines of global competition.

But for Dye, Ranald himself *is* capable of diplomacy: his mixed status as *both* an Asiatic American and a peer of Anglo-Saxon American explorers is another one of the ways that she seizes on his unfixed identity for her own narrative purposes. If on the one hand she casts his journey to Japan as the unselfconscious Asiatic instinct of the North American Indian, on the other hand his journey to Japan also nationalizes him as a modern U.S. American. Dye plays up his accomplishments in Japan as an important U.S. diplomatic contribution, borrowing from statements made in MacDonald's letters but never included by McLeod in the manuscript. Her character Ranald says in his old age:

Yes, I flatter myself that I was the instigator of Commodore Perry's expedition to Japan. You will find my depositions in executive document number fifty-nine of the Thirty-Second Congress. That started Perry. I suggested to Captain Glynn of the ship "Preble" that, in the event of another visit to Japan for the purpose of opening trade, models of Western ingenuity should be taken and exhibited. And Commodore Perry did that. . . . I broke the seal that made Japan a closed empire,—at all events cracked it; so it was easy for Commodore Perry to do the rest. (394)

By including MacDonald's own claims to fame and pointing out the location of his deposition, Dye literally writes Ranald into U.S. political history. Dye's Ranald serves not only as a guide for a broader Anglo-Saxon North American progress; more specifically, he exhibits what Dye represents as a key national characteristic *differentiating* U.S. American settlers from her British HBC fur traders: a desire for mobility and modernity. While MacDonald's dislocation on the U.S.-Canadian border inserts heterogeneous histories of competing empires into this text, Dye is careful to narrate the relationship between British and American influences in the Pacific Northwest as one where a more modern force displaces an older one, with the highly mobile Ranald allied with the more modern United States.

In her earlier work *The Conquest,* Dye describes the hospitality of the HBC men at Fort Vancouver toward the first U.S. settlers as an occasion of racial rapproachement: "Anglo Saxon greeted Anglo Saxon, to march henceforth hand in hand forever" (439). In *McDonald of Oregon,* however, when the first U.S. settlers cross the Oregon Trail to arrive at Fort Vancouver, HBC chief factor John McLoughlin announces what is different about them: "The Yankees are here, and the next thing we know they will yoke up their oxen, drive down to the mouth of the Columbia, and come out at Japan" (108). Their constant watchword is "a little farther on," causing McLoughlin to remark, "Beats anything I ever saw. . . . When I tell our Canadians to stop, they stop, but these Americans go on as if I had not spoken" (149). The text represents Ranald's father Archibald McDonald and other fur traders as loving the Oregon country for its similarity to their ancestral Scottish highlands and its reminders of their past; U.S. American settlers are instead characterized by an intense desire for mobility and change. Ranald bridges the two; he is drawn to Japan because he is drawn to an ancient ancestral past, but in doing so he makes the way for and predicts the stance of a specifically U.S. American chapter of Anglo-Saxon empire.

While MacDonald himself was ambivalent about how to figure his own racial identity as part of his story, Dye finds multiple meanings for Ranald's Chinook ancestry. She racializes him as a Sacagawea-like guide who sanctions North American and Pacific expansion; as an object of empire excluded from self-conscious understanding of the racial forces supposedly propelling world history; and as a harbinger of a specifically U.S. American domination in the Pacific. What is mixed and liminal in his identity is useful to Dye because he provides a bridge between British and American, "nomad" and "ruling race," Oregon and Japan. Global forces like contending empires and ancient migrations cohere in his body to illustrate a political moment of U.S. expansion in the Pacific.

I have said that Dye makes Ranald in part a Sacagawea figure, but in evaluating the influence of her text, it seems important to note that her vision of him failed to capture the American reading public's imagination in the way that her portrayal of Sacagawea did. Despite some similar narrative devices and patterns, McDonald of Oregon sold far fewer copies than The Conquest.[61] One can only speculate the reasons for this (Dye's biographer Sheri Bartlett Browne blames the Panic of 1907), but the reversal of U.S. enthusiasm for Japan that hurt Eaton's sales during these years might be another factor, especially if that reversal evoked from the association of Indians and Japanese another new kind of empowered yellow peril living "at home" on reservations. And it also seems possible that the heterogeneous histories that haunted MacDonald's efforts to write himself into national narratives may have hampered Dye's success. Reviews of McDonald of Oregon were favorable—the New York Times praised "the line of thought opened up by points of similarity between the Indians of the Northwest and the 'little brown men' of the opposite coast" as "fascinating"[62]—but popular historical narratives in the United States have tended to suppress rather than highlight the transnational dynamics that so appealed to Dye. U.S. Americans have preferred to forget, in Benedict Anderson's sense, the conflicted pre-national past of competing empires in the Pacific Northwest. And the idea of a continuity between continental and overseas expansion waited almost a century to displace the exceptionalist notion that American expansion was antithetical to overseas empire, despite the efforts by Dye and other imperialists to promote and celebrate a continuous series of examples to the contrary. Dye's effort to write MacDonald into national and imperial narratives was more successful than MacDonald's own insofar as Dye's made it into print, but perhaps hers was no less able to control the wandering meanings of MacDonald's identity and adventure.

Custer's and Dye's different efforts to translate MacDonald's claim to national and imperial agency head in opposite directions: one toward local immobility and the other toward a predetermined racialized orientation. The pattern resembles dynamics described in earlier chapters. For example, in the divergent efforts to control the meaning of African American soldiers fighting in the Spanish American and Filipino American Wars, African American soldiers were either denied modern mobility or fixed on the battlefield within essentialized racial stereotypes such as the minstrel or the loyal servant. These divergent routes chosen by Custer and Dye represent larger rhetorical and narrative strategies to manage the heterogeneity of the United States when imagining it as a world power, and such strategies are the ones that I argue Steward, Hopkins, Eaton, and MacDonald negotiated in their writing. Like Steward, MacDonald responds to these hegemonic strategies in part by establishing authority through linguistic expertise as a teacher of English and a cultural translator. But language always reveals more than one intends, and in both Steward's and MacDonald's cases, wielding the terms of imperial authority can also undermines those terms, as their writings exhibit divided urges to at once benefit from, direct, and criticize imperial politics and the various racialized narratives that drive them. In this way, Steward and MacDonald's writings, more so than the more romantic and fantastic works of Eaton and Hopkins, bear marks of ambiguity or incoherence—perhaps a result of straining against the very terms required for readability within national narratives of race and empire rather than using fantasy and romance to rewrite those terms.

All of these writers, however, reacted to living in the United States at a time of intense discussion and anxiety about the relationship of race, nation, and empire, and all wrote in terms that borrowed from, reinforced, and complicated those competing narratives, intentionally marking and questioning the meaning or centrality of whiteness as an explanation or justification of the place of the United States on the world's stage. Placing their writings together and reading them in the context of a culture at odds with competing narratives of race and empire, we begin to recognize the complexity of U.S. racialization as it manipulated and was shaped by global visions, transnational affinities, and international relations at the beginning of the twentieth century.

Conclusion

I began thinking about this book after an experience I had engaging freshmen writers in a discussion about historical perspective. I had shown my class a segment from the *Schoolhouse Rock!* educational series titled "Elbow Room," an animated musical short that narrates American westward expansion as a result of the naturalized need for space.[1] I especially wanted the students to note how the video's date of production, the early 1970s, influenced its particular interpretation of manifest destiny: the video ends with the suggestion that when future Americans need more "elbow room," they will secure it for themselves on the moon. But the students were more interested in the video's effacement of conflict and of nonwhite bodies in general; one student suggested that the audacity of the image of the astronauts waving around their elbows next to an American flag on the moon would be mitigated if some of these white astronauts were replaced by African American, Native American, and Asian American astronauts. A few students disagreed, pointing out that this would not alter the assumption that the natural destiny of the United States was to expand to the moon as its rightful territory, but most members of the class seemed to concur.

This was back in 1996, when I was a graduate student; it was a formative moment for me, as I was beginning, along with many other scholars in American literary studies, to think about ways that a disciplinary model of multicultural American studies had instituted a kind of horizon of the national on its discussions of race and gender, making inclusion in the rights and privileges of U.S. citizenship its shortsighted goal. As an origin for this book and a lesson in historical perspective for myself, the experience led me to consider both the limitations of narratives of U.S. multiculturalism in a global context and those narratives' interpretive possibilities.

Over a decade later, at a time when an African American man is president of the United States and people of color have served at the highest levels of federal government, the question still remains: Does it matter who represents the United States on the world's stage? No longer explicitly described or represented in terms of racial mission, visions of U.S. global influence embrace the language and imagery of multiculturalism, not whiteness.[2] In such a context, the strategy of shadowing the white man's burden that I have described in this book might seem a quaint relic of yesteryear. To figure a nonwhite person in the role of soldier, explorer, diplomat, or even president representing the United States to the rest of the world would seem to merely confirm the banal multiculturalism that my students had imbibed. And yet, I would like to suggest that the value of studying these century-old stories of shadowing the white man's burden is both to appreciate their role in bringing about our era of multicultural nationalism, with all its limitations, and to identify their unfinished business.

What remains new in these stories of national inclusion are their surprisingly destabilizing narrative effects. Some critics currently seek to uncover a cultural history of transnational identities and coalitions as models of resistance, reasoning that transnational forms of domination call for transnational resistance movements and that global histories of slave rebellion, labor radicalism, feminism, and anti-imperialism can provide valuable models for such movements. But of course the scale of international relations and the frame of national belonging have been and remain important grounds for imagining domination and resistance, and for this reason alone, narratives that adopt this scale should still command part of our attention. Even so, I have argued that in the case of such writings by Steward, Hopkins, Eaton, and MacDonald, their power comes not from their persuasive visions of multiracial national inclusion but from their complication of the mutually constitutive relationship between race and nation. By revealing interior frontiers, heterogeneous histories, fictive national ethnicities, and transnational comparisons, these writers' works do more than change the color of U.S. national power on the global stage; they also represent that power as fragmented, internally divided, and historically embedded in ongoing, multipolar, colonial processes. That is these writers' unfinished business: to globalize U.S. history from within by locating the dialectical relationship between race as a global and domestic system of meaning.

As a study of the narratives and discourses of empire, my point has not been to create an "exposé" refuting American exceptionalism, a claim that Susan Gillman argues has blinkered such studies. Rather than adjudicating denials of U.S. imperialism past and present, I analyze imperial narratives' internal contradictions, as they were harnessed and exploited by writers whose vacillating positions on war and global power cannot be reduced to "pro-imperialist" or "anti-imperialist."[3] My question about these writers has not been are they "for or against" U.S. empire but how did they use stories of U.S global power as devices to reflect on race domestically and globally, reflections that ultimately destabilize empire's racial grounding and open up possibilities for new kinds of transnational and cosmopolitan identifications.

Today the racial grounding of U.S. global power, which once stood uneasily on the construct of whiteness, seems to have been replaced with a neoliberal conception of clashing civilizations. But are today's conceptions of U.S. global power multiracial, or are they "de-raced," a term that I use in chapter 2 to describe the meaning of Steward's racially unidentified U.S. military officer? What we learn from Steward's fictional experimentation in representing de-raced U.S. power is its productive failure to ever fully forget U.S. racial history and its intersection with the fluid color lines continually being redrawn on the world's stage. In contrast, it is the pose of racelessness that would attempt to conceal those histories and intersections altogether. The destabilizing effect of seemingly de-raced global power might be comparable with what José E. Limón described in his response to Amy Kaplan's 2003 American Studies Association Presidential Address. Limón responds to Kaplan by questioning what he sees as her assumption of continuity between the so-called internal colonization of Mexican Americans and the U.S. occupation of Iraq. To disrupt this continuity, he describes the complicating position of Lieutenant General Ricardo S. Sanchez as the commander of all ground forces in Iraq during 2003–4. Linking Sanchez's "now devalued narrative of ethnic mobility" about growing up in Rio Grande City to the colonial history of the Texas borderlands, Limón sees Sanchez's position not as a sign that race no longer matters for today's multiracial U.S. military and its overseas mission but as a signifying opportunity to recall multipolar U.S. border conflict and the agency of Mexican Americans living in and writing about these borderlands. Despite Sanchez's subsequently revealed role overseeing interrogations during the Abu Gharaib abuses, Limón's narrative shadows the white man's burden by looking for unexpected moments where global conflicts evoke local histories, and "the very ideas of U.S. empire, U.S. violence, and U.S. minorities as well as the U.S. military become complicated sites with multivalent social and moral meanings and outcomes, frustrating any effort to give them a singular interpretation."[4]

My goal, like Limón's, is not to mitigate or justify extensions of U.S. global power because they provide a route to social mobility and authority for U.S. minorities, nor is it to expect the persons taking those positions of authority to transcend abuses of state power; instead, my goal in this book is to understand how these positions have created spaces for critical reflection and speculative imagination on racial formation, national identity, and colonial history. This role of imagination is why literature and narrative convention matter for these writers and for their interlocutors (including Kipling, Dixon, William Huntington Wilson, John Fox Jr., Thomas Nelson Page, John C. Freund, Wallace Irwin, Jack London, Elizabeth Bacon Custer, and Eva Emory Dye); all are engaged in a symbolic contest over the relationship of whiteness and U.S. national identity as it is defined against a global backdrop of colonial competition.

This symbolic contest is still with us today, as the reaction to Barack Obama's 2008 election to the U.S. presidency reminds us. Speaking about Obama's victory the day after the election, Bill Moyers claimed that whatever the failures or successes of Obama's actual presidency, "Symbolically, metaphorically, *and* politically, I think race is not going to have us by the throat the way it has for so long now."[5] But are we released from race's jaws, or does the symbolic meaning of the Obama presidency invite us back into history and out into the world from a new perspective? This book is about such symbolic possibilities: Louis Dalrymple's 1899 image of the white Uncle Sam leading the multiracial U.S. schoolroom (discussed in chapter 1) reflected and reinforced the idea of whiteness as a metonym for U.S. power, but the writers I study here engage in a symbolic strategy to exploit that formulation's contradictions and cast new light on racial and colonial history by changing the color of the nation's metonym.

By saying that whiteness has disappeared as an overt referent in contemporary narratives of America's global mission, I do not mean to imply that race is no longer an issue in American visions of U.S. global power. Islamophobia is, as Shu-mei Shih writes, still currently "looking to attach a vilifiable race to the immense racial, cultural, and national diversity of those who profess the Islamic faith," and the shifting racialization of Arabs and Muslims in legal decisions and in popular culture over the course of the twentieth century reveals the continuing processes in which changing landscapes of global politics alter racial categories and perceptions within the United States.[6] Behind the rhetoric of "homeland" security, we can still see, as Amy Kaplan argues, profoundly insecure appeals to "a sense of racial purity and ethnic homogeneity that even naturalization and citizenship cannot erase."[7]

The logic behind such racial appeals is highly contested and fragile, but what this book demonstrates is that insecurity about contradictory racial narratives and categories has its precedents at the turn of the twentieth century. When journalist and political commentator Michael Ignatieff argued in 2003 that "America's [current] empire is not like empires of times past, built on colonies, conquest and the white man's burden," he implied a recent break with the confident racialization of empires past.[8] But in this book, I uncover a history of anxious associations between whiteness and empire in U.S. public discourse and imagined incarnations of the white man's burden. A literary reading of Kipling's reception offers us the grounds from which to recognize his poem's role in a debate that reaches beyond the question of whether or not to pursue U.S. empire, to the question of how race and nation interact in imagining and re-imagining new kinds of agency on the world's stage. That is what the writers I discuss in this book offer us today: a sense of possibility pulled from the interstices between race and nation and pieced together from an imperial history more uncertain and internally divided than we often remember.

Notes

INTRODUCTION

1. John T. Bramhall, "The Red, Black and Yellow," *Overland Monthly* 37 (February 1901), 722.

2. Ibid., 726.

3. This period stands out not because the United States was actually domestically isolated prior to 1898 but because of the self-consciousness that writers exhibited during this period in their efforts to resituate the country culturally, economically, and diplomatically in the world. As I have argued elsewhere, expansion into the Pacific at the turn of the twentieth century was often seen as a break with a significant national tradition of continental expansion and hemispheric belonging; to administer the Philippines was frequently depicted as either a dangerous departure from the tradition and integrity associated with domestic isolation at home or an important step toward mature global responsibility and privilege (Gretchen Murphy, *Hemispheric Imaginings: The Monroe Doctrine and Narratives of U.S. Empire* [Durham, N.C.: Duke University Press, 2005]). These perceptions made the idea of Pacific empire a particularly evocative and explosive concept for a variety of U.S. Americans attempting to represent relations among race, nation, and imperial mission.

4. Both scholarly and popular sources used the phrase "world power" to name the newly perceived global influence of the United States. For example, Archibald Cary Coolidge, *The United States as a World Power* (New York: Macmillan, 1906); John Holladay Latané, *America as a World Power* (New York: Harper, 1907); and *The United States as a World Power,* a special issue of *The Annals of the American Academy of Political and Social Science* 36, no. 2 (1905).

5. Literary critics, historians, and legal scholars engaged in "whiteness studies" have examined this contested process of racial construction in the nineteenth and early twentieth centuries as it intersected with the changing demographics of urbanization and immigration and with the contingencies of developing industrial economic conditions. For example, Noel Ignatiev, *How the Irish Became White* (New York: Routledge, 1995); Matthew Frye Jacobson, *Whiteness of a Different Color: European Immigration and the Alchemy of Race* (Cambridge: Harvard University Press, 1998); Ian F. Haney-López, *White by Law: The*

Legal Construction of Race (New York: New York University Press, 2006 [1996]); and David Roediger, *Wages of Whiteness: Race and the Making of the American Working Class* (London: Verso, 1991). See also the discussion of Irish and Chinese racial formation in Robert G. Lee, *Orientals: Asian Americans in Popular Culture* (Philadelphia: Temple University Press, 1999), 51–82.

6. Quoted in Thomas F. Gossett, *Race: The History of an Idea in America* (New York: Schocken, 1973 [1963]), 37.

7. George Stocking Jr., *Race, Culture, and Anthropology: Essays on the History of Anthropology* (New York: Free Press, 1968), 163.

8. This focus on competing discourses comprising a dynamic network of power relations is of course the fundamental assumption of historicism after Michel Foucault. Following this historicist approach, I view knowledge of race at this time as at once a dominant episteme and the site of competing, contradictory claims to power that allow for conceptual instability in the poststructuralist sense.

9. Etienne Balibar, "Racism and Nationalism," in Etienne Balibar and Immanuel Wallerstein, *Race, Nation, Class: Ambiguous Identities* (London: Verso, 1991), 49.

10. Robert S. Levine, *Dislocating Race and Nation: Episodes in Nineteenth-Century American Literary Nationalism* (Chapel Hill: University of North Carolina Press, 2008), 7.

11. Amy Kaplan and Donald Pease, eds., *Cultures of United States Imperialism* (Durham, N.C.: Duke University Press, 1993); Andy Doolen, *Fugitive Empire: Locating Early American Imperialism* (Minneapolis: University of Minnesota Press, 2005); David Kazanjian, *The Colonizing Trick: National Culture and Imperial Citizenship in America* (Minneapolis: University of Minnesota Press, 2003); John Carlos Rowe, *Literary Culture and U.S. Imperialism: from the Revolution to World War II* (New York: Oxford University Press, 2000); and Laura Wexler, *Tender Violence: Domestic Visions in an Age of U.S. Imperialism* (Chapel Hill: University of North Carolina Press, 2000).

12. Claudia Sadowski-Smith, *Border Fictions: Globalization, Empire, and Writing at the Boundaries of the United States* (Charlottesville: University of Virginia Press, 2008), 7.

13. Sandhya Shukla and Heidi Tinsman, "Introduction: Across the Americas," in *Imagining Our Americas: Towards a Transnational Frame*, ed. Sandhya Shukla and Heidi Tinsman (Durham, N.C.: Duke University Press, 2007), 12.

14. Caroline Levander and Robert S. Levine, "Introduction: Essays Beyond the Nation," in *Hemispheric American Studies*, ed. Caroline Levander and Robert S. Levine (New Brunswick, N.J.: Rutgers University Press, 2008), 7.

15. Paul Giles, "The Deterritorialization of American Literature," in *Shades of the Planet: American Literature as World Literature*, ed. Wai Chi Dimock and Lawrence Buell (Princeton, N.J.: Princeton University Press, 2007), 57.

16. Vijay Prashad, *Everybody Was Kung Fu Fighting: Afro-Asian Connections and the Myth of Cultural Purity* (Boston: Beacon, 2001), 48.

17. Michelle Stephens, "Uprooted Bodies: Indigenous Subjects and Colonial Discourses in Atlantic American Studies," in *Imagining Our Americas: Towards a Transnational Frame*, ed. Sandhya Shukla and Heidi Tinsman (Durham, N.C.: Duke University Press, 2007), 191.

18. A number of studies examine relationships of identification and collaboration linking African Americans and other U.S. racial minorities to colonized and enslaved peoples of the Caribbean, Asia, Africa, and Central and South America in the nineteenth and twentieth centuries. Paul Gilroy's *The Black Atlantic: Modernity and Double Consciousness* (Cambridge: Harvard University Press, 1993) inspired studies of transatlantic and Caribbean black political identities, including Ifeoma Kiddoe Nwankwo, *Black Cosmopolitanism: Racial Consciousness and Transnational Identity in the Nineteenth-Century Americas* (Philadelphia: University of Pennsylvania, 2005); Michelle Ann Stephens, *Black Empire: The Masculine Global Imaginary of Caribbean Intellectuals in the United States, 1914–1962* (Durham, N.C.: Duke University Press, 2005); and David Luis-Brown, *Waves of Decolonization: Discourses of Race and Hemispheric Citizenship in Cuba, Mexico, and the United States* (Durham, N.C.: Duke University Press, 2008). Studies of Afro-Asian anticolonial coalitions include Bill V. Mullins, *Afro-Orientalism* (Minneapolis: University of Minnesota Press, 2004); Prashad, *Everybody Was Kung Fu Fighting*; and Crystal S. Anderson, "When *Were* We Colored? Blacks, Asians and Racial Discourse," in *Blacks and Asians: Crossings, Conflict, and Commonality*, ed. Hazel M. McFerson (Durham, N.C.: Carolina Academic Press, 2006), 59–77.

19. Nwankwo, *Black Cosmopolitanism*, 7

20. Homi K. Bhabha, "Of Mimicry and Man," *October* 28, no. 1 (1984), 125–33.

21. On the importance of recognizing the enduring power of nation in global social identities, power structures, and social movements, see Peter Fritzche, "Global History and Bounded Subjects: A Response to Thomas Bender," *American Literary History* 18, no. 2 (2006), 283–87.

22. Ann Laura Stoler, "Tense and Tender Ties: The Politics of Comparison in North American History," *Journal of American History* 88 (December 2001), 862; emphasis in original. My approach is also influenced by the historical scholarship of Paul A. Kramer, who echoes Stoler's call in his book, *The Blood of Government: Race, Empire, the United States, and the Philippines* (Chapel Hill: University of North Carolina Press, 2006). Kramer recommends studying rather than making colonial comparisons as a way to access previous eras' scales of global thinking, explaining that "when historians establish 'connections' based on perceived structural similarities, they risk obstructing the actual ways that historical actors compared, contrasted, and connected their own and other societies, substituting for these criteria ones that are artifacts of the contemporary sociology of knowledge" (368).

23. Stephens, "Uprooted Bodies," 191.

24. Kramer, *Blood of Government,* 19.

25. Rowe, *Literary Culture and U. S. Imperialism,* 8.

26. Richard Drinnon, *Facing West: The Metaphysics of Indian Hating and Empire Building* (Minneapolis: University of Minnesota Press, 1980), xiii, xvi.

27. Works exploring interactions and comparisons among racializations or meztizos or mulattos in a hemispheric context include Anna Brickhouse, *Transamerican Literary Relations and the Nineteenth-Century Public Sphere* (Cambridge: Cambridge University Press, 2004), 37–83; Suzanne Bost, *Mulattas and Mestizas: Representing Mixed Identities in the Americas, 1850–2000* (Athens: University of Georgia Press, 2003); and Debra J. Rosenthal, *Race Mixture in Nineteenth-Century U.S. and Spanish American Fictions: Gender, Culture and Nation Building* (Chapel Hill: University of North Carolina Press, 2004).

28. Eric T. L. Love argues for the discrete functioning of race and empire in *Race over Empire: Racism and Imperialism, 1865–1900* (Chapel Hill: University of North Carolina Press, 2004), xi, 6. I address Love's argument directly in chapter 1.

29. For example, Brent Edward Hayes, *The Practice of Diaspora: Literature, Translation, and the Rise of Black Internationalism* (Cambridge: Harvard University Press, 2003), 1–2; Luis-Brown, *Waves of Decolonization,* 1–4; Kramer, *Blood of Government,* 13–15; Nwankwo, *Black Cosmopolitanism,* 18; and Heike Raphael-Hernandez and Shannon Steen, eds., introduction to *AfroAsian Encounters: Culture, History, Politics* (New York: New York University Press, 2006), 1.

30. Eric J. Sundquist, *To Wake the Nations: Race and the Making of American Literature* (Cambridge, Mass.: Belknap, 1993), 547.

31. W. E. B. Du Bois, "The Present Outlook for the Dark Races of Mankind," in *The Oxford W. E. B. Du Bois Reader,* ed. Eric J. Sundquist (New York: Oxford University Press, 1996), 47. Subsequent page citations appear parenthetically in the text.

32. Kramer, *Blood of Government,* 13.

33. Nancy Leys Stephen and Sander Gilman, "Appropriating the Idioms of Science: The Rejection of Scientific Rationalism," in *The Bounds of Race: Perspectives on Hegemony and Resistance,* ed. Dominick LaCapra (Ithaca, N.Y.: Cornell University Press, 1991), 92. Anthony Appiah calls this strategy "the antithesis in the classic dialectic reaction to prejudice" because Du Bois's anti-racist strategy insists on valuable racial differences instead of racial equality (Anthony Appiah, "The Uncompleted Argument: Du Bois and the Illusion of Race," *Critical Inquiry* 12 [Autumn 1985], 25).

34. W. E. B. Du Bois, "The Conservation of Races," in *The Oxford W. E. B. Du Bois Reader,* ed. Eric J. Sundquist (New York: Oxford University Press, 1996), 40. Subsequent page citations appear parenthetically in the text.

35. Appiah, "Uncompleted Argument," 28.

36. For one, see Rachel Adams, "The Worlding of American Studies," *American Quarterly* 53, no. 4 (2001), 723–24.

37. Kaplan made a version of this argument in an essay published in the premier journal for historians of U.S. foreign policy: "Commentary: Domesticating Foreign Policy," *Diplomatic History* 18, no. 1 (1994), 97–105. She argues for extending this extradisciplinary audience by articulating a version of American studies that can engage with policy efforts by administrative entities such as the U.S. State Department in "Violent Belongings and the Question of Empire Today: Presidential Address to the American Studies Association, October 17, 2003," *American Quarterly* 56, no. 1 (2004), 11.

38. This is the case in Sandhya Shukla and Heidi Tinsman's interdisciplinary anthology *Imagining Our Americas,* which brings together essays from scholars in epidemiology, literature, and political science, all showing transnational and colonial or postcolonial relations among the Americas, but none attempting to gauge the importance of literature for political science and epidemiology or of medical and historical evidence for literary study.

PART I

1. In *The Life of Rudyard Kipling* (Garden City, N.Y.: Doubleday, 1955), Kipling's biographer C. E. Carrington briefly mischaracterizes the poem's reception in the United States as hostile, describing only the opinions of selected elites and intellectuals such as Henry James and the *Nation*'s E. L. Godkin (408–9). Carrington uses his account of these critics' distaste for the poem as evidence that widespread anti-imperialist sentiment in the United States permanently hurt Kipling's literary reputation there, a point that I contest. Thomas F. Gossett's *Race: The History of an Idea in America* (New York: Schocken, 1973 [1963]) is an exception to the tendency to mischaracterize the poem's readership. Gossett's brief discussion of the poem's reception (332–38) provided a starting point for my research for this chapter, as did Jim Zwick's excellent collection of American responses to the poem on Boondocks.net. Susan K. Harris, "Kipling's 'White Man's Burden' and the British Newspaper Context, 1898-9," *Comparative American Studies* 5, no. 3 (2007), 243–63, focuses on reception among pro-imperialist newspapers in London, which almost univocally interpreted the poem as recommending Anglo-Saxon imperial partnership. In contrast to Harris, who sees a "symbiotic relationship" (245) between the ideologies promoted by the poem and those promoted by its British commentators and reviewers, I demonstrate that a wide-ranging study of reception in the United States shows the contradictory sweep of American thinking about race and empire and calls the meaning of the poem itself into question.

2. Charles A. Johanningsmeier estimates the readership of a typical piece distributed through the McClure's newspaper syndicate by noting that "McClure

syndicated individual works to anywhere from 20 to 40 newspapers. . . . If each of the papers with whom McClure . . . dealt had an average circulation of 30,000 (a low estimate, given that a large paper such as the *Boston Globe* often sold 100,000 copies and more of each edition), individual fictions had at the very least a potential readership of 600,000; actual readership, however, most certainly numbered in the millions" (Charles A. Johanningsmeier, *Fiction and the American Literary Marketplace: The Role of Newspaper Syndicates in America, 1860-1900* [Cambridge University Press, 1997], 202).

3. Evidence of the sudden burst of publications devoted to Kipling in 1899 includes the *Kipling Handbook,* a supplement put out by the *San Francisco Examiner* (March 5, 1899); Will M. Clemens, *A Ken of Kipling: Being a Biographical Sketch of Rudyard Kipling* (New York: New Amsterdam, 1899); Charles Eliot Norton, *Rudyard Kipling: A Biographical Sketch* (New York: Doubleday and McClure, 1899), which reproduced in pamphlet form an essay that previously appeared in *McClure's Magazine;* and the short run of a journal titled *A Kipling Notebook,* which was later that year bound and published under the title *Kiplingiana: Biographical and Bibliographical Notes anent Rudyard Kipling* (New York: M.F. Mansfield and A. Wessels, 1899). The quoted phrase "The Kipling Boom" comes from an article with that title in *A Kipling Notebook* 8 (September 1899), 128–30.

4. "Kipling in America," *Review of Reviews* 19 (April 1899), 421.

5. "Kipling (Limited)," *Kipling Notebook* 8 (September 1899), 118.

6. E. S. Martin, "This Busy World," *Harper's Weekly* 185 (February 25, 1899), 185. Parodies of the poem proliferated in Britain as well (David Gilmour, *The Long Congressional: The Imperial Life of Rudyard Kipling* [New York: Farrar, Straus and Giroux, 2002], 128), and some British parodies such as Henry Labouchere's "The Brown Man's Burden" were widely reprinted in American newspapers. However, not all parodies were oppositional; they ranged from serious criticisms of imperialism to comedic reinventions of the "white man's burden" as the difficult trial of having a visit from one's in-laws. A poem in one newspaper parodies the phenomenon of parodying Kipling:

> Take up "The White Man's Burden,"
> Then put it down again;
> Don't touch it with your pencil,
> Typewriter or your pen"

(Hobart, "Lagniappe," *New Oreans Daily Picayune* [February 19, 1899], 6)

7. Bertrand Shadwell, "The Gospel of Force," in *Republic or Empire: The Philippine Question,* ed. William Jennings Bryan (Chicago: Independence, 1899): 713–15.

8. Robert Underwood Johnson, "The White Man's Burden," *Current Literature* 31 (July 1901), 64.

9. Ernest Crosby, "The Real 'White Man's Burden,'" *Swords and Ploughshares* (New York: Funk and Wagnalls, 1906 [1902]), 33–35.

10. Albert K. Weinberg, *Manifest Destiny: A Study of Nationalist Exceptionalism in American History* (Gloucester, Mass.: Peter Smith, 1958 [1935]), 71.

11. Jabez T. Sunderland, "The Religion of Rudyard Kipling," *New England Magazine* 20 (July 1899), 610.

CHAPTER 1

1. "Chappy," *Milwaukee Journal* (February 18, 1899), 6.

2. For example, Andrew Hagiioannu, *The Man Who Would Be Kipling: The Colonial Fiction and the Frontiers of Exile* (London: Palgrave, 2003), interprets the poem primarily to highlight its similarities with other works (86), as does Harry Ricketts, *The Unforgiving Minute: A Life of Rudyard Kipling* (London: Chatto and Windus, 1999), 235. Vasant Shahane's book-length study of Kipling's poetry and prose, *Rudyard Kipling: Activist and Artist* (Carbondale: Southern Illinois University Press, 1973), does not mention the poem at all, while Ann Parry, *The Poetry of Rudyard Kipling: Rousing the Nation* (Buckingham: Open University Press, 1992) refers to it only briefly as a familiar, obvious case not meriting lengthy analysis.

3. "Chappy," 6.

4. This perception of Kipling's influence on U.S. foreign policy is found in Albert K. Weinberg, *Manifest Destiny: A Study of Nationalist Expansionism in American History* (Gloucester, Mass.: Peter Smith, 1958 [1935]), 301; and Thomas F. Gossett, *Race: The History of an American Idea* (New York: Schocken, 1973), 302. In recent decades the poem has also received renewed attention as an early precedent of neoliberal efforts to expand global democracy with U.S. military power. For example, John Bellamy Foster, Harry Magdoff, and Robert W. McChesney, "Kipling, 'The White Man's Burden,' and U.S. Imperialism," in *Pox Americana: Exposing the American Empire,* ed. John Bellamy Foster (New York: Monthly Review Press, 2004), 12–21; and Rahul Mahajan, *The New Crusade: America's War on Terrorism* (New York: Monthly Review Press, 2002), 99–100.

5. In "Pairing Empires: Britain and the United States, 1857–1947," Paul Kramer and John Plotz use the poem to introduce the comparative approaches taken in their special issue of *Journal of Colonialism and Colonial History* 2, no. 1 (2001). See also Victor Bascara's notion of "unburdening empire" as a play on Kipling's cloaking of imperial self-interest in *Model-Minority Imperialism* (Minneapolis: University of Minnesota Press, 2006), xxxiii.

6. The location of meaning in a literary work is the theoretical question behind reception study, with antifoundationalists such as Stanley Fish contending that the text itself has no power to constrain meaning and that, instead, the assumptions, practices, and expectations of "interpretive communities" create meanings that readers construct rather than find. In my reading, the text does constrain the reader's interpretation, insofar as certain ambiguities in Kipling's

language evoked controversies and anxieties in response to the poem. Furthermore, in my reading the poem also has the determinative power to jar readers' interpretive assumptions by crossing into the political sphere of foreign policy and ethnology in ways that readers of the day found unfamiliar, thereby altering audiences' "horizons of expectation" through its impact. For example, see James L. Machor, introduction to *Reception Study: From Literary Theory to Cultural Studies,* ed. James L. Machor and Philip Goldstein (New York: Routledge, 2001), ix–xvii; Stanley Fish, *Is There a Text in This Class? The Authority of Interpretive Communities* (Cambridge: Harvard University Press, 1980); and Hans Robert Jauss, *Toward an Aesthetic of Reception,* trans. Timothy Bahti (Minneapolis: University of Minnesota Press, 1982), 20–45.

7. Frederick Laurence Knowles, *A Kipling Primer* (Boston: Brown, 1899), 187; Walter L. Shelden, *Two Sides of Kipling* (Philadelphia: S. Burns Weston, 1900), 129; "Rudyard Kipling," *Outlook* 61 (March 4, 1899), 490; and Paul Elmer More, "The Seven Seas and the Rubáiyát," *Atlantic Monthly* 84 (December 1899), 801. See also W. J. Peddicord, *Rudyard Reviewed* (Portland, Ore.: Marsh, 1900), a self-published pamphlet complaining that the widespread tendency to read Kipling's "The White Man's Burden" as policy rather than poetry hides its aesthetic failures.

8. Quoted in C. E. Carrington, *The Life of Rudyard Kipling* (Garden City, N.Y.: Doubleday, 1955), 216–17.

9. Essays in Machor and Goldstein, *Reception Study,* demonstrate this range.

10. "This White Man's Burden," *Atchison Daily Globe* (February 10, 1899), 4.

11. Numbers in parentheses in the text are poetry line numbers. Because of my emphasis on reception, I am quoting the version of Kipling's poem that appeared in *McClure's* ("The White Man's Burden," *McClure's Magazine* 12, no. 4 [February 1899], 1–2), not the definitive version based on later revisions. Kipling made a number of revisions to the poem after its first publication in the United States, mostly in punctuation or capitalization, but a few in wording. For the later revision, see *Rudyard Kipling's Verse: Definitive Edition* (London: Hodder and Stoughton, 1949), 323–34.

12. Rudyard Kipling, *The Letters of Rudyard Kipling,* vol. 2, ed. Thomas Pinney (Ames: University of Iowa Press, 1990), 346–47. See also Kipling's letters to Charles Roswell Bacon and Theodore Roosevelt reprinted in the same volume, 344–45, 350.

13. Ashley Dawson and Malini Johar Schueller, eds., *Exceptional State: Contemporary U.S. Culture and the New Imperialism* (Durham, N.C.: Duke University Press, 2007), 3.

14. Kipling, *Letters,* 347.

15. Hamlin Garland, *Roadside Meetings* (St. Clair Shores, Mich: Scholarly Press, 1977 [1930]), 410, 411.

16. Kipling, *Letters*, 347.

17. Gail Bederman, *Manliness and Civilization: A Cultural History of Gender and Race in the United States, 1880–1917* (Chicago: University of Chicago Press, 1995).

18. Kristen Hogansen, *Fighting for American Manhood* (New Haven, Conn.: Yale University Press, 1998); and Amy Kaplan, *The Anarchy of American Empire* (Cambridge: Harvard University Press, 2002).

19. Walter L. Sheldon likens Kipling's poetry to Roosevelt's "Strenuous Life" in *Two Sides of Kipling*, 142. Here I am engaging with Bradley Deane's interpretation of the poem in "Rethinking Race and Masculinity in Kipling's Verse," Kipling Conference 2007, University of Kent (Canterbury, U.K.), September 7, 2007. In one of the more nuanced readings of "The White Man's Burden," Deane convincingly makes the case that more than a desire to elevate whiteness, the desire to recommend an abject form of martyred manhood structures Kipling's imperialist thought and poetry. But the readiness with which whiteness became the main concern of the poem's readers in the United States only sharpens Deane's point about generations of readers missing one of Kipling's major obsessions. I am arguing that readers interpreted the poem to reflect primarily on whiteness because of both their culture's intense anxieties surrounding the issue and Kipling's own oblique invocation of the idea of racial maturation, a concept intertwined with evolutionary discourses about racial progress and degeneracy.

20. Ann Parry, *The Poetry of Rudyard Kipling: Rousing the Nation* (Buckingham: Open University Press, 1992), 87; and Martin Seymour-Smith, *Rudyard Kipling* (New York: St. Martin's, 1989), 283.

21. Carrington, *Life of Rudyard Kipling*, 334. See also Alice Moore, *Kipling and the White Man's Burden* (London: Faber and Faber, 1969), who explains that "it was easy enough to misunderstand Kipling's use of the words 'white man' by which he himself meant a man of right feeling and civilized moral standards, whatever his colour" (51), and David Gilmour, *The Long Congressional: The Imperial Life of Rudyard Kipling* (New York: Farrar, Straus Giroux, 2002), 128.

22. P. J. Keating, *Kipling the Poet* (London: Seeker and Warburg, 1994), 87; John McBratney, *Imperial Subjects, Imperial Spaces: Rudyard Kipling's Fiction of the Native Born* (Columbus: Ohio State University Press, 2002) argues that Kipling's own sense of whiteness was complicated by his status as an Indian-born creole, which gave him a sense of ethnic difference that made him, in part, a "subtle rebel against a doctrine of white supremacy" (12–13). Readers in the United States did not call Kipling's own whiteness into question, but his poem's reception there reveals that the poem spotlighted a set of conflicting standards and definitions of whiteness different from those that concerned the Indo-British Kipling.

23. Henry Austin, "The Kipling Hysteria," *Dial* 310 (May 16, 1899), 327.

24. William Ferguson, "Effect of His Illness on the Book Market," in *Kipling Handbook* (San Francisco: San Francisco Examiner, 1899), 30. The connection

between Kipling's illness and his sudden surge in popularity was widely remarked; for example, Austin, "Kipling Hysteria." Also contributing to Kipling's popularity in the United States might have been his marriage to an American and his residence for several years in Vermont.

25. Stuart Anderson, *Race and Rapproachement: Anglo-Saxonism and Anglo-American Relations, 1895–1904* (East Brunswick, N.J.: Associated University Presses, 1981), discusses and gives examples of the equation of Kipling's phrase "white man's burden" with Anglo-Saxonism (127). See also Gossett, *Race,* 332–38.

26. "Rudyard Kipling," *Living Age* 220 (March 1899), 786.

27. Quoted in "Is Kipling on the Downward Track?" *Literary Digest* 19 (July 15, 1899), 71.

28. Sunderland, "Religion of Rudyard Kipling," 604; and Johnson Brigham, "Kipling as a World Prophet," *Optimist* 1 (September 1900), 28.

29. Helen Knuth, "The Climax of American Anglo-Saxonism, 1898–1905," Ph.D. dissertation, University of Illinois, Evanston, 1958 (Ann Arbor: University Microfilms, 1970). On the emergence of Anglo-Saxonism and U.S. imperialism in the Mexican American War, see Reginald Horsman, *Race and Manifest Destiny* (Cambridge: Harvard University Press, 1981). On Anglo-Saxonism's rise and fall in policy circles at the turn of the century, see Anderson *Race and Rapproachement;* Gossett, *Race,* 324–28; and Paul A. Kramer, "Empires, Exceptions, and Anglo-Saxons," in *The American Colonial State in the Philippines: Global Perspectives,* ed. Julian Go and Anne L. Foster (Durham, N.C.: Duke University Press, 2003), 43–91.

30. William Dean Howells, "The Laureate of the Larger England," *McClure's Magazine* 8 (March 1897), 453.

31. William Dean Howells, "The New Poetry," *North American Review* 168 (May 1899), 583.

32. Peddicord, *Rudyard Reviewed,* 110–11.

33. U.S. Congress, *Congressional Record,* 55th Congress, Third Session, Vol. 32 (Washington, D.C.: Government Printing Office, 1899), 1531, 1532.

34. On racism as an anti-imperialist motivation in these senate debates, see Christopher Lasch, *The World of Nations: Reflections on American History, Politics, and Culture* (New York: Knopf, 1973), 74.

35. U.S. Congress, *Congressional Record,* 55th Congress, Third Session, 1532.

36. I observed this phenomenon in honors courses taught in 2003–2005 at the University of Minnesota–Morris. Undertaking this exercise during the U.S. invasion and occupation of Iraq no doubt also influenced my students' interpretations.

37. "A Talk with Howells," *Milwaukee Sentinel* (April 30, 1899), 3.

38. Howells, "New Poetry," 538.

39. Editorial, "The White Man's Burden," *San Francisco Bulletin* (February 7, 1899).

40. Eric T. L. Love, *Race over Empire: Racism and Imperialism, 1865–1900* (Chapel Hill: University of North Carolina Press, 2004), xi, 6.

41. Ibid., 6.

42. On this chronology, see Carrington, *Life of Rudyard Kipling,* 217.

43. While Love does not present literary evidence for his conclusion that the poem contains "too much" irony and cynicism, the poem is treated as though such meaning is contained in it before its contact with readers.

44. Editorial, "White Man's Burden," 1.

45. Sunderland, "Religion of Rudyard Kipling," 609.

46. David Starr Jordan, *Imperial Democracy* (New York: Appleton, 1899), 106, 96, 171.

47. "The Black Man's Burden," *Harper's Weekly* 42 (February 18, 1899), 182.

48. Anna Manning Comfort, "Home Burdens of Uncle Sam," *Public* 2 (May 13, 1899), 14.

49. Alice Smith-Travers, "The White Man's Burden," *Indianapolis Freeman* (March 4, 1899), 3. In *The Signifying Monkey: A Theory of Afro-American Literary Criticism* (New York: Oxford University Press, 1988), Henry Louis Gates quotes T. Thomas Fortune's "The Black Man's Burden":

> What is the Black Man's Burden
> Ye Gentile parasites
> Who crush and rob your brother
> Of his manhood and his rights?

Gates considers this to be a paradigmatic example of African American signifyin(g), but the similarity of Fortune's verse to this broad strand of Kipling parody penned by whites and blacks raises the question of whether and how to differentiate black and white oppositional parody (103). Focusing on the similarities, I see both as part of a broader cultural response to the problem of calibrating race and nation in envisioning a global role for the United States.

50. In *Sitting in Darkness: New South Fiction, Education, and the Rise of Jim Crow Colonialism, 1865–1920* (Jackson: University of Mississippi, 2008), Peter Schmidt interprets this cartoon as a sincere statement about the necessity of operating without the consent of the governed in light of obvious racial inferiority (7–9). Schmidt points to *Puck's* pro-McKinley bias to support his reading, but I read the cartoon as a more ambiguous satire of U.S. imperial mission, despite the magazine's and cartoonist Louis Dalrymple's usual politics.

51. Susan Gillman, *Blood Talk: American Race Melodrama and the Culture of the Occult* (Chicago: University of Chicago 2003), 102.

52. Peter MacQueen, "When Will the War Cease?" *Arena* 20 (May 1899), 702.

53. Willard B. Gatewood, *Black Americans and the White Man's Burden, 1898–1903* (Urbana: University of Illinois Press, 1975).

54. Bruce Grit, "Why Talk of the White Man's Burden?" *Washington (D.C.) Colored American* (February 25, 1899), 1.

55. Peter Dunne Finley, *Mr. Dooley in the Hearts of His Countrymen* (New York: Greenwood, 1969), 225.

56. Quoted in Elmer Ellis, *Mr. Dooley's America: A Life of Finley Peter Dunne* (New York: Knopf, 1941), 146–47.

57. On Roosevelt's representation of African American soldiers in *The Rough Riders*, see Kaplan, *Anarchy of Empire*, 125–42. I call Roosevelt's representations of the black soldiers notorious because numerous angry rebuttals appeared in the black press; Willard B. Gatewood includes examples of these in *Smoked Yankees and the Struggle for Empire: Letters from Negro Soldiers, 1898–1902* (Urbana: University of Illinois Press, 1971), 92–97.

58. J. D. O'Connell, "'Anglo-Saxon' Humbug," *New York Irish World and American Liberator* (April 29, 1899), 1.

59. Jacobson, *Whiteness of a Different Color*, 13–14.

60. "Rudyard Kipling," *Living Age* 220 (March 1899), 787.

61. See also More, "The Seven Seas and the Rubáiyát," 801–2.

62. Henry C. Ide, "The Imbroglio in Samoa," *North American Review* 168 (June 1899), 687.

63. Anderson, *Race and Rapprochement*, 175–76.

64. Kramer, "Empires, Exceptions, and Anglo-Saxons," 70.

65. Advertisement, *Boston Daily Advertiser* 55 (March 6, 1899), 1.

CHAPTER 2

1. *Bookman* began listing *The Leopard's Spots* as one of ten "top sellers" around the country in its sales report for the month of March and continued to do so monthly until the middle of 1903 (*Bookman* 15 [May 1902], 298). See also Maxwell Bloomfield "Dixon's 'The Leopard's Spots': A Study in Popular Racism" *American Quarterly* 16.3 (1964), 399.

2. Scott Romine, "Things Fall Apart: The Postcolonial Condition of *Red Rock* and *The Leopard's Spots*," in *Look Away: The U.S. South in New World Studies*, ed. John Smith and Deborah Cohn (Durham, N.C.: Duke University Press, 2004), 129.

3. Sandra Gunning, *Race, Rape and Lynching: The Red Record of American Literature, 1890–1912* (New York: Oxford University Press, 1996), 28.

4. Kim Magowan, "Coming between the 'Black Beast' and the 'White Virgin': The Pressures of Liminality in Thomas Dixon," *Studies in American Fiction* 27, no. 1 (1999), 4.

5. Susan Gillman, *Blood Talk: American Race Melodrama and the Culture of the Occult* (Chicago: University of Chicago 2003), 112.

6. In *Our America: Nativism, Modernism, and Pluralism* (Durham, N.C.: Duke University Press, 1995), Walter Benn Michaels calls *The Leopard's Spots* an

example of "the major anti-imperialist literature of the turn of the century" (17), a claim that is profoundly weakened when readers pay any attention to Dixon's own imperialist leanings in his political life and writing. Michaels errs by not observing that the defense of the south against colonizing Northern conquerors after the Civil War was for Dixon a necessary precondition for the fantasy driving *The Leopard's Spot's*: a White Man's Burden carried out on a global scale. As Scott Romine has argued, "To Michael's assertion that *The Leopard's Spots* is an anti-imperial novel, one must add the crucial qualification that Dixon sanctions normative imperialism, in contrast to the reverse colonization of Reconstruction, as a cultural imperative" ("Things Fall Apart," 193). Dixon's figuratively postcolonial South is represented in his novel as a model for burgeoning white nationalism poised to join in a wider race mission of global proportions. A similar argument is elaborated in Harilaos Stecopoulos, *Reconstructing the World: Southern Fictions and U.S. Imperialisms, 1898–1976* (Ithaca, N.Y.: Cornell University Press, 2008), 19–38.

7. Stecopoulos, *Reconstructing the World,* 28.

8. Thomas Dixon, *The Leopard's Spots: A Romance of the White Man's Burden, 1865–1900* (Ridgewood, N.J.: Gregg, 1967), 200. Subsequent page citations appear parenthetically in the text.

9. In "'One of the Meanest Books': Thomas Dixon Jr. and *The Leopard's Spots,*" *North Carolina Literary Review* 2, no. 1 (1994), Glenda Gilmore argues that Dixon's scientific racism was based on the Teutonic germ theory of Herbert Baxter Adams, a respected professor of Dixon's in his days as a young graduate student at Johns Hopkins. Germ theory interpreted history through race, contending that a sort of genetic capacity of self-government had spread from the forests of Germany to Britain and America (92). However, while this idea is not irreconcilable with the novel's racial theories, Dixon does not specifically include it there. Germ theory was out of favor by the 1890s, and in its place Dixon adapts more modern understandings of evolutionary racial science in his protagonist's ideas.

10. U.S. Congress, *Congressional Record,* 55th Congress, Third Session, Vol. 32 (Washington, D.C.: Government Printing Office, 1899), 1424.

11. Ibid., 1423.

12. Editorial, "The White Man's Duty," *American Missionary* 53 (July 1899), 51.

13. Mrs. Jefferson Davis, "The White Man's Problem: Why We Do Not Want the Philippines," *Arena* 23 (January 1900), 2.

14. Charles Minor Blackford, "The White Man's Problem: Negro Education," *Arena* 23 (January 1900), 26–27.

15. On Dixon and the Social Gospel movement, see W. Fitzhugh Brundage, "Thomas Dixon: American Proteus," in *Thomas Dixon Jr. and the Birth of Modern America,* ed. Michele K. Gillespie and Randal L. Hall (Baton Rouge: Louisiana State University Press, 2006), 26–27. On Dixon's similarities with Strong, see David Stricklin, "'Ours Is a Century of Light': Dixon's Strange Consistency" in the same volume, 112.

16. Raymond Cook, *Thomas Dixon* (New York: Twayne, 1974), 46.

17. Thomas Dixon, *Southern Horizons: The Autobiography of Thomas Dixon* (Alexandria, Va.: I. W. V. Publishing, 1984), 243–44.

18. Ibid., 244.

19. W. H. Johnson, "The Case of the Negro," *Dial* 35 (May 1903), 301.

20. W. H. Johnson, "The Ku Klux Klan in Fiction," *Critic* 46 (1905), 278.

21. Johnson, "Case of the Negro," 301.

22. Sutton Griggs makes this argument in an essay appended to the third edition of his 1905 novel, *The Hindered Hand, or the Reign of the Repressionist* (Nashville, Tenn.: Orion, 1905), 325, 326. The argument is made more implicitly in the novel itself, in a scene where characters converse about "the book of a rather conspicuous Southern man, who had set for himself the task of turning the entire Negro population out of America" (206).

23. Marcus Cunliffe, "Stephen Crane and the American Background of Maggie," *American Quarterly* 7, no. 1 (1955), 33.

24. Thomas Dixon, *The Failure of Protestantism in New York and Its Causes* (New York: Victor O. Stauss, 1896), 58–59.

25. Michael Rogin, *Ronald Reagan, the Movie and other Episodes on Political Demonology* (Berkeley: University of California Press, 1987), 194; and Bloomfield, "Dixon's 'The Leopard's Spots,'" 392.

26. Thomas Dixon, *Dixon's Sermons Delivered in the Grand Opera House, 1898–99* (New York: F. L. Bussey, 1899), 114.

27. Amy Kaplan, *The Anarchy of Empire* (Cambridge: Harvard University Press, 2002), 121–23; and Gillman, *Blood Talk*, 81, 106.

28. Michaels, *Our America*, 20.

29. Gillman, *Blood Talk*, 106–7.

30. B. O. Flower, "Books of the Day," *Arena* 28 (August 1902), 218.

31. Benjamin Kidd, *The Control of the Tropics* (New York: Macmillan, 1898), 53.

32. Dixon, *Dixon's Sermons*, 34.

33. Ibid., 29, 85.

PART II

1. William Huntington Wilson, "The Return of the Sergeant," *Harper's Weekly* (September 15, 1900), 871, 873.

2. Amy Kaplan, *The Anarchy of Empire* (Cambridge: Harvard University Press, 2002), 127.

3. Jim Cullen, "'I's a Man Now': Gender and African American Men," in *Divided Houses: Gender and the Civil War*, ed. Catherine Clinton and Nina Silber (New York: Oxford University Press, 1992), 76–96.

4. In 1902, the *CAM* was estimated to have a circulation of 17,840 readers, which places it well below *Harper's Weekly's* 150,000 readers but not far below the *Atlantic Monthly,* estimated at 25,000 readers. Circulation figures are from N. W. Ayer and Son's *American Newspaper Annual* (Philadelphia: N. W. Ayer and Son, 1903), 1435, 604.

5. On the magazine's sale, see Hannah Wallinger, *Pauline E. Hopkins: A Literary Biography* (Athens: University of Georgia Press, 2005), 79–86.

6. In "Diversity, Cosmopolitanism and the Emergence of the American Liberal Intelligentsia," *American Quarterly* 27, no. 2 (1975), David Hollinger describes this tension in cosmopolitan thought in the United States (135). Ross Posnock, *Color and Culture: Black Writers and the Making of the Modern Intellectual* (Cambridge: Harvard University Press, 1998), defines the cosmopolitanism of early black intellectuals such as W. E. B. Du Bois and Pauline Hopkins as one seeking to construct identity apart from racialized essentialisms and bodily categories, a goal claimed more recently by Paul Gilroy in *Against Race: Imagining Political Culture beyond the Color Line* (Cambridge, Mass.: Belknap, 2000), 15. See also Robert F. Reid-Pharr, "Cosmopolitan Afrocentric Mulatto Intellectual," *American Literary History* 13, no. 1 (2001), 169–79.

7. Ifeoma Kiddoe Nwankwo, *Black Cosmopolitanism: Racial Consciousness and Transnational Identity in the Nineteenth Century Americas* (Philadelphia: University of Pennsylvania Press, 2005), 7

8. Willard B. Gatewood, *Black Americans and the White Man's Burden, 1898–1903* (Urbana: University of Illinois Press, 1975), v–x, 11–12.

9. George P. Marks, *The Black Press Views Imperialism, 1898–1900* (New York: Arno, 1971), 172–73.

10. Kelly Miller, "The Effect of Imperialism upon the Negro Race," *Howard's American Magazine* 5 (October 1900), 90, 92.

11. In "The Varieties of Cosmopolitan Experience," Scott L. Malcolmson has observed that, in contrast to cosmopolitanism as a philosophical ideal, certain "actually existing cosmopolitanisms" have historically emerged from and contributed to religious and military expansion, as well as from the thinking of "more normal people, left and right, who look outside their situations for social or political models" (238–39). Malcolmson's essay appears in *Cosmopolitics: Thinking and Feeling beyond the Nation,* ed. Pheng Cheah and Bruce Robbins (Minneapolis: University of Minnesota Press, 1998). See also Walter D. Mignolo, "The Many Faces of Cosmo-Polis: Border Thinking and Critical Cosmopolitanism," *Public Culture* 12, no. 3 (2000), 721–48.

12. Mignolo, "Many Faces of Cosmo-Polis," 723.

13. The lines are from W. E. B. Du Bois's "The Riddle of the Sphinx," a response to Kipling's poem "The White Man's Burden" that appeared in his book *Darkwater: Voices from Within the Veil* (New York: Harcourt, Brace and Howe, 1920), 54, lines 60–61.

14. J. Shirley Shadrach, "Charles Winter Woods: From Bootblack to Professor," *CAM* 5, no. 5 (1902), 348.

15. Jennifer C. James, *A Freedom Bought with Blood: African American War Literature from the Civil War to World War II* (Chapel Hill: University of North Carolina Press, 2007), 129.

16. "Editorial and Publisher's Announcements," *CAM* 6, no. 1 (1902), 77.

17. Homi K. Bhabha, "Of Mimicry and Man," *October* 28, no. 1 (1984), 125–33.

18. Kaplan, *Anarchy of Empire*, 144.

CHAPTER 3

1. "Here and There," *CAM* 6, no. 10 (1903), 750.

2. Ibid., 744.

3. "Here and There," *CAM* 2, no. 3 (1901), 202, 199.

4. Helen Jun, "Black Orientalism: Nineteenth Century Narratives of Race and U.S. Citizenship," *American Quarterly* 58, no. 4 (2006), 1047–66. Jun's argument is a counterweight to Bill V. Mullin's definition of "Afro-Orientalism" as a discourse opposing colonialism and imperialism, one that at times shares certain features with Edward Said's conception of Orientalism but "primarily constitutes an independent critical trajectory of thought on the practice and ideological weight of Orientalism in the Western world" (Bill V.Mullin, *Afro-Orientalism* [Minneapolis: University of Minnesota Press, 2004], xv). For Jun, Mullins's model for theorizing Afro-Asian rhetorical encounters overestimates the power wielded by black writers to transcend the limiting terms of national belonging and thereby allows a teleological investment in "interracial solidarity" to overshadow the heterogeneous and historically contingent meanings that arise when Asia is used to negotiate "the limits and disappointments of black citizenship" (Jun, "Black Orientalism," 1050).

5. Susan Gillman, *Blood Talk: American Race Melodrama and the Culture of the Occult* (Chicago: University of Chicago 2003), 102, 98–113. See also Amy Kaplan, *The Anarchy of Empire* (Cambridge: Harvard University Press, 2002), 121–45; Kevin Gaines, "Black Americans' Racial Uplift Ideology as 'Civilizing Mission': Pauline E. Hopkins on Race and Imperialism," in *Cultures of United States Imperialism*, ed. Amy Kaplan and Donald Pease (Durham, N.C.: Duke University Press, 1993), 433–55; and Jennifer C. James, *A Freedom Bought with Blood: African American War Literature from the Civil War to World War II* (Chapel Hill: University of North Carolina Press, 2007), 125–66.

6. The novels of Sutton Griggs, including *Imperium in Imperio* (1899), *Unfettered* (1902), and *The Hindered Hand* (1905), currently comprise the known body of African American fictional responses to this conflict; for criticism on these, see Kaplan *Anarchy of Empire*, 123–24, and Gillman, *Blood Talk*, 73–116.

James (*Freedom Bought with Blood,* 128) adds Prince Hall Mason F. Grant Gilmore's *The Problem: A Military Novel* (1915) about black soldiers in Cuba and the Philippines to this list, despite its later publication date and composition during World War I. Analysis of Steward's writing is an important supplement to these, because while Griggs's novels explore insurgent black nationalism and the divided loyalties of race and nation at home, Steward explores African American authority to carry out and lead a U.S. civilizing mission. Most other fictional narratives studied in this context are authored by whites, such as Robert L. Bridgeman's *Loyal Traitors: A Story of Friendship for the Filipinos* (Boston: J. H. West, 1903), or they make only oblique reference to U.S. imperialism, such as Charles Chesnutt's *The Marrow of Tradition* (Boston: Houghton Mifflin, 1901).

7. Lists of Steward's writings are incomplete in even the few basic reference texts that mention Steward, such as Rayford Logan and Michael W. Winston, *Dictionary of American Negro Biography* (New York: W. W. Norton, 1982), 569, and Thomas Truxton Moeb, *Black Soldiers—Black Sailors—Black Ink: A Research Guide on African Americans in U.S. Military History* (Chesapeake Bay, Md.: Moebs, 1994), 166. Furthermore, Logan and Winston overlook Steward's fiction entirely while mentioning his other accomplishments.

8. My profile of T. G Steward is drawn from Alan K. Lamm, *Five Black Preachers in Army Blue* (Lewiston, N.Y.: Edwin Mellen, 1998); George Albert Miller, *Elevating the Race: Theophilus G. Steward, Black Theology, and the Making of an African American Civil Society, 1865–1924* (Knoxville: University of Tennessee Press, 2003); and William Seraile, *Voice of Dissent: Theophilus Gould Steward (1843–1924) and Black America* (Brooklyn: Carlson, 1991). Steward's *The Colored Regulars in the United States Army* (1904) is also the subject of one chapter in James, *Freedom Bought with Blood,* 123–66.

9. On Steward's postgraduate legal career, see the entry by Logan, in *Dictionary of American Negro Biography,* which draws its information from Harvard University publications intended to update alumni on the class of 1896. Examining university records, Logan reports that Steward did not receive honors at Harvard but took classes with some of Du Bois's professors, including George Herbert Palmer, George Santayana, and Albert Bushnell Hart. Steward's unsuccessful bid for state office is mentioned in passing in Constance A. Cunningham, "Homer S. Brown: The First Black Political Leader in Pittsburgh," *Journal of Negro History* 66, no. 4 (1981), 316. Information on Steward's applications to the State Department can be found in the National Archives, College Park, Md., State Department Series, "Applications and Recommendations for Appointment to the Consular and Diplomatic Services, 1901–24," A1 Entry 764, box 238. Other biographical sources on Steward include Willard B. Gatewood's *Smoked Yankees and the Struggle for Empire: Letters from Negro Soldiers, 1898–1902* (Urbana: University of Illinois Press, 1971), which reproduces a letter that appeared in the *Washington Bee* written by Steward describing his military service (294–96).

Based on the similarity of information contained, this letter appears to be the source for the *CAM*'s 1901 profile on Steward, suggesting that Steward sent the same letter from the Philippines to both publications. Gatewood cites the same letter in passing in *Black Americans and the White Man's Burden, 1898–1903* (Urbana: University of Illinois Press, 1975), 271.

10. The book review is the only one of Steward's publications that I do not discuss later in this essay: Frank Rudolph Steward, "Roosevelt and Haiti," *Voice of the Negro* 3, no. 6 (1906), 434–37.

11. Frank R. Steward, "Colored Officers," in *The Colored Regulars in the United States Army*, ed. T. G. Steward (New York: Arno, 1969 [1904]), 304.

12. Ibid., 305, 321, 306.

13. James, *Freedom Bought with Blood*, 129.

14. Kaplan, *Anarchy of Empire*, 122; Nina Silber, *The Romance of Reunion: Northerners and the South, 1865–1900* (Chapel Hill: University of North Carolina Press, 1993).

15. John Fox Jr., *Crittenden: A Kentucky Story of Love and War* (New York: Scribners, 1913 [1900]), 170, 212.

16. Ibid., 158–59, 165.

17. Ibid., 220, 223.

18. John T. Bramhall, "Red, Black and Yellow," *Overland Monthly* 37 (February 1901), 725.

19. Poultney Bigelow, *The Children of Nations: A Study of Colonization and Its Problems* (New York: McClure, Phillips, 1901), 105.

20. Major General Joseph Wheeler, introduction to *Under Fire with the Tenth U.S. Calvary*, by Herschel V. Cashin, Charles Alexander, William T. Anderson, Arthur M Brown, and Horace W. Bivins (New York: F. Tennyson Neely, 1899), xv.

21. Steward, "Colored Officers," 327. James mistakenly attributes this quotation to T. G. Steward, Frank's father, in her discussion of *The Colored Regulars* (*Freedom Bought with Blood*, 147–48). Her error underscores my point about Frank Steward being unknown even to specialists of African American war literature.

22. As I have argued elsewhere, this genre of romance explored the possibilities of modernity, global interconnection, and U.S. formal and informal empire through gendered stories of romance and friendship across the Pacific (Gretchen Murphy, "The New Woman and the New Pacific," *Prospects: An Annual of American Cultural Studies* 29 [2005], 395–418). While Long and Winnifred Eaton (the subject of chapter 5) dominated this genre at the turn of the century, other examples appear in Frances Little, *The Lady of the Decoration* (New York: Century, 1906), and Archibald Clavering Gunter, *My Japanese Prince* (New York: Home, 1904).

23. On the use of the outsider as first-person narrator in local color writing, see Tom Lutz, *Cosmopolitan Vistas: American Regionalism and Literary Value* (Ithaca, N.Y.: Cornell University Press, 2004), 30–31; and Brad Evans, *Before*

Cultures: The Ethnographic Imagination in American Literature, 1865–1920 (Chicago: University of Chicago Press, 2005), 11.

24. Nancy Glazener, *Reading for Realism: The History of a U.S. Literary Institution* (Durham, N.C.: Duke University Press, 1997), 191.

25. Stephanie Foote, *Regional Fictions: Culture and Identity in Nineteenth-Century American Literature* (Madison: University of Wisconsin Press, 2001), 11.

26. Amy Kaplan, "Nation, Region, Empire," in *The Columbia History of the American Novel,* ed. Emory Elliott (New York: Columbia University Press, 1991), 225.

27. Lisa Lowe discusses the importance of recognizing the heterogeneous constituencies and effects of Orientalism in *Critical Terrains: French and British Orientalisms* (Ithaca, N.Y.: Cornell University Press, 1991). On the variability of Orientalist binaries in turn of the century U.S. romances, see Murphy, "New Woman and the New Pacific."

28. For example, Kaplan, "Nation, Region, Empire," 251–52; Foote, *Regional Fictions,* 1–14; and Glazener, *Reading for Realism,* 193.

29. Lutz, *Cosmopolitan Vistas,* 30–31; Glazener, *Reading for Realism,* 193; and Kaplan, "Nation, Region, Empire," 256.

30. Nancy Glazener in *Reading for Realism* particularly identifies Pauline Hopkins as one such writer and the *CAM* as a publication engaged in this dialogue (11).

31. The complexity of moving "beyond race" in such writings is the impetus behind Gene Andrew Garrett's anthology of black imaginative writing about white characters, *African American Literature beyond Race: An Alternative Reader* (New York: New York University Press, 1996).

32. J. Saunders Redding, *To Make a Poet Black* (Chapel Hill: University of North Carolina, 1939), 61. In making this assumption, readers might also assume that the "Tales of Laguna" are partly autobiographical, which they may indeed be. The narrator and Steward have a number of similarities, including rank and station in the Philippines and education at Harvard. However, the style of characterization and dialogue and the dramatic plots clearly mark the works as efforts at fiction, not reportage or memoir.

33. Ross Posnock, *Color and Culture: Black Writers and the Making of the Modern Intellectual* (Cambridge: Harvard University Press, 1998), 3–9.

34. Ann duCille, *The Coupling Convention: Sex, Text, and Tradition in Black Women's Fiction* (New York: Oxford University Press, 1993), 54. See also Claudia Tate, *Psychoanalysis and Black Novels: Desire and the Protocols of Race* (New York: Oxford University Press, 1988), 24. DuCille proposes reading Kelly's characters as "*raceless*" (54), but I would argue that *de-raced* is the better term for the device that duCille and Tate thought they had found in Kelly's work, for it indicates that identification with blackness (or any overtly identified, and thus nondominant, racial identity) is being conjured up and suppressed rather than remaining merely unmarked as whiteness tends to be in writing by whites.

35. While I read Kelly as leaving whiteness unmarked, Holly Jackson in "Identifying Emma Dunham Kelly: Rethinking Race and Authorship," *PMLA* 122, no. 3 (2007), 728–41, argues convincingly that even when we assume that the characters in Kelly's novels are white, the works do not take race for granted; rather, they argue implicitly for an ethnic construction of whiteness that includes the Irish. In this way, to call her Irish characters white was a form of de-racing, of placing under erasure a mode of ethnic identity that Kelly wanted not to matter.

36. The story's sidestepping of race might seem like a form of literary "passing," an issue that probably mattered to Steward because of his family history. Steward descended from a family famous for its mixed race heritage: his father grew up in Gouldtown, New Jersey, which was founded in 1683 when Elizabeth Adams, the white granddaughter of Lord John Fenwick, married Benjamin Gould, a free African. The nine subsequent generations took great pride in this heritage and continued intermarrying with whites and light-skinned blacks. According to T. G. Steward's family history, *Gouldtown: A Very Remarkable Settlement of Ancient Date* (Philadelphia: J. B. Lippencott, 1913), they held themselves above the surrounding communities of darker-skinned African Americans. T. G. Steward was light enough in appearance that he was at one time encouraged to pass as Cuban in order to secure lodging in Brooklyn, New York, where he was serving as a pastor, and, according to his biographer, T. G. Steward struggled with issues of color throughout his life (William Seraile, *Voice of Dissent: Theophilus Gould Steward [1843–1924] and Black America* [Brooklyn: Carlson, 1991], 1–2, 59). It is possible that sidestepping his narrator's racial identity was one way that Frank Steward addressed this conflict in his own family's racial identity.

37. On the dialect writing and the reception of Dunbar's poetry, see Gene Andrew Jarrett, *Deans and Truants: Race and Realism in African American Literature* (Philadelphia: University of Pennsylvania Press, 2007), 1–51.

38. Frank R. Steward, "Starlik: A Tale of Laguna," *CAM* 6, no. 5 (1903), 387. Subsequent page references to this story are cited parenthetically in the text.

39. Richard Brodhead compares the relationship of Chesnutt's white narrator John with the generic white framing narrator of "Marse Chan" and other regionist writings, demonstrating how Chesnutt reveals and inverts the power relations of white narrator and black interlocutor (Richard Brodhead, *Cultures of Letters: Scenes of Reading and Writing in the United States* [Chicago: University of Chicago Press, 1993], 197–209). In *To Wake the Nations: Race and the Making of American Literature* (Cambridge: Harvard University Press, 1993), Eric Sundquist similarly argues that Chesnutt undercuts John's rational perception of the ex-slave Uncle Julius's tales of conjure and magic in order to "give a 'voice' to those who had been so misrepresented in the plantation tradition" (372, 359–88).

40. Frank R. Steward, "Pepe's Anting Anting," *CAM* 5 (September 1902), 360. Subsequent page references to this story are cited parenthetically in the text. A

familiar element of Filipino traditions, Anting-Antings are talismans that appear in several U.S. fictional works about the occupation of the Philippines. For example, in Charles E. Meyers's "The Anting-Anting of Maga," *Overland Monthly* 46 (March 1905), 301–5, American passengers on a steamship to Singapore listen to a tale of "Oriental superstitions" from an American war correspondent, in which a Filipino's "charm" necklace turns out to contain a pirate treasure map. A 1901 collection of Filipino war stories by "Sergeant Kayme" took its title, *Anting-Anting Stories and Other Strange Tales of the Filipinos,* from the charms, explaining that "no more curious fetich can be found in the history of folk lore. A button, a coin, a bit of paper with unintelligible words scribbled upon it, a bone, a stone, a garment, anything, almost—often a thing of no intrinsic value—any of these can be imagined to protect its possessor from physical harm in battle" ([Boston: Small, Maynard, 1901], vi). While outside the scope of my discussion here, the figure of the Anting-Anting more broadly in U.S. writing about the Philippines during this period invites further analysis as a particular strand of western fascination with the fetish.

41. Willard Gatewood describes this suspicion of divided African American loyalties in the Philippines, of which in at least one instance Filipino insurgents attempted to take advantage. A placard created by the insurgents and directed at the 24th infantry read, "It is without honor that you are spilling your costly blood. Your masters have thrown you into the most iniquitous fight with double purpose—to make you the instruments of their ambition and also your hard work will soon make the extinction of your race. Your friends, the Filipinos, give you this good warning" (quoted in Gatewood, *Black Americans and the White Man's Burden,* 287).

42. Stephen Bonsal, "The Negro Soldier in War and Peace," *North American Review* 186 (June 1907), 325.

43. Ann Laura Stoler, *Carnal Knowledge and Imperial Power: Race and Intimate in Colonial Rule* (Berkeley: University of California Press, 2002), 80. On the concept of interior frontiers, Stoler writes: "When coupled with the word *interior,* frontier carries the sense of internal distinctions within a territory (or empire). At the level of the individual, frontier marks the moral predicates by which a subject retains his or her national identity despite location outside of the national frontier and despite heterogeneity within the nation-state" (80). Through the racial markers of mixture surrounding Enriqueta, Steward invokes such racial heterogeneity within the United States, creating a potentially threatening breach of internal frontiers.

44. Following Wernor Sollors, recent criticism has reexamined the figure of the mulatta in American fiction to challenge the assumption voiced by Sterling Brown that mixed-race characters served accommodationist ends in fiction by endlessly repeating a stereotyped character who was simultaneously white enough to attract the sympathy of white readers and yet doomed to death as a

forbidding symbol of the tragic results of miscegenation. New approaches take note of varying meanings of mulattas and other mixed-race characters, paying attention to how they are often used to trouble rather than reify a black/white binary and its racist assumptions. I am arguing that Steward's use of the figure would fall in the latter category for its interrogation of white imperialist practices. See Sollors, *Neither Black nor White Yet Both: Thematic Explorations of Interracial Literature* (New York: Oxford University Press, 1997), 234.

45. New York Public Libraries, Schomburg Library, New York, Theophilus Gould Steward Papers, box 5, folder 2. T. G. Steward later cut this reference to Dona Victorina, perhaps to soften his criticism of Charleston, when he published the essay in *Fifty Years in the Gospel Ministry, 1864–1914* (Philadelphia: A.M.E. Book Concern, 1921), 345.

46. R. B. Lemus, "The Negro and the Philippines," *CAM* 6, no. 4 (1903), 315.

47. Pauline E. Hopkins, "Talma Gordon," in *Short Fiction by Black Women, 1900–1920*, ed. Elizabeth Ammons (New York: Oxford University Press, 1991), 50. Subsequent page references to this story are cited parenthetically in the text.

48. U.S. Congress, *Congressional Record,* 55th Congress, Third Session, Vol. 32 (Washington, D.C.: Government Printing Office, 1899), 923.

49. John Nickel, "Eugenics and the Fiction of Pauline Hopkins," in *Evolution and Eugenics in American Literature and Culture: Essays on Ideological Conflict and Complicity, 1880–1940,* ed. Lois A. Cuddy and Claire M. Roche (Lewisberg, Pa.: Bucknell University Press, 2003), 133–47. My reading here takes issue with Hazel Carby's argument in *Reconstructing Womanhood: The Emergence of the Afro-American Woman Novelist* (New York: Oxford University Press, 1987) that "Talma Gorden" is an anti-imperialist story (133–36), a point that she overstates in her otherwise successful effort to recover Hopkins as a political thinker with a global perspective.

50. Gertrude Atherton, *Senator North* (Ridgewood, N.J.: Gregg, 1967), 260.

51. The *CAM* identifies the author of "The Men Who Prey" as Capt. Frank R. *Stewart,* not Capt. Frank R. Steward, the stated author of the "Tales of Laguna." However, stylistic and thematic similarities present overwhelming evidence that the author is the same person. Some of the most obvious commonalities are the setting in Laguna; the protagonist holding the rank of captain; the presence of a character named Flora, who chews buyo, is described as a hag, and is a laundress; the liberal use of Spanish; and the subject of casual and erotic interaction among American soldiers and Filipinas in a garrisoned town. The *CAM* frequently altered frequent contributors' names in order to create the appearance of a more varied range of contents, but this inconsistency in spelling seems more likely to be a typographical error, as it is not an effective effort to conceal Steward's identity. In *Smoked Yankees,* Gatewood corrects a similarly obvious misspelling of Steward's name in a letter printed in the *Washington Bee* attributed to "Frank R. Stuart, Captain, 49th US Volunteer Infantry" (296). Similarly, Robert

Ewell Greene mislabels a photograph of Steward, calling him "Frank Rudolph Stewart," in *Black Defenders of America, 1775–1973: A Reference and Pictorial History* (Chicago: Johnson, 1974), 151.

52. Frank R. Stewart [*sic*], "The Men Who Prey," *CAM* 6, no.10 (1903), 720. Subsequent page references to this story are cited parenthetically in the text.

53. On African American voices in dialect and the politics of choosing or rejecting dialect, see Gavin Jones, *Strange Talk: The Politics of Dialect Literature in Gilded Age America*. (Berkeley: University of California Press, 1999), 98–101, 182–86.

54. "Conservation of Races," *Oxford W. E. B. Du Bois Reader,* ed. Eric J. Sundquist (New York: Oxford University Press, 1996), 43.

55. Norma Alarcón, "Traddutora, Traditora: A Paradigmatic Figure of Chicana Feminism," *Cultural Critique* 13 (Autumn 1989), 57–87.

CHAPTER 4

1. Pauline Hopkins, *The Magazine Novels of Pauline Hopkins* (New York: Oxford University Press, 1988), 509; emphasis added. Subsequent page references to this story are cited parenthetically in the text.

2. For example, Hannah Wallinger in *Pauline E. Hopkins: A Literary Biography* (Athens: University of Georgia Press, 2005) extensively interprets this passage as revealing Reuel's temporary perspective as a colonizer and explorer who has internalized dominant scientific and ideological assumptions of western mastery over the feminized African landscape (212–14). Wallinger made a similar point about this passage in an earlier essay, "Voyage into the Heart of Africa: Pauline Hopkins and *Of One Blood*" in *Black Imagination and the Middle Passage,* ed. Maria Diedrich, Henry Louis Gates Jr., and Carl Pedersen (New York: Oxford University Press, 1999), 208–9.

3. Nicholas Campbell, "Some Foreign Cities I Have Seen," *CAM* 6, no. 1 (1902), 4. Subsequent page references to this story are cited parenthetically in the text.

4. Interrogating the role of conventional tropes in Hopkins's writing has been a central theme in Hopkins criticism since Thomas J. Otten chose not to apologize for Hopkins's sensational plots and popular generic devices but, instead, to view them as self-conscious elements that her fiction analyzes for their power to shape or displace racial identity and revises to rewrite racial history ("Pauline Hopkins and the Hidden Self of Race," *English Literary History* 59, no. 1 [1992], 246–47). In *To Wake the Nations: Race and the Making of American Literature* (Cambridge: Harvard University Press, 1993), Eric Sundquist follows this suggestion by calling *Of One Blood* a "signifying inversion of the colonial adventure story widely popular in the work of H. Rider Haggard and others" (570). And in *Black Women Intellectuals: Strategies of Nation, Family, and Neighborhood*

in the Works of Pauline Hopkins, Jessie Fauset, and Marita Bonner (New York: Garland Press, 1998), Carol Allen interprets Reuel's travels more specifically as a revisionist rewriting of H. Rider Haggard's 1887 novel *She* (41–44).

5. John Gruesser, "Pauline Hopkins' *Of One Blood*: Creating an Afrocentric Fantasy for a Black Middle Class Audience," in *Modes of the Fantastic: Selected Essays from the Twelfth International Conference on the Fantastic in the Arts,* ed. Robert Latham and Robert A. Collins (Westport, Conn.: Greenwood, 1995), 78.

6. Kevin Gaines, "Black Americans' Racial Uplift Ideology as 'Civilizing Mission': Pauline E. Hopkins on Race and Empire," in *Cultures of United States Imperialism,* ed. Amy Kaplan and Donald Pease (Durham, N.C.: Duke University Press, 1993), 435.

7. Gruesser, "Pauline Hopkins," 80; and Martin Japtok, "Pauline Hopkins's *Of One Blood,* Africa, and the Darwinist Trap," in *African American Review* 36, no. 3 (2002), 404–15.

8. Ross Posnock, *Color and Culture: Black Writers and the Making of the Modern Intellectual* (Cambridge: Harvard University Press, 1998), 66–69.

9. Campbell most directly confronts racial prejudice in the U.S. Navy in "The Negro in the Navy," *CAM* 6, no. 6 (May–June 1903), 406–13. Here Campbell justifies the importance of his topic because the "future welfare of the United States and her newly acquired possessions depends largely, if not entirely, on the ability of her navy to protect her" (406).

10. For more, see Lois Brown, *Pauline Elizabeth Hopkins: Black Daughter of the Revolution* (Chapel Hill: University of North Carolina Press, 2008), 407–41; and Wallinger, *Pauline E. Hopkins,* 70–96.

11. This now-familiar and suggestive evidence about the role of Hopkins in the magazine's takeover includes an account, possibly written by W. E. B. Du Bois, called "The Colored Magazine in America," *Crisis* 5 (November 1912), 33–35; and a 1947 account by William Stanley Braithwaite titled "Negro America's First Magazine," in *The William Stanley Braithwaite Reader,* ed. Philip Butcher (Ann Arbor: University of Michigan Press, 1972), 114–21.

12. Some of Hopkins's theory about Washington's role has not been proven. For example, she speculates that Freund, who claimed to not yet have met Booker T. Washington when he first approached the magazine, actually did so at Washington's bidding, an accusation for which the letters do not provide evidence. (Indeed, it may be that Freund got involved with the *CAM* to gratify his wish to meet Washington, to whom he seems to have been highly attracted.) However, Hopkins's theory about a conspiracy directed by Washington is not far-fetched; Washington used such covert efforts in other documented cases. Louis Harlan, *Booker T. Washington: The Wizard of Tuskegee, 1901–1915* (New York: Oxford University Press, 1983) details the "tactics of repression and espionage" (86) that Booker T. Washington and his followers used to deal with African American publishers who challenged Washington's ideas about racial uplift.

13. Hopkins-Trotter letter, April 5, 1905, 4, in Fisk University Library, Memphis, Pauline Hopkins Letters, box 1, file 1.

14. Ibid., 6.

15. Soga specifically credits Hopkins in a passage from *Uzwi Labantu* quoted in "Editorial and Publishers Announcements," *CAM* 6, no. 11 (1903), 831.

16. A. Kirkland Soga, "Ethiopians of the Twentieth Century I: Questions Affecting the Natives and Colored People Resident in British South Africa," *CAM* 6, no. 6 (1903), 432–39; A. Kirkland Soga, "Ethiopians in the Twentieth Century II: Questions Affecting the Natives and Colored People Resident in British South Africa. To the Right Honorable Joseph Chamberlain P.S.M.P, His Majesty's Secretary of State for the Colonies," *CAM* 6, no. 8 (1903), 562–67.

17. "Editorial and Publishers Announcements," *CAM* 6, no. 6 (1903), 467.

18. Hopkins's political and intellectual interest in Africa has been extensively described in interpretations of her novel *Of One Blood* as a powerful expression of her ideas about Pan-Africanism, the concealed greatness of past African civilization, and the proud role of the American Negro in returning Africa to its ancient glory. In *To Wake the Nations,* Sundquist places Hopkins in the context of Pan-Africanism of her era (569–73). See also Allen, *Black Women Intellectuals,* 26, 31–34; Brown, *Pauline Elizabeth Hopkins,* 386–406; Hazel Carby, *Reconstructing Womanhood: The Emergence of the Afro-American Woman Novelist* (New York: Oxford University Press, 1987), 161; and Jennie A. Kassanoff, "Fate Has Linked Us Together: Blood, Gender and the Politics of Representations in *Of One Blood,*" in *The Unruly Voice: Rediscovering Pauline Hopkins,* ed. John Cullen Gruesser (Urbana: University of Illinois Press, 1996), 170–71.

19. Freund-Dupree letter, April 6, 1904, 1, in Fisk University Library, Memphis, Pauline Hopkins Letters , box 1, file 1.

20. Hopkins-Trotter letter, 6.

21. Prof. S. E. F. C. Hamadoe, "El Sr. Don Jose Rizal," *CAM* (April 1904), 253–57, 274–76.

22. Hopkins-Trotter letter, 9.

23. These are Benjamin Griffith Brawley's poem, "New Wars," *CAM* 1, no. 5 (1900), 290–91; and Frank Putnam's essay "The Negro's Part in National Problems," *CAM* 1, no. 2 (1900), 69–72.

24. "Editorial and Publisher's Announcements," *CAM* 7, no.2 (1903), 832–33.

25. Examining the content of the *CAM* in relation to the era's racial politics, one critic similarly notes that the magazine, like Hopkins's fiction, contains an ambiguous mixture of the era's radical and conservative ideas about racial uplift (Sigred Anderson Cordell, "The Case Was Very Black Against Her: Pauline Hopkins and the Politics of Racial Ambiguity at the *Colored American Magazine,*" *American Periodicals* 16, no. 1 (2006), 52–73.

26. Charles Steward, "Manila and Its Opportunities," *CAM* 3, no. 4 (1901), 253, 259, 255.

27. Rev. A. L. Demond, "The Negro Element in American Life," *CAM* 4, no. 5 (1902), 363, 365–66.

28. Hopkins-Trotter letter, 2.

29. On this conventional antebellum view of Jamaica, see Matthew Pratt Guterl, "An American Mediterranean: Haiti, Cuba, and the American South," in *Hemispheric American Studies*, ed. Caroline F. Levander and Robert S. Levine (New Brunswick, N.J.: Rutgers University Press, 2008), 104–5.

30. Hopkins-Trotter letter, 3.

31. John C. Freund, "A Trip to Paradise: Being the Experiences of a New Yorker in the Island of Jamaica," *CAM* 7, no. 1 (1904), 1.

32. John C. Freund, "A Trip to Paradise: Being the Experiences of a New Yorker in the Island of Jamaica; Third Letter," *CAM* 7, no. 3 (1904), 171.

33. John C. Freund, "A Trip to Paradise: Being the Experiences of a New Yorker in the Island of Jamaica; Second Letter," *CAM* 7, no. 2 (1904), 85.

34. John C. Freund, "A Trip to Paradise: Being the Experiences of a New Yorker in the Island of Jamaica; Fourth Letter," *CAM* 7, no. 4 (1904), 230.

35. In *Barbarian Virtues: The United States Encounters Foreign Peoples at Home and Abroad* (New York: Hill and Wang, 2000), Matthew Frye Jacobson mentions the *Dixie* in passing while discussing U.S. involvement in the Panama Revolution (44–45).

36. Nicholas H. Campbell, "Panama: The New Black Republic," *CAM* 7, no. 4 (1904), 270–73.

37. See especially Carby, *Reconstructing Womanhood*, and Elizabeth Ammons, *Conflicting Stories: American Women Writers at the Turn into the Twentieth Century* (New York: Oxford University Press, 1992), 81–85.

38. On Ethiopianism, see Sundquist, *To Wake the Nations*, 551–55; and Susan Gillman *Blood Talk: American Race Melodrama and the Culture of the Occult* (Chicago: University of Chicago, 2003), 50–55.

39. Debra Bernardi infers Hopkins's anti-imperialism from this quotation in "Narratives of Domestic Imperialism: The African-American Home in the *Colored American Magazine* and the Novels of Pauline Hopkins, 1900–1903," in *Separate Spheres No More: Gender Convergences in American Literature, 1830–1930*, ed. Monika Elbert (Tuscaloosa: University of Alabama Press, 2000), 220. See also Carby, *Reconstructing Womanhood*, 161.

40. That Hopkins makes God's will rather than a supposedly natural force such as evolution the fundamental and unfathomable cause here seems on the surface to contradict some of her other writings. "Talma Gordon," as described in chapter 3, seems more optimistic about man's ability to harness racial mixing for positive eugenicism, and *Contending Forces: A Romance Illustrative of Negro Life North and South* (New York: Oxford University Press, 1988) explicitly refers to evolution and genetics as forces shaping human destiny and character. But *Contending Forces* also continually reminds the reader that these forces are

incompletely understood by all except God, making the important opposition in Hopkins not science versus religion but man's inadequate knowledge versus religion and the unknown. For example, the narrator states: "Man has said that from lack of means and social caste the Negro shall remain in a position of serfdom all of his days, but the mighty working of cause and effect, the mighty unexpected results of the law of evolution, seem to point to a different solution to the Negro question than any worked out by the most fertile brain of the highly cultured Caucasian" (87). To Hopkins, evolution and God's will are not mutually exclusive ways of describing fate, and as the narrator makes clear: "With all the centuries of civilization and culture that have come to this grand old world, no man has yet been found to trace the workings of God's inscrutable ways" (157).

41. Pauline Hopkins, "The Dark Races of the Twentieth Century, Part I," *Voice of the Negro* 2, no. 4 (1905), 108.

42. Gaines, "Black Americans' Racial Uplift Ideology as 'Civilizing Mission,'" 447.

43. Pauline Hopkins, *Contending Forces: A Romance Illustrative of Negro Life North and South* (New York: Oxford University Press, 1988), 151.

44. This is a point that Hopkins seems to retreat from in her series on "The Dark Races of the Twentieth Century," where mulattos are represented as an always-disappearing social element. There she draws on Martin R. Delany's *The Origins of Races and Color* to assert that mixed races will tend to "revert" to the "original standard of pure white or pure black" by continued reproduction with pure bloodlines, and that mixed races of the Pacific islands will "become extinct by the resolvent European and Mongolian races settling among them" (Hopkins, "Dark Races of the Twentieth Century, Part I," 110).

PART III

1. Ronald Spector, *Admiral of the New Empire: The Life and Career of George Dewey* (Baton Rouge: Louisiana State University Press, 1974), 105.

2. "The City a Mass of Color," *New York Times* (September 29, 1899), 4.

3. Dewey's official correspondence is reprinted in "Dewey's Chinese Seamen," *New York Times* (February 23, 1899), 7.

4. Dewey is quoted calling for their right to citizenship in "Dewey's Chinese," *New York Times* (September 21, 1899), 6.

5. Almost nothing has been written about Dewey's requests on behalf of these Chinese seamen since 1899. These details about place of birth and length of time in service are gleaned from newspaper coverage of Dewey's requests. Dewey gave some of these details in a letter he wrote in reply to Miss Ellen C. Parsons, a Protestant missionary involved in the Presbyterian Board of Foreign Missions established in San Francisco in 1853. Parsons had learned of Dewey's Chinese seamen and believed that she had known some of them as pupils of the San

Francisco Mission ("Letter from Admiral Dewey," *Woman's Work* 14, no. 3 [1899], 63; and "Our Chinese Helpers," *New York Evangelist* [March 2, 1899], 7). Another informative source is the news article "Dewey's Chinese Seamen"(7), which reprints some of the official correspondence and gives details about one sailor whose birthplace, with Dewey's help, was confirmed to be in San Francisco, giving him the right to reenter the United States.

6. Laura Wexler, *Tender Violence: Domestic Visions of U.S. Imperialism* (Chapel Hill: University of North Carolina Press, 2000), 33, 21.

7. This reply from the Treasury Department is reproduced in "Dewey's Chinese Seamen," 7

8. Rev. S. L. Baldwin, "Dewey's Chinese Sailors," *Zion's Herald* (April 12, 1899), 15.

9. "Letter from Admiral Dewey," 63; and "Our Chinese Helpers," 7.

10. "The Chinese Who Served with Dewey," *Morning Oregonian* (July 30, 1898), 6.

11. "Dewey's Chinese," 6.

12. "Dewey's Chinamen, From *The Tacoma News,*" *New York Times* (September 18, 1899), 2.

13. On the linkage between Dewey's victory and whiteness in the popular imagination, see Wexler, *Tender Violence,* 31–32, and Ann McClintock's discussion of Dewey's image in a Pear's Soap advertisement in *Imperial Leather: Race, Gender and Sexuality in the Colonial Conquest* (New York: Routledge 1995), 32–33.

14. Erika Lee, *At America's Gates: Chinese Immigration during the Exclusion Era, 1882–1943* (Chapel Hill: University of North Carolina Press, 2003), 174.

15. The play opened in New York on August 19, 1899 ("News of the Theaters," *New York Times* [August 9, 1899], 7).

16. The legal proceedings leading up to Driscoll's execution were minutely followed in New York, but for an overview of the entire story, see "Hanged: Dan Driscoll, the Whyo Chief, on the Gallows," *Atchison (Kans.) Daily Champion* (January 24, 1888), 1. Reviews of *The Queen of Chinatown* in regional theaters typically note its basis on the sensational Driscoll-Garrity murder ("At the Theaters," *Wilkes-Barre Times* [August 14, 1899], 3).

17. This plot pattern and the topical interest of returning sailors attending to domestic problems was repeated in a similar play in George Macdonald, *Lays of Chinatown and Other Verses* (New York: H. I. Kimball, 1899), titled *Flotsam and Jetsam: A Bowery Tragedy,* which features two naval officers returning from Santiago to encounter mistreated white prostitutes in a Chinatown dive bar.

18. Joseph Jarrow, *The Queen of Chinatown,* in *The Chinese Other, 1850–1925: An Anthology of Plays,* ed. Dave Williams (Lanham, Md.: University Press of America, 1997), 179. Subsequent page references are cited parenthetically in the text.

19. Wexler, *Tender Violence,* 44.

CHAPTER 5

1. Winnifred Eaton, *A Japanese Blossom* (New York: Harper, 1906), 112. Subsequent page references to this work are cited parenthetically in the text.

2. Lafcadio Hearn, *Japan: An Attempt at Interpretation* [1904] (Rutland, Vt.: Charles E. Tuttle, 1955), 6–10.

3. According to Noel Ignatiev's influential study *How the Irish Became White* (New York: Routledge, 1995), Irish immigrants found themselves in a racial landscape structured most powerfully by its distinction between black and white, and consequently they asserted their whiteness by putting distance between themselves and African Americans. My study suggests that the process of claiming whiteness—for Irish, as well as Japanese—took place on a field of racial difference more complex than one framed by only domestic absorption in the white/black binary.

4. Matthew Frye Jacobson, *Whiteness of a Different Color: European Immigration and the Alchemy of Race* (Cambridge: Harvard University Press, 1998), 17, 222.

5. Examples include Ignatiev, *How the Irish Became White*; David Roediger, *Wages of Whiteness: Race and the Making of the American Working Class* (London: Verso, 1991); and Robert G. Lee's discussion of Irish and Chinese racial formation in *Orientals: Asian Americans in Popular Culture* (Philadelphia: Temple University Press, 1999), 51–82.

6. By referring to this conception of empire as a "frontier model," I am drawing on insights from new western studies that complicate Frederick Jackson Turner's characterization of western expansion as an escape from European conflicts by describing the actual imperial competition that accompanied U.S. expansion. For example, see Patricia Limerick, *The Legacy of Conquest: The Unbroken Past of the American West* (New York: Norton, 1988 [1987]), 26–27; and Richard White, *It's Our Misfortune and None of My Own: A History of the American West* (Norman: University of Oklahoma Press, 1991). For an exploration of the continental west as a space-marked colonial competition in the nineteenth-century U.S. imagination, see Stephanie LeMenager, *Manifest and Other Destinies: Territorial Fictions of the Nineteenth-Century United States* (Lincoln: University of Nebraska Press, 2004), 8–12.

7. Richard Drinnon, *Facing West: The Metaphysics of Indian Hating and Empire Building* (Minneapolis: University of Minnesota Press, 1980), xiii, xvi.

8. Paul Giles, "Transnationalism and Classic American Literature," *PMLA* 118, no. 1 (2003), 62–77.

9. For example, see Yuko Matsukawa, "Cross-Dressing and Cross-Naming: Decoding Onoto Watanna," in *Tricksterism in Turn-of-the-Century American Literature: A Multicultural Perspective*, ed. Elizabeth Ammons and Annette White-Parks (Medford, Mass.: Tufts University Press, 1995), and the introduction to Samina Najmi, *The Heart of Hyacinth* (Seattle: University of Washington Press, 2000), v–xlvi.

10. David Palumbo-Liu, "The Ethnic as 'Post-': Reading *Reading the Literatures of Asian America*," *American Literary History* 7, no. 1 (1995), 165, 163. For more recent consideration of this weakness in Eaton criticism, see Jean Lee Cole, *The Literary Voices of Winnifred Eaton: Redefining Ethnicity and Authenticity* (New Bunswick, N.J.: Rutgers University Press, 2002); and Dominika Ferens, *Edith and Winnifred Eaton: Chinatown Missions and Japanese Romances* (Urbana: University of Illinois Press, 2002).

11. Here I am paraphrasing Kandice Chuh's description of one aspect of this project to denationalize Asian American literature in "Imaginary Borders," *Orientations: Mapping Studies in the Asian Daispora*, ed. Kandice Chuh and Karen Shimakawa (Durham, N.C.: Duke University Press, 2001), 279. On this critical project, see also Sau-Ling C. Wong, "Denationalization Reconsidered: Asian American Cultural Criticism at a Crossroads," *Amerasia Journal* 21, no. 1–2 (1995), 1–27; and Rachel Lee, *The Americas of Asian American Literature: Gendered Fictions of Nation and Transnation* (Princeton, N.J.: Princeton University Press, 1999).

12. Walter LaFeber, *The Clash: U.S.-Japanese Relations throughout History* (New York: Norton, 1997), 32–64.

13. T. R. Jernigan, "Japan's Entry into the Family of Nations," *North American Review* 169 (August 1899), 266.

14. Joseph M. Henning, *Outposts of Civilization: Race, Religion and the Formative Years of American-Japanese Relations* (New York: New York University Press, 2000), 159–64.

15. Arthur May Knapp, "Who Are the Japanese?" *Atlantic Monthly* 110 (September 1912), 340.

16. Henning, *Outposts of Civlization*, 161.

17. "Japan and the Jingoes," *Nation* 79 (September 1904), 255.

18. As Ian F. Haney-López points out in *White by Law: The Legal Construction of Race* (New York: New York University Press, 2006 [1996]), such early-twentieth-century efforts to define or redefine something as seemingly obvious as the boundaries of whiteness seem "quaint" and strained only if they are viewed from a contemporary vantage point "built on the assumption that races are fixed, transhistorical categories" (55).

19. Jacobson, *Whiteness of a Different Color*, 241.

20. John Wigmore, "American Naturalization and the Japanese," *American Law Review* 28 (November–December 1894), 827.

21. Takuji Yamashita, "Applicant's Reply Brief in the Supreme Court of the State of Washington, in the Matter of the Application of Takuji Yamashita for Admission to the Bar," *Washington State Supreme Court Briefs*, Vol. 50, May Session (Olympia: Washington State Supreme Court, 1902), 26.

22. "The American Sentiment concerning Japan and Russia," *Century* 68 (September 1904), 815.

23. "Why America Sympathizes with Japan," *Arena* 31 (May 1904), 519.

24. Edwin Maxey, "Why We Favor Japan in the Present War," *Arena* 32 (August 1904), 132.

25. "American Sentiment concerning Japan and Russia," 815.

26. Josiah Strong, *Expansion under New World Conditions* (New York: Baker and Taylor, 1900), 186.

27. Wolf von Schierbrand, *America, Asia and the Pacific, with Special Reference to the Russo-Japanese War and Its Effects* (New York: Henry Holt, 1904), 5, 4.

28. O. Eltzbacher, "The Yellow Peril," *Living Age* 242 (July 1904), 235.

29. Karl Blind, "Does Russia Represent Aryan Civilization?" *North American Review* 177 (June 1904), 806.

30. Sidney Lewis Gulick, *The White Peril in the Far East: An Interpretation of the Significance of the Russo-Japanese War* (New York: Fleming Revell, 1905), 155.

31. For example, Kaneko Kentaro, "Japan's Position in the Far East," *Annals of the Academy of Political and Social Science* 26 (July 1905), 75–82.

32. Prescott F. Hall, *Immigration and Its Effects upon the United States* (New York: Henry Holt, 1907 [pub. 1906]), 63–65, 123.

33. "The Daughters of Nijo," review of *Daughters of Nijo: A Romance of Japan,* by Onoto Watanna, *Philadelphia Public Ledger* (May 15, 1904), newspaper clipping in scrapbook belonging to Winnifred Eaton, in University of Calgary Library, Calgary, Alberta, Winnifred Reeve Fonds Special Collections, box 19. Eaton's scrapbook also contains newspaper clippings from booksellers listing the novel among top-sellers for May 1904.

34. "Natural Fighters, She Says of Japs: Woman Who Writes Books on Eastern Nation Talks on the War with Russia," clipping from a New York newspaper (title obscured) (February 12, 1904), in University of Calgary Library, Calgary, Alberta, Winnifred Reeve Fonds Special Collections, box 16, file 17.

35. Hall, *Immigration and Its Effects,* 46.

36. Michael H. Hunt, *Ideology and U.S. Foreign Policy* (New Haven, Conn.: Yale University Press, 1987), 78, 79.

37. Alfred Thayer Mahan, *The Problem of Asia and Its Effect upon International Policies* (New York: Little, Brown, 1900), 108.

38. In *Literary Voices,* Jean Lee Cole argues that Ellen's maternal influence holds the real power in the family as it domesticates Japanese militarism (50–57). But in my assessment, Japanese militarism is softened but not significantly transformed in the story, suggesting that the two are merely represented as compatible in a balance of power.

39. Archibald Clavering Gunter, *My Japanese Prince* (New York: Home, 1904), 42. Subsequent page references to this novel are noted parenthetically in the text.

40. Frederick William Wells, introduction to K. Asakura, *The Russo-Japanese War: Its Causes and Issues* (New York: Houghton Mifflin, 1904), vii.

41. Winnifred Eaton, "The Wrench of Chance," in *"A Half Caste" and Other Writings*, ed. Linda Trinh Moser and Elizabeth Rooney (Urbana: University of Illinois Press, 2003), 78. Subsequent page references to this story are noted parenthetically in the text.

42. Mark Twain, *Collected Tales, Sketches, Speeches and Essays* (New York: Library of America), 466.

43. Stuart Anderson, *Race and Rapprochement: Anglo-Saxonism and Anglo-American Relations, 1895–1904* (East Brunswick, N.J.: Associated University Presses, 1981), 148–73.

44. Cole, *Literary Voices*, 60.

45. Ferens, *Edith and Winnifred Eaton*, 165.

46. LaFeber, *The Clash*, 65–73.

47. Thomas F. Millard, *The New Far East* (New York: Scribners, 1906), 16, 29.

48. Roger Daniels, *The Politics of Prejudice: The Anti-Japanese Movement in California and the Struggle for Japanese Exclusion* (New York: Atheneum, 1969), 16–30.

49. Wallace Irwin, *The Letters of a Japanese Schoolboy* (New York: Doubleday, Page, 1909), 21–22, 23.

50. Theodore Roosevelt, *Message of the President of the United States Communicated to the Two Houses of Congress* (Washington, D.C.: U.S. Government Printing Office, 1906), 36–37.

51. David Starr Jordan, "Japanese Exclusion," *Independent* 61 (1906), 1426.

52. L. O'Connell, "The Little Man from Nippon: A Californian's View of the Issue Raised by the Presence and Practices of Japanese in This Country," *New York Times* (December 2, 1906), 2; "California Defends Hostility to Japanese: State Officers Say East Doesn't Understand the Situation," *New York Times* (December 7, 1906), 3.

53. M. E. C., "California Race Issue Seen at Close Range: A Woman Tells Why the Japanese Meet with Opposition," *New York Times* (December 16, 1906), 7.

54. Onoto Watanna, "The Japanese in America," in *"A Half Caste" and Other Writings*, ed. Linda Trinh Moser and Elizabeth Rooney (Urbana: University of Illinois Press, 2003), 175.

55. M. E. C., "California Race Issue," 7.

56. Watanna, "Japanese in America," 175–76.

57. Jack London, *Jack London Reports: War Correspondences, Sports Articles and Miscellaneous Writings*, ed. King Hendricks and Irving Shepard (Garden City, N.Y.: Doubleday, 1970), 105. Subsequent page references to London's war correspondence are noted parenthetically in the text.

58. Colleen Lye, *America's Asia: Racial Formation and American Literature, 1893–1945* (Princeton, N.J.: Princeton University Press, 2005), 32–44.

59. John Fox Jr., author of the novel *Crittenden* discussed in chapter 3, offers a similar account of being shocked by the reality of visual whiteness upon seeing his first Russian prisoner while following Japanese troops as a war correspondent in *Following the Sun Flag: A Vain Pursuit through Manchuria* (New York: Scribner's, 1905), 117–18. For analysis of Fox and of U.S. ambivalence toward the popular spectacle of Japanese militarism, see Gregory A. Waller, "Narrating the New Japan: Biograph's *The Hero of Liao Yang* (1904)," *Screen* 47, no. 1 (2006), 43–65.

60. Eaton, "Japanese in America," 177.

61. Gary Okihiro, *Margins and Mainstreams: Asian American History and Culture* (Seattle: University of Washington Press, 1994), xiii.

62. Lye, *America's Asia*, 9.

CHAPTER 6

1. Peter Booth Wiley and Korogi Ichiro's diplomatic history *Yankees in the Lands of the Gods: Commodore Perry and the Opening of Japan* (New York: Viking, 1990) introduces its subject with MacDonald's story and claims that MacDonald's experiences and those of other shipwrecked U.S. sailors "would ultimately shape" Commodore Perry's plans. Memorials built by historical societies in Astoria, Oregon; Kettle Falls, Washington; and Rishiri and Nagasaki all make various claims for MacDonald's influence on international relations. Frederik L. Schodt describes these memorials and makes similar claims for MacDonald's diplomatic contributions in *Native American in the Land of the Shogun: Ranald MacDonald and the Opening of Japan* (Berkeley: Stone Bridge, 2003), 204, 280, 361, 375.

2. This account is told most fully in the two book-length studies of MacDonald that have appeared to date: Schodt's *Native American in the Land of the Shogun* and JoAnn Roe's *Ranald MacDonald: Pacific Rim Adventurer* (Pullman: Washington State University Press, 1997).

3. The first two chapters were published in the *Kettle Falls Pioneer* on November 23, 1893. The first full printing was edited by William S. Lewis and Naojiro Murakami and printed as part of a volume titled, rather comprehensively, *Ranald MacDonald: The Narrative of His Early Life on the Columbia under the Hudson's Bay Company's Regime, of His Experiences in the Pacific Whale Fishery; and of His Great Adventure to Japan; with a Sketch of His Later Life on the Western Frontier, 1824–1894* (Spokane, Wash.: Inland-American, 1923). The edition included MacDonald's manuscript under the separate title of "Japan Story of Adventure of Ranald MacDonald, First Teacher of English in Japan, a.d. 1848–1849," as well as a biographical essay and appendices corroborating his story. The Oregon Historical Society printed a facsimile edition of Lewis and Murakami's version in 1990 and distributed it widely to libraries and other institutions, funded by the electronics company Epson Portland on behalf of the

Friends of MacDonald, a committee of the Clatsop Country Historical Society. A previously published article examines the appeal of MacDonald's story in the 1990s for transnational corporate interests and the geographical discourse of the Pacific Rim (Gretchen Murphy, "A Home Which Is Still Not a Home: Finding a Place for Ranald MacDonald," *ATQ: Nineteenth Century Literature and Culture* 15, no. 3 [2001], 225–44).

    4. For example, see the chapter on "Native Border Theory" in Claudia Sadowski-Smith, *Border Fictions: Globalization, Empire, and Writing at the Boundaries of the United States* (Charlottesville: University of Virginia Press, 2008), 72–97.

    5. "Japan Story of Adventure" in Lewis and Murakami, *Ranald MacDonald,* 73–74. By "the 1893 edition," I refer to the most updated version of the manuscript that was prepared to appear in the *Kettle Falls Pioneer* that year and that was published by Lewis and Murakami in its entirety in 1923. All subsequent page citations to this edition appear parenthetically in the text.

    6. *Japan Story of Adventure* typescript, 3, in Royal BC Museum, Victoria, British Columbia Archives [hereafter cited as BCA], MS 1249, box 6, folder 1. For accuracy, I have checked all the quotations that I take from the typescript against the handwritten manuscript in BCA MS 1249, box 7, vols. I–IV.

    7. Ibid., box 8, folder 6.

    8. In this literary partnership, McLeod took a major authorial role in crafting the sections of the book that explained the significance of MacDonald's adventures. While the core sections of the narrative describing MacDonald's time in Japan adhere closely to an account recorded in MacDonald's handwriting in the 1850s, and to descriptions that MacDonald later sent to McLeod for the purpose of fleshing out his written record, much of the book's framing material that I analyze in this chapter was produced by McLeod. McLeod informed prospective publishers that in editing he had "adhered most strictly to [MacDonald's] text" (*Japan Story of Adventure,* BCA, MS 1249, box 1, folder 4), but other letters and drafts reveal McLeod's extensive additions. Thus, although I refer to the narrative voice they created as "MacDonald's" throughout this chapter, I do view the two men as coauthors.

    9. Malcolm McLeod, *Pacific Railway, Canada: Britannicus Letters &c. Thereon* (Ottawa: A. S. Woodburn, 1875), 18.

    10. Ibid., 23.

    11. MacDonald to McLeod, July 18, 1892, and MacDonald to McLeod, December 25, 1891, both in BCA, MS 1249, box 9, folder 13.

    12. Draft letter, McLeod to MacDonald, n.d., in BCA, MS 1249, box 8, folder 2. The draft letter is written in the back of a notebook McLeod used to compose the "true American" revisions.

    13. *Japan Story of Adventure* typescript, 199, 198, in BCA, MS 1249, box 6, folder 1.

14. MacDonald to McLeod, May 24, 1889, in BCA, MS 1249, box 9, folder 13.

15. Schodt, *Native American in the Land of the Shogun*, 328–30.

16. Mary Louise Pratt, *Imperial Eyes: Travel Writing and Transculturation* (New York: Routledge, 1992), 3–7.

17. Donald Bartholomae, "Inventing the University," in *Cross Talk in Comp Theory: A Reader*, ed. Victor Villanueva Jr. (Urbana, Ill.: National Council of Teachers of English, 1994), 593.

18. Juliet Thelma Pollard, "The Making of the Métis in the Pacific Northwest Fur Trade Children: Race, Class, and Gender," Ph.D. dissertation, University of British Columbia, 1990, vi.

19. Gloria Anzaldúa, *Borderlands / La Frontera: The New Mestiza* (San Francisco: Aunt Lute, 1987), 3.

20. For example, in *Indian Nation: Native American Literature and Nineteeth-Century Nationalisms* (Durham, N.C.: Duke University Press, 1997), Cheryl Walker argues that although critics have typically seen Native American autobiographers William Apess, George Copway, and Sarah Winnemucca as either assimilated to or alienated from nationalist discourses, these writers in fact appropriated dominant discourses of nation in order to participate with whites in a dialogic project of defining America. However, MacDonald's autobiography significantly differs from these earlier examples as Walker reads them because his border crossing complicates her pragmatic use of the term "America" to refer to, as she explains, "the United States as a symbolic construct" (221). While MacDonald could be seen as employing what Walker calls "the trope of personification, in which an Indian is placed at the center of the nation known as America" (23), MacDonald also complicates this trope through his representation of heterogeneous colonial histories.

21. *Japan Story of Adventure* typescript, 6, in BCA, MS 1249, box 6, folder 1.

22. Homi K. Bhabha, *The Location of Culture* (New York: Routledge, 1994), 148.

23. Jennifer S. H. Brown, *Strangers in Blood: Fur Trade Company Families in Indian Country* (Vancouver: University of British Columbia Press, 1980), xi–xxi; and Sylvia Van Kirk, *Many Tender Ties: Women in Fur Trade Society, 1670–1870* (Norman: University of Oklahoma Press, 1983), 4. These historians write specifically about British fur trade families, whose views of race and mixed marriages were distinct from those of French Canadians. It is for this reason that I use the term "half-breed," a term with derogatory and pseudobiological connotations, rather than *métis* in this essay. In the nineteenth century, the term *métis* referred to people of French and Indian descent, and often more specifically to the cultural and political identity adopted by French-Cree descendents living in Red River (in modern-day Manitoba). Mixed people of English-Indian descent were called "half-breed." In recent decades, however, "métis" has become even more broadly used to apply to people with Indian and either French or English

descent in Canada. On this terminology, see Jaqueline Peterson and Jennifer S. H. Brown, introduction to *The New Peoples: Being and Becoming Métis in North America* (Manitoba: University of Manitoba Press, 1985), 5–7.

24. Ranald actually signed his last name "Macdonald," but I will follow the convention set by other scholars in standardizing the capitalization to MacDonald.

25. Quoted in Myron Eells, *Father Eells; or, The Results of Fifty Five Years of Missionary Labors in Washington and Oregon: A Biography of Rev. Cushing Eells* (Boston: Congregational Sunday School and Publishing, 1894), 108–9.

26. Pollard, "Making of the Métis," 460–67.

27. Ibid., 436.

28. M. Nicholls, "Jane Klyne McDonald, 1810–1879," *British Columbia Historical News* 21, no. 4 (1988), 2–5; and Van Kirk, *Many Tender Ties*, 209–10.

29. Lois Halliday McDonald, ed., *Fur Trade Letters of Francis Ermatinger* (Glendale, Calif.: Arthur H. Clark, 1980), 128.

30. Eells, *Father Eells*, 86; and Clifford Merrill Drury, *Elkanah and Mary Walker, Pioneers among the Spokanes* (Caldwell, Id.: Caxton, 1940), 104, 258.

31. Brown, *Strangers in Blood*, 11–12, 51.

32. Van Kirk, *Many Tender Ties*, 4, 28–29.

33. Schodt, *Native American in the Land of the Shogun*, 376.

34. Van Kirk, *Many Tender Ties*, 237; and Pollard, "Making of the Métis," 462.

35. *Japan Story of Adventure* ms., 33, in Northwest Museum of Culture (formerly Eastern Washington State Historical Society), Spokane, William S. Lewis Collection, MS 24, box 2, folder 16. This is the 1893 manuscript that Lewis used to prepare the 1923 version.

36. *Japan Story of Adventure* typescript, 183, in BCA, MS 1249, box 6, folder 3.

37. McDonald, *Fur Trade Letters of Francis Ermatiger*, 254.

38. Quoted in Lewis and Murakami, *Ranald MacDonald*, 39.

39. Quoted in Schodt, *Native American in the Land of the Shogun*, 47.

40. Brown, *Strangers in Blood*, 190.

41. Elizabeth Bacon Custer, "An Out of the Way 'Outing,'" *Harper's Weekly* (July 18, 1891), 534. Subsequent page citations to this article are noted parenthetically in the text.

42. MacDonald to McLeod, August 29, 1891, in BCA, MS 1249, box 9, folder 13.

43. Letter to Editor, *Kettle Falls Pioneer* (September 3, 1891), 4.

44. Editorial, "Was Uncalled For," *Kettle Falls Pioneer* (September 3, 1891), 4.

45. Ranald MacDonald to Eva Emery Dye, July 24, 1892, in Oregon Historical Society, MS 1089, box 2, folder 5.

46. Schodt, *Native American in the Land of the Shogun*, 349. See also MacDonald to Dye, July 24, 1892.

47. Thomas W. Prosch, "McDonald of Oregon" (Review), *Washington Historical Quarterly* 1, no. 2 (1907), 66–70. See also Sheri Bartlett Browne, *Eva Emery*

Dye: Romance with the West (Covallis: Oregon State University Press, 2004), 130. Browne mistakenly refers to the manuscript as a "diary."

48. Some of the many sources that credit Dye for this invention of Sacagawea include Ella E. Clark and Margot Edmunds, *Sacagawea of the Lewis and Clark Expedition* (Berkeley: University of California Press, 1979), 90–92; Harold P. Norman, *Sacagawea* (Norman: University of Oklahoma Press, 1971), 182; and Donna Kessler, *The Making of Sacagawea: A Euro-American Legend* (Tuscaloosa: University of Alabama Press, 1996), 67. Browne (*Eva Emery Dye*, 163) includes a longer list of sources corroborating this claim.

49. Of course Pocahontas as a Euro-American literary figure begins in John Smith's accounts, but her mythic meaning was not elaborated until later popular plays such as James Nelson Barker's *The Indian Princess* (1808).

50. Eva Emery Dye, *The Conquest: The True Story of Lewis and Clark* (Chicago: A. C. McClurg, 1902), 290.

51. This strategy is also seen in Dye's earlier writing. An avid supporter of Theodore Roosevelt and his vision of U.S. commercial and military power in the Pacific, Dye concludes *The Conquest* by placing Lewis and Clark's exploratory and diplomatic mission (rendered as "conquest") in a continuous line with overseas colonial expansion. The last line of the book reads, "Five transcontinental lines bear rushing armies westward, ever westward into the sea. Bewildered a moment they pause, then turn—to the conquest of the Poles and the Tropics. The frontiersman? He is hewing the forests of the Philippines" (Dye, *The Conquest*, 442–43). Railroad lines bear "armies" (literally of soldiers, but also metaphorically of settlers and builders) westward "into" the sea, leaving them nothing to do but continue colonizing elsewhere. On Dye's political views and Roosevelt, see Browne, *Eva Emery Dye*, 78, 126; and John Spencer, "'We Are Not Dealing Entirely with the Past': Americans Remember Lewis and Clark," in *Lewis and Clark: Legacies, Memories, and New Perspectives*, ed. Kris Fresonke and Mark Spence (Berkeley: University of California, 2004), 169.

52. Alexander W. Bradford, *American Antiquities and Researches into the Origin and History of the Red Race* (New York: Dayton and Saxton, 1841), 239.

53. John T. Short, *The North Americans of Antiquity: Their Origin, Migration, and Type of Civilization Considered* (New York: Harper, 1880). See also Justin Winsor, "The Progress of Opinion Respecting the Origin and Antiquity of Man in America," in *Narrative and Critical History of America*, vol. 1 (Boston: Houghton Mifflin, 1889); Daniel G. Brinton, *The American Race: A Linguistic Classification and Ethnographic Description of the Native Tribes of North and South America* (New York: David McKay, 1901); Clark W. Wissler, "Ethnological Diversity in America and Its Significance," in *The American Aborigines: Their Origins and Antiquity*, ed. Diamond Jenness (New York: Cooper Square, 1973 [1933], 169; and Robert Wauchope, *Lost Tribes and Sunken Continents: Myth and Method in the Study of American Indians* (Chicago: University of Chicago Press, 1964), 1–2.

54. Vine Deloria Jr., *Red Earth, White Lies: Native Americans and the Myth of Scientific Fact* (New York: Scribner's, 1995), 61–107. See also Vine Deloria Jr., afterword to *America in 1492: The World of the Indian Peoples before the Arrival of Columbus*, ed. Alvin M. Josephy Jr. (New York: Knopf, 1992), 429–43.

55. David B. Madsen, "Colonization of the Americas before the Last Glacial Maximum: Issues and Problems," in *Entering America: Northeast Asia and Beringia before the Last Glacial Maximum*, ed. David B. Madsen (Salt Lake City: University of Utah Press, 2004), 1–26; J. M. Adovasio, *The First Americans: In Pursuit of Archaeology's Greatest Mystery* (New York: Random House, 2002); Elaine Dewar, *Bones: Discovering the First Americans* (New York: Carroll and Graff, 2001); James E. Dixon, *Bones, Boats, and Bison: Archeology and the First Colonization of Western North America* (Albuquerque: University of New Mexico Press, 1999); and Joseph F. Powell, *The First Americans: Race, Evolution, and the Origin of Native Americans* (Cambridge: Cambridge University Press, 2005), 229–36.

56. *Japan Story of Adventure* typescript, 161, in BCA, MS 1249, box 6, folder 1.

57. Short, *North Americans of Antiquity*, 148.

58. Edward Sylvester Morse, "Was Middle America Peopled from Asia?" *Appleton's Popular Science Monthly* 53 (November 1898), 6.

59. Daniel G. Brinton describes de Quatrefages's theory critically in *The American Race: A Linguistic Classification and Ethnographic Description of the Native Tribes of North and South America* (New York: David McKay, 1901), 19, 32. Against de Quatrefages, Brinton argues for a western European migration predating any subsequent Asian migration.

60. McLeod explained these ethnological theories at length in his manuscript "Japan, with the Narrative of Ranald MacDonald, the First Teacher of English in Japan, ad 1848–9, with a Compendium of History &c. of Japan, Old and New, by Malcolm McLeod," in BCA, MS 1249, box 7. On this version, see Schodt, *Native American in the Land of the Shogun*, 342–44.

61. Browne (*Eva Emery Dye*) notes that by 1919, *The Conquest* had sold more than thirty thousand copies (it would continue to be reprinted into the 1930s), while *McDonald of Oregon* only went through two editions to sell a total of fifty-three hundred copies (132).

62. "Oregon and Japan" (Review of *McDonald of Oregon*), *New York Times* (October 27, 1906), 703.

CONCLUSION

1. *Schoolhouse Rock!* was a staple on Saturday morning ABC-TV between 1973 and 1985. "Elbow Room" first aired in 1974.

2. Melani McAlister examines new multicultural articulations in conservative fundamentalist Christian visions of U.S. global power in "Left Behind and the Politics of Prophecy Talk," in *Exceptional State: Contemporary U.S. Culture*

and the New Imperialism, ed. Ashley Dawson and Malini Johar Schueller (Durham, N.C.: Duke University Press, 2007), 206–12.

3. Susan Gillman criticizes studies of American imperialism as a project "conceived as an exposé" and bound up in the question of "whether to celebrate or condemn [its] subjects" as "for or against" U.S. empire in "The New, Newest Thing: Have American Studies Gone Imperial?" *American Literary History* 17, no. 1 (2005), 196, 199, 198.

4. José E. Limón, "Translating Empire: The Border Homeland of Rio Grande City, Texas," *American Quarterly* 56, no. 1 (2004), 31.

5. "Bill Moyers' View of Contemporary America," *Fresh Air,* National Public Radio, November 5, 2008.

6. Shu-mei Shih, "Comparative Racialization: An Introduction," *PMLA* 132, no. 5 (2009), 1357.

7. Amy Kaplan, "Violent Belonging and the Question of Empire Today; Presidential Address to the American Studies Association, October 17, 2003," *American Quarterly* 56, no. 1 (2004), 9.

8. Michael Ignatieff, "The American Empire: The Burden," *New York Times Magazine* (January 5, 2003), 22.

Index

Adams, Herbert Baxter, 241n9
Africa, images in Hopkins's fiction of, 121–46, 251n2, 251n4
African Americans: black cosmopolitan image of, 78–85; black "Orientalism" and, 89–90, 244n4; deracialized fiction by, 98–105; divided loyalties suspected among, 104–5, 249n41; Dixon's view of, 60–76; Filipino-American war fiction by, 87–120; military service of, 2, 7–8, 19–20, 51–57, 78, 87, 90–97; patriotism of, 77–78; transnational affiliations of, 8–9; U. S. imperialism and role of, 48–52, 128–36, 223–27, 239n49
Africanist genre, Hopkins fiction as, 121–46
African Methodist Episcopal (AME) Church, 89–90
agency, imperialism and, 11
Aguinaldo, Emilio, 131
Alarcón, Norma, 120
Allen, Carol, 251n4
Americanist ideology: local color writing and, 96–97; in Steward's fiction, 102–5
American Missionary, 62
American Negro Academy, 13
Anderson, Benedict, 220
Anderson, Stuart, 55–56
Anglo-Saxonism: black cosmopolitanism and, 84–85; Dye's narrative of MacDonald and, 210–21; emergence and popularity of, 38–41; in Hopkins's "Talma Gordon," 111; Japanese racial identity and, 166–68, 171–73; MacDonald's travels and role of, 190, 196–205, 210–21; race relations and, 32–38, 54–57; as transnational racial identity, 3–4; transnational racial identity and, 161; white man's burden ideology and, 67–74; white supremacy and, 59, 64–67

"An Out of the Way 'Outing'" (Custer), 205–10
anthropological research, racial categories and, 4
anti-imperialism: *CAM* articles on, 129–33; in Hopkins's *Of One Blood,* 136–46, 254n39; in literature, 24–25; racial ideology and, 41–46, 110–13; white supremacy and, 59–60, 240n6
Anting Anting fetish, 101–2, 248n40
"Anting-Anting of Maga, The" (Meyers), 248n40
Anting-Anting Stories and Other Strange Tales of the Filipinos, 248n40
Anzaldúa, Gloria, 195–96
Apess, William, 263n20
Appiah, Anthony, 14–15
Arena, 52, 62–63
Asian Americans: fiction by, 151–57; immigration policies concerning, 152–57, 165–68, 178–86; transnational racial identity of, 161–86
Asian Exclusion Leagues, 178
Astor, John Jacob, 196–97
Astoria (Irving), 196–97
At America's Gates: Chinese Immigration during the Exclusion Era, 1882-1943 (Lee), 152–53
Atchison Daily Globe, 32
Atherton, Gertrude, 112–13
Atlantic Monthly, 31

Baker, Houston, 83
Balibar, Etienne, 4
Barnston, George, Mrs., 201
Bartholomae, Donald, 195
Bederman, Gail, 37–38
Bering Strait theory, research concerning, 214–21

About the Author

GRETCHEN MURPHY is Associate Professor of English at the University of Texas–Austin. She is the author of *Hemispheric Imaginings: The Monroe Doctrine and Narratives of U.S. Empire.*